CONTENTS

BODIES AND SOULS: A SAFE RETURN PASSAGE

FOR HEAVEN'S SAKE

PRACTICAL PARENTING

YE SHALL

*B*EAR

*R*ECORD

OF ME

TALKS FROM THE 2001 BYU WOMEN'S CONFERENCE

© 2002 Brigham Young University

Bookcraft is a registered trademark of Deseret Book Company.

Visit us at www.deseretbook.com

Library of Congress Cataloging-in-Publication Data

Women's Conference (2001 : Brigham Young University)
    Ye shall bear record of me : talks from the 2001 BYU Women's Conference.
       p.   cm.
Includes bibliographical references and index.
    ISBN 1-57008-781-4 (alk. paper)
    1. Mormon women—Religious life—Congresses.   2. Witness bearing (Christianity)—Congresses.   I. Title.
BX8641 .W74 2002
289.3'32'082—dc21   2001008614

Printed in the United States of America   54459-6918
Malloy Lithographing Inc., Ann Arbor, MI

10   9   8   7   6   5   4   3   2   1

YE SHALL BEAR RECORD OF ME

LOVE AT HOME: RELATIONSHIP WORK

WE'LL ALL WORK TOGETHER: LEADERSHIP LESSONS

EDUCATING OUR CONSCIENCE

WHO AM I? LEARNING OUR IDENTITY

PREFACE

This volume, the sixteenth in the series, is a compilation of selected addresses from the 2001 BYU Women's Conference. We are grateful for the time, energy, and prayer the authors put into preparing their presentations at the conference, and we are pleased to share in this volume a sampling of their ideas and feelings.

The book has been divided into specific sections that will appeal to sisters throughout this worldwide church. In each section sisters will find helpful insights about reaching out to those of other faiths, working together as families and wards, drawing hope and faith from scripture study and temple worship, living as women of God, and developing meaningful relationships with children and spouses, among other topics.

We are grateful for the efforts of the conference planning committee, who made both the conference and this volume possible. We acknowledge the dedication and skill of our editorial team—Dawn Hall Anderson, Suzanne Brady, Rebecca Chambers, Dlora Dalton, and Susette Green—who compiled this work.

As you read this volume, may you receive strength and encouragement from our Savior's message—and the theme of this conference— to "be of good cheer, and do not fear, for I the Lord am with you, and will stand by you; and ye shall bear record of me, even Jesus Christ, that I am the Son of the living God, that I was, that I am, and that I am to come" (D&C 68:6).

—Janet S. Scharman
Chair, 2001 BYU Women's Conference

THREE GUIDELINES FOR OUR TIMES

Thomas S. Monson

Sister Monson and I met at a Hello Day dance when we were freshmen at the University of Utah. In my home, my family was quite informal, so when my older sister, Marjorie, had a date, we would hide in the darkened kitchen where we could see through a window into the dining room and the living room beyond. We took turns standing on chairs to see if we approved of the boyfriends. In the home of the young lady who would become my wife, Frances Johnson, I found a more formal environment. She was the only daughter. When I arrived to pick her up for our first date, her mother and father were dressed up for the occasion. She introduced me to her mother and father, and her father said, "*Monson*. That's a Swedish name, isn't it?"

I said, "Yes, sir."

He said, "So is mine. *Johnson*. My wife and I were born in Sweden."

Then he went into the bedroom and brought from the bureau drawer a picture of two missionaries, formally dressed. You've seen the pose. He said, pointing to one of the missionaries in the picture, "Are you related to this Monson?" To my surprise, I recognized the face. "Oh yes," I said, "that's my father's uncle, Elias Monson." Then Frances's father began to shed tears. He said, "He's one of the missionaries who brought the gospel to our family in Sweden." Then he threw his arms

President Thomas S. Monson is the first counselor in the First Presidency of The Church of Jesus Christ of Latter-day Saints. He graduated cum laude from the University of Utah in business management and received an MBA degree from Brigham Young University. Before being called as a General Authority, he was general manager of Deseret Press and chairman of the Deseret News. He is a member of the National Executive Board of Boy Scouts of America. He and his wife, Frances Beverly Johnson, are the parents of three and grandparents of eight.

around my neck and embraced me. Afterwards Frances's mother did likewise. Then I looked to Frances. She said, "I'll go get my coat."

Four years later, in 1948, we were married in the Salt Lake Temple. I had felt it necessary to serve my enlistment in the United States Navy, graduate from the university, and be employed before getting married. My, how today the sequence has changed!

It's been a wonderful marriage. We have three choice children, eight wonderful grandchildren, and our first great-grandchild—beautiful two-months-old Emily Ann.

Our lives have been somewhat different from many others as a result of my early Church service. I was serving as the ward clerk when Frances and I were married. Not long after, I was called as a counselor in the bishopric, and then six weeks later as the bishop. All of this was in the ward in which I had grown up, a ward of more than a thousand members, including eighty widows.

After I had served five years in that assignment, there came a call to the stake presidency, followed by an assignment to serve as president of the Canadian Mission, with headquarters in Toronto, Canada. My wife was expecting our third child. We'd never been to Canada. When President Stephen L Richards extended the call, he said, "Can you be there in three weeks?"

I said, "Yes, sir."

With our little family, we journeyed through the falling snow to Canada, to us a foreign land. Oh, how we came to love Canada and the many wonderful people we met there! My heart still stirs to a line of the Canadian national anthem: "O Canada, I stand on guard for thee."

In October 1963 came my call from the Lord through President David O. McKay to serve as a member of the Council of the Twelve, followed by service in the First Presidency to three presidents of the Church. Frequently, my assignments took me away for weeks at a time; Frances usually remained at home with the children.

I relate this chronicle of Church responsibility only that you may appreciate Frances, who has shouldered considerable responsibility over the years and with never a complaint. Rarely have we sat together in a sacrament meeting during our married lives.

Grocery shopping is not one of my areas of competence. In fact, Frances pleads with me not to go grocery shopping with her. I can count on the fingers of both hands the times I've ever entered a supermarket since our marriage.

One example will illustrate why: Frances had been hospitalized after suffering a devastating fall some time ago. She asked me to go to the grocery store for a few items. Her shopping list included potatoes. As I walked through the aisles, I was enthralled by the beautiful array of fruits and vegetables. I didn't think of a cart at first, but since I couldn't carry all of the potatoes, and knew nothing of the plastic bags that potatoes can be placed in, I went back for a cart. I placed a number of potatoes in the small upper basket. As I moved along, the potatoes fell out of the cart and onto the floor, exiting through two openings in the back of the cart. A dutiful young lady, one of the store clerks, hurried to my aid, calling out, "Let me help you."

When I tried to explain that my cart was defective, she told me that all the carts had those two holes in the back, that they were meant for the legs of small children. The young clerk then took my list and I followed her to the canned food area for spaghetti. She asked, "Do you want plain spaghetti, spaghetti with meat sauce, or spaghetti with meat balls?" Not knowing, I replied, "Oh . . . ah . . . give me two of each." Difficult choices accompanied each item on the list. I was very happy to finish my task.

When we were done, the young lady said, "You are Bishop Monson, aren't you?"

I answered that I had indeed been a bishop many years ago. She said, "At that time, I was not a member of the Church. I lived on Gale Street in your ward, and you made certain the other girls who were members brought me out to MIA. I just wanted to let you know that the fellowshipping you arranged for me led to my becoming a member of the Church. I thank you for your kindness." I smiled and said to her, "I think I'd better go grocery shopping more often."

Perhaps our lives as a young married couple did not follow the usual course. But great rewards have followed for both of us from even our smallest acts of service or kindness, as in the case of this young lady in the grocery store.

As Latter-day Saints, we know that we lived before we came to earth, that mortality is a probationary period wherein we might prove ourselves obedient to God's command and therefore worthy of celestial glory. From God's revealed word we learn who we are. Now, what does God expect us to become? The way will not be easy. The path of life has its pitfalls; the battleground, its ambushes. Dear sisters, may I suggest three guidelines for our times? First, strengthen your home and family. Second, share your talents. Third, serve your God.

STRENGTHEN YOUR HOME AND FAMILY

To strengthen your home and family, you need to know how vital you are to this process. A favorite quote of President David O. McKay's is also one of mine: "Woman was made of a rib out of the side of Adam; not out of his feet to be trampled upon by him, but out of his side to be equal with him, under his arm to be protected, and near his heart to be loved."[1] Honor his priesthood, and he will honor your womanhood.

On one occasion a writer referred to the family dwelling as "that ghetto called home." I reply, "Home is what the mother makes of it." Home, that beautiful word in our language, was never meant to be a ghetto but rather a haven called heaven, where the Spirit of the Lord might dwell.

Too frequently women underestimate their influence for good. Well could you follow the formula given by the Lord in the Doctrine and Covenants: "Establish a house, even a house of prayer, a house of fasting, a house of faith, a house of learning, a house of glory, a house of order, a house of God" (D&C 88:119). In such a house will be found happy, smiling children who have been taught the truth by precept and example. In a Latter-day Saint home, children are not simply tolerated but welcomed, not commanded but encouraged, not driven but guided, not neglected but loved.

I recognize there are times when Mother's nerves are frayed, her patience exhausted, and her energies consumed, times when she says, "My children don't appreciate a single thing I do." Have you heard that phrase? Have you uttered it? On a school science quiz, after a study of magnets, was this question: "What begins with 'm' and picks things up?" The obvious answer, of course, was *magnet;* however, more than a third of the school students answered *mother*. I think they do appreciate you.

They notice more than you think. Historians of war state that frequently the last word spoken by a dying combatant on battlefields is *Mama* or *Mother*. Love of mother and her teachings prompts bad men to be good and good men to be better more often than any other motivational force. When a son or a daughter is far away from home and the family hearth, can you reach them? A telephone call is good; a letter is also welcome. A sincere mother's prayer is perhaps best of all. Prayers are heard; prayers are answered.

Heartwarming is the story of a mother who prayed daily for her son's well-being in World War II as the vessel on which he served sailed into the bloody cauldron known as the Pacific Theater of the war. Each morning she knelt in prayer for her son, then left home to serve as a volunteer on those production lines that became lifelines to men in battle. Could a mother's own handiwork somehow directly affect the life of her loved one? Her seaman son's name was Elgin Staples. His ship went down off Guadalcanal. Staples was swept over the side; but he survived, thanks to a lifebelt that proved, on later examination, to have been inspected, packed, and stamped back home in Akron, Ohio, by his own mother.[2]

In peacetime, lifebelts and safety nets are often financial. Wise money management is a crucial aspect of strengthening your home and family. Feelings become strained, quarrels more frequent, and nerves frayed when excessive debt knocks on the family door. When emergency situations arise, making ends meet may become impossible if resources are already stretched to pay for the rent, the food, the clothing, and in addition, the debt. Payment on a debt does not put one crumb on the table, provide one degree of warmth in the house, or bring one thread into a garment. Elder Richard L. Evans once said, "That which is beyond our ability to pay ultimately proves to be beyond our enjoyment also. . . . No matter how good or how bad the reasons, no matter how avoidable or unavoidable, trying to figure out how to pay for yesterday's expenditures with tomorrow's prospects is a discouraging picture."[3] Many more people could ride out the storm-tossed waves in their economic lives if they had their year's supply of food and clothing and were debt free.

Today many follow this counsel in reverse. They have at least a year's supply of debt and are food free.

Some years ago President N. Eldon Tanner suggested five financial guidelines: (1) pay an honest tithing, (2) live on less than you earn, (3) learn to distinguish between needs and wants, (4) develop and live within a budget, (5) be honest in all your financial affairs.[4] These are pearls of great price, my dear sisters. Some families have numerous members; others are composed of single mothers and children; and yet others, an unmarried person only. All can benefit from President Tanner's wise counsel.

SHARE YOUR TALENTS

Attending Sunday services at a nursing home, I spoke with a young girl who had come to play her violin. She confided to me that she was nervous but hoped to do her best. As she played, an elderly patient exclaimed, "Oh, you are pretty, and you play so beautifully!" The bow moved elegantly across the strings, and the young girl's agile fingers seemed inspired by the impromptu outburst. She played magnificently. Afterward, I congratulated her and her equally gifted accompanist—whose talents often go unpraised. They responded, "We came to cheer the frail, the sick, and the elderly and found that our own fears vanished as we played, our own cares and concerns were forgotten. We may have cheered them, but they truly did inspire us."

Teaching is another talent we are frequently called on to develop and share in various Church-related assignments. Henry Brooks Adams observed, "A teacher affects eternity; [she] can never tell where [her] influence stops."[5] An example from my boyhood was my Sunday School teacher in the Sixth-Seventh Ward of the Pioneer Stake. The ward population was somewhat transient, which led to a high turnover rate among teachers. Just as we boys and girls became acquainted with and grew to appreciate a particular teacher, the Sunday School superintendent would visit the class and say, "You have a new teacher." Disappointment prevailed, and a breakdown of discipline resulted.

Our class soon developed an unsavory reputation, and prospective teachers would graciously decline to serve or suggest the possibility of teaching a different class in which the students were more manageable. Rather than feeling penitent, we took delight in our newfound status as the problem class and determined to live up to the fears of the faculty.

One Sunday the Sunday School superintendent came, accompanied by a young woman who had, he said, requested the opportunity to teach us. Can you imagine? She asked for us! Her name was Lucy Gertsch. She told us that she had been a missionary and loved young people. She was beautiful, soft-spoken, and interested in us. She asked each of us questions about ourselves and our backgrounds. She told us of her childhood in Midway, Utah, and the beautiful valley and green fields she loved so much.

Those first weeks were not easy. Boys don't become gentlemen overnight. You mothers know that. Yet she never raised her voice, and our rudeness and boisterousness soon ebbed away as we grew more and more interested in her lessons. She made the scriptures actually live. Through her teaching, we became personally acquainted with Samuel, Peter, Paul, Nephi, Alma, and the Lord Jesus Christ. Our gospel scholarship grew. Our deportment improved. Our love for Lucy Gertsch knew no bounds.

That summer we undertook a project to save nickels and dimes for what was to be a gigantic Christmas party. Sister Gertsch kept a careful record of our progress, and being typical teenagers, in our minds we boys instantly converted the monetary totals into cakes, cookies, pies, and ice cream. This was to be a glorious event. No previous teacher had even suggested a social event like this was to be. The summer months faded into autumn, autumn to winter, and at last the party goal was reached.

Not long after, on a cloudy, gray Sunday morning none of us will ever forget, our beloved teacher told us that the mother of one of our classmates had passed away. We thought of our own mothers and how much they meant to us. Our hearts ached for Billy Devenport. That Sunday our lesson was from Acts 20:35: "Remember the words of the Lord Jesus, how he said, It is more blessed to give than to receive." To end her lesson, Sister Gertsch commented on the economic plight of Billy's family. These were depression times, and money was scarce. She paused, then asked, "How would you like to follow this teaching of our Lord? How would you feel about taking our party fund, and, as a class, visiting the Devenports to give it to them as an expression of our love?"

The decision was unanimous. We counted the money carefully, then placed it in a large envelope. We inscribed a beautiful card with our names, and we were on our way.

This simple act of generosity welded us together as a class and taught us that it is indeed more blessed to give than to receive. The years have flown. The old chapel is gone, a victim of industrialization. The boys and girls who learned, who laughed, who grew under the direction of that inspired teacher of truth have never forgotten her love or her lessons.

James, a servant of God and of the Lord Jesus Christ, advised, "Be ye doers of the word, and not hearers only, deceiving your own selves" (James 1:22). Thomas Huxley observed, "The end of life is not knowledge, but action."[6] To the Philippians, the apostle Paul said, "Whatsoever things are true, whatsoever things are honest, whatsoever things are just, whatsoever things are pure, whatsoever things are lovely, whatsoever things are of good report; if there be any virtue, and if there be any praise, think on these things" (Philippians 4:8).

But what comes next? What beyond thinking did James advise? He wrote, "Those things, which ye have both learned, and received, and heard, and seen in me, do: and the God of peace shall be with you" (Philippians 4:9). What a blessing: the God of peace shall be with you. With Paul, as he wrote to the Philippians, I plead with you to be doers as well as thinkers. Let your thoughts dwell on all that is virtuous, pure, and true, and then translate your thoughts into deeds. Our beloved Savior beckons us to follow him.

Remember the parable of the talents, how one was given five talents, another two, and another one? How pleased the Master was with those individuals who multiplied their talents and had put them to good use. How unhappy he was with the person who had one talent and who, fearful of losing it, buried it in the ground. Oh, how that rebuke would sting were we to hear these words from our Lord and Master: "Cast ye the unprofitable servant into outer darkness" (Matthew 25:30).

SERVE YOUR GOD

When I was newly called as a member of the Council of the Twelve, after a meeting in the Salt Lake Temple, the First Presidency and the Twelve were seated around a luncheon table. I was sitting close to President McKay because the seniority started on the other side of the table. President McKay led me into conversation. "Brother Monson, do you think William Shakespeare really wrote the sonnets attributed to him?"

I replied, "Yes, I do."

He said, "Good. So do I." Then he asked, "Do you read Shakespeare?"

I had to be truthful, so I answered, "Occasionally."

He inquired, "What is your favorite play?"

I responded, "*Henry VIII.*"

He asked further, "What is your favorite verse?"

I said, "My favorite verse from Shakespeare is when Cardinal Wolsey, stripped of his power and his glory, laments from the depth of his soul, 'Had I but served my God with half the zeal I served my king, he would not . . . have left me naked to mine enemies.'"[7]

President McKay then said, "Brother Monson, that was wonderful. Would you pass the potatoes?" No one has ever passed the potatoes with greater alacrity than I passed those potatoes.

On the topic of service, let me add to Shakespeare this truth penned by Albert Schweitzer: "I do not know where all of you are going or what you will do, but let me tell you simply this: unless you set aside some portion of your lives to help and serve those less fortunate than yourselves, you will really not be happy."[8] And as king Benjamin from the Book of Mormon writes, inspiring our compliance: "When ye are in the service of your fellow beings ye are only in the service of your God" (Mosiah 2:17).

A few years ago, I visited a ward in Leeds, Utah. The newly called ward Primary president had been assigned to speak in sacrament meeting. Opening her remarks, she said, "I was on the verge of a nervous breakdown before I saw President Monson come into the meeting. Now, I am well into it." She went on to tell of her call to be the president of the Primary. She had said to her bishop at the time, "Oh, I really don't know if I can do this." In reply he had asked, "Who are you?" Thinking, *He lives only a few streets away. He knows who I am*, she responded, "I don't quite know what you mean, Bishop. You know me."

He replied, "You are a daughter of God called to teach his precious children. To be a successful Primary president you need only to prepare yourself and your material and go to your Heavenly Father in prayer."

That fine new Primary president continued, "I'll never forget who I am and the help which is available to me."

Her remarks brought to mind a request made by Elder Marion G. Romney: "Will you please pray for me that no enemy shall dent the small sector of the line which I am assigned to defend?"[9] It matters little in which organization of the Church we are called to labor. We have each been given a portion of the line to defend, and it is our responsibility to do so. May all of us pray to God that no enemy will breach that portion of the line assigned to us.

Let me encourage you today to heed these three guidelines (perhaps I will call it the "S" formula): Strengthen your home and family, share your talents, and serve your God.

If you want to see the light of heaven, if you want to feel the inspiration of Almighty God, if you want to have that feeling within your bosom that your Heavenly Father is guiding you to the left or guiding you to the right, then, "Stand ye in holy places, and be not moved" (D&C 87:8). And then the Spirit of our Heavenly Father will be yours. He will guide and bless you in the important decisions which each one of you will be called upon to make.

I bear this testimony to you, and I invoke upon you the promise of the Lord when he said, "I, the Lord, am merciful and gracious unto those who fear me, and delight to honor those who serve me in righteousness and in truth unto the end. Great shall be their reward and eternal shall be their glory" (D&C 76:5–6).

Notes

1. Matthew Henry, as quoted in Thomas S. Monson, comp., *Favorite Quotations from the Collection of Thomas S. Monson* (Salt Lake City: Deseret Book, 1985), 33.
2. Ronald H. Bailey, in Monson, *Favorite Quotations*, 158.
3. Richard L. Evans, "The Spoken Word from Temple Square," *Improvement Era*, January 1948.
4. N. Eldon Tanner, *Constancy amid Change* [pamphlet] (Salt Lake City: The Church of Jesus Christ of Latter-day Saints, 1979).
5. Henry Brooks Adams, *The Education of Henry Adams* (1907; reprinted, New York: Modern Library, 1931), 20; see also Richard L. Evans, Conference Report, April 1969, 74.
6. Thomas Huxley, as quoted in Thomas S. Monson, *Pathways to Perfection* (Salt Lake City: Deseret Book, 1973), 253–54.
7. William Shakespeare, *Henry VIII*, III, ii, 539–41.
8. Albert Schweitzer, as quoted in Marvin J. Ashton, *Be of Good Cheer* (Salt Lake City: Deseret Book, 1987), 44–45.
9. Marion G. Romney, *Look to God and Live* (Salt Lake City: Deseret Book, 1971), 288.

CHOSEN TO WITNESS FOR HIS NAME

Janet S. Scharman

Our beloved prophet, Gordon B. Hinckley, recently said: "This is the greatest day—the greatest season—in the history of The Church of Jesus Christ of Latter-day Saints. How wonderful to be alive today. How wonderful to be a part of this great cause at this time in the history of the world and in the history of this church. . . . I simply say that things are getting better and better. And I feel profoundly grateful for that."[1]

I too am grateful, grateful to know that in our midst lives a man who is not only the president of the eleven million members of The Church of Jesus Christ of Latter-day Saints but is a modern-day prophet, called of God, for the entire world. Our prophet has said that in spite of the obvious trials and challenges confronting each of us, we need to remember that things *are* getting better and better. This volume's scriptural theme also begins with a message of optimism: "Wherefore, be of good cheer, and do not fear, for I the Lord am with you, and will stand by you; and ye shall bear record of me, even Jesus Christ, that I am the Son of the living God, that I was, that I am, and that I am to come" (D&C 68:6).

Note that being of good cheer and not fearing are prerequisite to our ability to bear record of him. To be of good cheer and not to fear are the very essence of Jesus Christ's message to the world—a message that fills our souls with hope and allows us to see beyond the drama of

Janet S. Scharman is vice-president of Student Life at Brigham Young University. She and her husband, Brent, have a blended family of one son and nine daughters. She is the Laurel adviser in her ward and served as chair of the 2001 BYU–Relief Society Women's Conference.

the moment, beyond the pain and disappointment that inevitably invade our lives. To be of good cheer is not simply to put on a happy face. Good cheer radiates. It is a friendly warmth that reaches out and lifts, illuminates, and encourages. It begins with our willingness to trust in his will and to be an emissary for his cause.

We can be of good cheer even when life's circumstances are less than we had hoped. When negative, immobilizing emotions come to us uninvited, we can remind ourselves that the Lord wants us to succeed and has promised to stand by, sustain, and support us. We can remember that Jesus is the Christ who atoned for our sins, our children's sins, and the sins of those who have hurt us. Even feelings of grief, sorrow, or disappointment do not nullify cheer. In fact, our most challenging times may be when our knowledge that the Lord is with us and will stand by us cheers us most—providing strength, ability, and will to continue.

President Hinckley reiterated his message of good cheer and optimism recently when he said that the "work [of the Church] is possessed of a vitality which has never been evidenced before to such a degree."[2] *Never before.* That's quite a statement, given what we know about the commitment and passion demonstrated by our forefathers.

I believe President Hinckley; I trust his perspective because I see that vitality in the faithful women of the Church. Elder B. H. Roberts, in his account of Church history, said, "Never was a greater mistake made than when it has been supposed that the women of the church were weak, and ignorant, and spiritless."[3] Sisters, we have spirit, and we have the Spirit, a winning combination that enables us to be truly of good cheer. I believe it is because not only do we value *who* we are as women of strength and courage but, as Truman Madsen has said, we understand *whose* we are.[4] We are daughters of God.

Something powerful happens when righteous women unite together, aligning our lives, our purposes, and our efforts. We are strengthened by knowing that we are part of something grand, something divine, which is directed by the priesthood of God.

It is not by accident that we are where we are right now. The Lord has chosen each one of us to do his work on earth during this winding-up season. We have been chosen not because we are better but because he would have us make our contribution when the world needs our particular abilities. We each have been uniquely positioned to participate in specific, significant ways in the building of his kingdom. And all have been called to witness for his name. As Elder Jeffrey R. Holland reminded us, "Asking every member to be a missionary is not nearly as crucial as asking every member to be a member!"[5]

The Lord has confidence in us. He knows our capabilities and our desires; he knows that with his help we can successfully do his bidding. Living in the fulness of times, when the gospel of Jesus Christ has been restored, we have the organization, the priesthood authority, the ordinances, the scriptures, and modern-day revelation to guide us. We have the gift of the Holy Ghost to comfort us, prompt us, and help us to be more than we think we can be.

In July 1830, only a few months after the Church was organized, the Lord, through Joseph Smith, gave a revelation to his wife, Emma. The revelation ends: "This is my voice unto all" (D&C 25:16). In other words, the Lord is really speaking to all women—to you and to me.

This revelation begins with the expression, "If thou art faithful" (D&C 25:2). Beyond our usual sense of what being faithful means, President Hinckley, speaking to the women of the Church in 1984, said that in this particular verse the Lord was referring to our being "faithful to ourselves, to the very best that is within us. No woman can afford to demean herself, to belittle herself, to downgrade her abilities or her capacities. Let each be faithful to the great, divine attributes that are within her."[6] How do we know what our divine attributes are and how we can best use them?

Not long ago a passage in the Book of Mormon enlarged my understanding of what constitutes the divine within us. In 3 Nephi 10, the Lord compares himself to a hen gathering her chicks. For a long time, this analogy seemed very odd. I didn't understand its power or its relevance to me, although I assumed it was important because the Lord repeats it four times. Verse 4 begins, "O ye people . . . how oft have I gathered you as a hen gathereth her chickens under her wings"; verse 5 repeats, "And again, how oft would I have gathered you as a hen gathereth her chickens under her wings." At the end of the same verse, the Lord again says, "How oft would I have gathered you as a hen gathereth her chickens," and in verse 6 yet again: "How oft will I gather you as a hen gathereth her chickens under her wings."

Not being a farm girl, I had never seen this happen. I wondered what circumstances would cause a mother hen to gather her chicks, and what would encourage lively chicks to be gathered. And why would the Lord repeat this image four times in three verses?

Then a friend shared with me this story from a magazine. A group of college students were helping measure range damage after a wildfire had raged across the prairie outside their university town. As they walked over the expanse of blackened earth, they noticed a cluster of small, smoldering mounds. One curious volunteer asked a range manager what they were. This veteran of many range fires suggested that the young man turn over one of the unidentifiable heaps. He did. To his great surprise several sage grouse chicks ran out from under the upturned mound. He was fascinated. *How incredible*, he thought, *that these little chicks had known to find and run underneath this mysterious shelter.*

What was the mound, the young man asked, and how did the chicks know to take refuge there? To his amazement, he was told that the smoldering heap was the remains of their mother. When there is danger, the mother hen instinctively calls out to her young ones and stretches out her wings for them to run under and find protection in her embrace. The young man was profoundly moved by this symbol of a mother's innate love and desire to protect her young.[7]

I was moved as well by this image. This divine attribute—that loving impulse to gather and protect—is within all of us. I reflected back many years to an experience of my own. When I was a young mother, our family moved to Germany for three years. I felt there the intense responsibility of holding my little ones close to me, of protecting and nurturing, so they could face a world quite strange to them. None of us spoke a word of German, and we felt very alone in a little village where we were the only Americans and the only Latter-day Saints.

I had never undertaken such an overwhelming adventure, and many lessons awaited us. Our first visit to the local market must have been extremely entertaining for the residents as I thumbed through my dictionary, trying to determine the contents of certain packages. I felt like a preschooler as I tried to figure out which bills and coins to use to pay for our goods. And then, as if dictionary struggles and lack of knowledge of the local currency were not enough, we had not brought baskets with us. Our village market had no bags. So, my three young children and I scurried home through the town, our arms full of loose food items, looking rather ridiculous, I suspect.

I registered my children in the local elementary school with the hope that they would soon make some friends and learn the basics of the language. I remember those early days very clearly. I so much wanted this to be a good experience for my children, and yet I could tell they were suffering. In response to my cheerful "How was school today?" my ten-year-old son routinely answered: "How do you think it would be if you had no friends and couldn't understand anything anyone was saying to you?"

My seven-year-old daughter, who had been a happy, self-confident child in Utah, became fearful whenever I was out of sight. After many tears and much clinging, I finally learned that she worried if she had a problem, no one would be able to understand and help her.

We spent a lot of time during those early days talking, reading books together, playing games, and going on outings—much more than we ever had before. I wasn't particularly brave and was often close to tears, but we went on because it was the only thing to do. I gathered my chicks under my wings, not because I was especially noble or good but because I was their mother and I needed them as much as they needed me. We summoned our strength, and then all ventured out to face the world again. My insecurities and initial lack of German survival skills did not remove my responsibility to those children nor did it diminish the bonds that grew in the time we spent together. Our time abroad evolved into one of our most treasured experiences, not because the way was easy, or because we navigated the course particularly well, but because we navigated it together.

Now my children are all grown, and our "nest" is usually empty. Spontaneous gathering has given way to more predictable events. Dinner on Sunday evenings at our home is when children and grandchildren gather. We celebrate birthdays or purchases of new homes, announce due dates of new little children, rehearse talks for Primary, share talents, and play games. It is also a time for revealing disappointments, discussing fears, and talking about life. Those who live some distance from us are gathered with e-mail, phone calls, and small packages in the mail.

Gathering one with another in righteousness, as well as gathering those we love under our wings, is critical in this day and time. The world is not neutral. Neither can we be. Obvious challenges are relatively easy to resist. Subtle, distracting messages, though, touch on how we dress, what we eat, how we spend our money. It can become confusing to know when to reach out and when to turn away. I believe guidance comes from staying connected, being together, and listening to the promptings of the Spirit.

Again I reflect on the question posed in 3 Nephi: How oft have I gathered my chicks under my wings? In following the Savior's example, as righteous women we seek to gather and protect our own and one another. In that regard, I am struck that the verses do not say: How often have I gathered my chicks with confidence, having a clear plan, feeling happy and secure every single time. Nor does it say: Remember the *one* really great time I gathered you together? Each repetition begins "how oft"; being together often, strengthening the family bonds, seems to be the key. Something both comforting and fortifying occurs when we gather with others who are important to us. Gathering implies more than just sitting next to someone in the same room. It means smiling, reaching out, belonging, sharing a part of ourselves, and inviting a reciprocal response. Sometimes we nurture, and sometimes we seek nurturing. It also means trusting in and sustaining those who have stewardship for us.

When we gather in worship, we are inspired as we realize once again that we are part of something grand and glorious, that the Lord has a plan for his children, and that we have been privileged to participate in his work. For a brief time together, we feel protected from the raging fires of the world as we fill our cups to go back to lives we love and the divine roles the Lord has chosen to assign to us, and which we, in turn, have chosen to accept.

The Lord himself has commissioned each of us to help prepare the earth for the return of our Savior. Given all that, we must remember an important point. He has chosen us not only because *he* needs us to do his work but because *we* need to do his work. In 2 Nephi 32:9, Nephi teaches us: "Pray unto the Father in the name of Christ, that he will consecrate thy performance unto thee, that *thy performance may be for the welfare of thy soul*" (emphasis added). As we bear record of Christ in the way we think, what we do, and the words we choose to profess— in our very beings—we become perfected and progress on the journey to exaltation, our own exaltation.

The Lord's promise, "I am with you, and will stand by you," is the surest protection from the firestorms of life. "As a hen gathereth her chicks," he stretches out his arms to us with the unequaled power of the Atonement, which can purify our souls. He calls us to him, promising, "I go to prepare a place for you . . . ; that where I am, there ye may be also" (John 14:2–3). As we align our lives with the Lord's purposes, we can feel reassured of his love for us and can know for a surety in our hearts that Jesus Christ is the Son of the living God, that he was, that he is, and that he will come again.

Notes

1. Gordon B. Hinckley, "The Lord Is at the Helm," *Brigham Young University Speeches, 1993–94* (Provo, Utah: Brigham Young University Press, 1994), 110–11.
2. Gordon B. Hinckley, "This Great Millennial Year," *Ensign*, November 2000, 67.

3. B. H. Roberts, *A Comprehensive History of The Church of Jesus Christ of Latter-day Saints*, 6 vols. (Provo, Utah: Brigham Young University Press, 1965), 5:253.

4. See, for example, *Five Classics by Truman G. Madsen* (Salt Lake City: Deseret Book, 2001), 147.

5. Jeffrey R. Holland, "'Witnesses unto Me,'" *Ensign*, May 2001, 14–15.

6. Gordon B. Hinckley, "If Thou Art Faithful," *Ensign*, November 1984, 90.

7. Phillip A. Allred, "Whosoever Will Come, Him Will I Receive," *Meridian Magazine* [online] www.meridianmagazine.com; copy in possession of the author.

BEARING RECORD: NOTHING COMPARES TO IT!

Bonnie D. Parkin

Nearly four years ago, on a sweltering June afternoon, my husband and I stood at gate C–11 in the Salt Lake International Airport, surrounded by our children, grandchildren, mother, brothers, sisters, and friends. All our hearts were tender that day as we said our good-byes. Two months earlier, we had packed half our empty nest into boxes and shipped them 4,860 miles from the Colonies to the Mother Country. In case of emergency, we'd added angel food cake mixes, instant vanilla pudding, and pounds of chocolate chips. Chocolate chip cookies are a great motivator! That day, I looked around at so many I loved and wondered how I could possibly leave for three years to become what one friend described as "chaperones of a three-year youth conference."

As the plane rocketed into the summer blue sky, I thought of all I was leaving behind. Then I saw my nametag: Sister Parkin. It struck me that not only was I leaving behind the people, places, and things I loved, but I was leaving behind my very identity and replacing it with a black plastic plaque. In England, nobody knew me: I was no longer Bonnie, whose car whipping around the corner was often mistaken for an errant space shuttle; Bonnie, a longtime member of the Parleys Third Ward family; Bonnie, a volunteer, teacher, friend, neighbor, sister, mother.

Peter described my feelings perfectly when he said, "It is a fearful thing to fall into the hands of the living God" (Hebrews 10:31).

Bonnie Dansie Parkin, former second counselor in the Young Women General Presidency, recently returned from serving with her husband, James L. Parkin, while he presided over the England London South Mission. They are the parents of four sons and the grandparents of fourteen grandchildren.

I glanced again at my nametag and only then noticed the rest: England London South Mission, The Church of Jesus Christ of Latter-day Saints. There was another name on my tag, one more important than my own. It was the name I took upon myself at baptism, the name of him who calmed the seas and fed the masses, the name of God's Only Begotten, the name of my Savior. My identity was secondary; I was there to bear record of him, even Jesus Christ, that he is the Son of the living God, that he was, that he is, and that he is to come (D&C 68:6).

A few months ago, we received a letter from one of our missionaries—Elder Riebe from Germany. When he arrived in the mission, he was shy, self-conscious, and barely able to express himself in English. During his first meeting at the mission home, he declined even to talk. (Bearing record of the Savior is somewhat difficult when you don't open your mouth.) But Elder Riebe's heart was right. He worked hard, he was obedient, he was humble; he became an effective teacher and an inspiring mission leader. In his letter he wrote: "I loved my mission. Of course it wasn't all fun. I took my assignment very sincere. The memories I have of my mission make my heart burn. I feel very deeply about it. It has been a school of excellence! It refined my skills to teach, to serve, to love, and to listen. Nothing compares to it."[1]

In bearing record of the Savior, I agree with Elder Riebe: Nothing compares to it! Yet despite the singularity of the experience, too often we allow inhibitions and fears, unexpected obstacles, uncertainty, tenacious distractions, misinformed others—the list is endless—to inhibit our sharing of the truths we hold so dear.

We had been in London for two months when one morning at 4:00 the phone rang. It was our son Brett calling to announce the birth of twin babies, Andrew and Eliza. He was emotional and overjoyed at their arrival, grateful that they were well and healthy. "I wish you could see them," he said. After I hung up the phone, I sat looking out at that misty English morning, and I cried until 6:00. *I should be there to help with those new babies*, I thought. *This is not fair.*

Then I remembered the advice I had given our missionaries at zone conference a few days earlier. When President Gordon B. Hinckley was a missionary in England, he became so discouraged that he finally wrote his father, saying that he was not doing any good and might as well return home. His father's reply was straightforward and wise: "Gordon, . . . forget yourself and go to work."[2]

As I sat pitying myself, feeling so homesick for those twins, I knew I had to personalize Brother Hinckley's advice. We had made his statement the motto of our mission, so at each zone conference we stood and substituted our own name, saying aloud, "Sister Parkin, forget yourself and go to work." We can remember that all of us who lose our lives for Jesus' sake shall find them (Matthew 16:25).

I hope all of us are praying for opportunities to bear record of him. When Elder M. Russell Ballard visited our mission, he encouraged us to keep in mind that as we pray to find people to share the gospel with, there are also people praying to find the gospel. I love Peter's be-prepared admonition: "Be ready always to give an answer to every man that asketh you a reason of the hope that is in you" (1 Peter 3:15). Peter is saying, "If people ask you why they sense something different about you, be ready to unapologetically bear record of Jesus." President Hinckley also challenged us to "become a vast army with enthusiasm for this work."[3]

We received an elder who frequently complained. He found half-empty glasses everywhere. As the principle of opposition in all things would have it, we also had a missionary with just the opposite gift: finding full glasses everywhere. Now, as the Lord would have it (and sometimes I think he must find some delight in this), my husband was inspired to call these two ends of the spectrum to serve as companions.

At the next president's interview with the pessimistic elder, five minutes passed without a complaint. This was nothing short of a record. Surprised, Jim asked what had happened. "It's my companion," the elder said. "Whenever a door was slammed in our faces, I'd start complaining; my companion would say, 'What a great idea, Elder! Complaining always helps! Why don't you complain for five minutes;

then I'll complain for five minutes; then we can both complain for five minutes. I'm sure things will get better.'"

Oh, the genius of nineteen-year-old elders! It didn't take long for the young man to recognize the futility of complaining. When his attitude changed, so did his experiences.

One of our newer sister missionaries was quite vocal about not liking to tract. In a visit several months later, she mentioned how much she enjoyed tracting. Doing a double take, I asked what had caused this radical change. "My companion," she explained. "She loves to tract. Even when someone gets angry and slams the door on us, she says, 'Did you see her cute apron?' or 'Did you look at her lovely garden?'" One sister's attitude blessed her companion as well as everyone they met.

Attitude and testimony are connected in the scripture: "Wherefore, be of good cheer, and do not fear, for I the Lord am with you, and will stand by you; and ye shall bear record of me, even Jesus Christ" (D&C 68:6). Attitude determines altitude; happily obeying the commandments helps others to do likewise.

In his departing testimony, Elder Riebe said, "I have learned three things in the mission field: one, be obedient, two, be happy, and three, if you can't be happy, be obedient." After three years and nearly six hundred missionaries, I realized happy missionaries were obedient missionaries. We can teach our future missionaries to find happiness through obedience.

The Apostle Paul wrote, "For as by one man's disobedience many were made sinners, so by the obedience of one shall many be made righteous" (Romans 5:19). The obedience of our children will help others become righteous.

Parents with a testimony of obedience can help their missionaries in the field improve their obedience. Late one evening, the phone rang in the mission home. My husband answered it. A father from the United States asked whether his son was an obedient missionary. When Jim asked why the father was curious, the father replied that his older sons had served missions and were allowed to call home only on Christmas and Mother's Day. His son in England, he noted, was calling family and friends much more frequently. Jim replied that the rules regarding phone calls were the same in the London South mission as in every other mission. The father responded, "Are you telling me that my son is a disobedient missionary?" Jim replied, "I am not telling you that; your son already has."

Jim told that story in a zone conference. Afterward a missionary approached him saying, "That was my father, wasn't it?" It was, and his father's call helped that elder become more obedient.

Following zone conferences, while my husband was interviewing, I'd visit with the elders and sisters. I'd often say to them, "Tell me about your mother." From their answers, I gained a humbling vision of great women around the world lovingly, carefully teaching children, grand-children, nieces, nephews, students, and neighbors how to live the gospel of Jesus Christ and bear record of Jesus. We must help our children know that they were valiant in their first estate, that they were obedient to Heavenly Father's plan, that they can influence others to follow that plan.

Preparing missionaries to serve is merely one of the ways we testify of Jesus. But we must become missionaries, too. Have you ever heard the missionary discussions? Do you know how simple, beautiful, and inspired they are? I am embarrassed to say that it was only after two of my sons had returned from missions and another was in the mission field that I heard the discussions.

Some time ago I was a Relief Society advisor to a group of young adult women. Lisa was a member of our group. She was getting married to Rick—a great guy who was that unusual Utah commodity: a non-member. He and Lisa often came to our home, forming friendships with our sons. One day I asked Lisa if Rick had heard the discussions.

"Bonnie," she said, "I can't ask him! I can't do that yet."

I said, "How would you feel if I asked him?"

"Oh, would you?" she responded.

Only then did I wonder, *What have I gotten myself into?* because I didn't know how to ask him, either!

I asked one of our returned-missionary sons, who said, "Mom, it's easy. You just say, 'Rick, is there a day next week that would be good for you to meet with the missionaries in our home?'"

That didn't sound too hard, so the following Sunday we invited Lisa and Rick over for dinner. I practiced my line over and over again. As they were leaving, I said to Rick, as casually as I could manage, "Is there a day next week, Rick, when you could meet with the missionaries here in our home?"

I don't know if I expected him to run off screaming or just laugh in my face. But sisters, do you know what he said?

"Wednesday would be great."

Now that wasn't so hard, was it?

Of course, some friends are not quite ready for the discussions. But bearing record does not just mean an invitation to be baptized. It was my friend Louise Nelson's turn to host her neighborhood stock market study group for lunch. Louise was the only Church member in the group. When it came time to eat, Louise asked if it was all right if she blessed the food. It was her home and her food, so no one objected. She prayed. The following month, at another friend's home, Louise was asked to bless the food. When she agreed, the hostess said, "Thank you; I liked the way that made me feel last time." Several others felt the same. What finer way to bear record of the Savior than through prayer in his holy name?

No matter how we share the gospel, such sacred moments leave lasting memories. Elder Maxwell wrote: "Sharing is like gathering around conversational bonfires that glow warm and bright against the horizon. You will find the memories of these bonfires will achieve a lastingness—not of what you wore or of what the menu was, but rather because of shared expressions of love and testimony."[4] The Lord promises that when we bear record of him, we are edified as well as those who hear us (D&C 50:22); our faith is strengthened with their faith;[5] and our sins are forgiven us (D&C 62:3).

As we prepare missionaries and share the gospel with our friends and families, we receive these spiritual gifts. But, my dear sisters, how marvelous would it be to receive these blessings daily? Those of you who are nervous about impending retirement, about nothing meaningful to do, about endless spare time on your hands—or worse, about a husband with endless spare time on his hands—what better way to transition into the next phase of life than a mission? Young missionaries, especially those who have never seen a happy marriage, are fortified by the experienced examples of senior couples. One young elder told of watching Brother and Sister Thiriot from Coalville, Utah, skipping toward the temple holding hands. "They did not know I was watching them," he said, "but someday, my wife and I are going to serve a mission and do just what the Thiriots are doing."

Sisters, now is the time to plan a mission as a senior missionary or as a couple. You'll need to ready yourself financially, physically, spiritually. And you know what? Heavenly Father will watch over you and your family while you are in his service. At 4,860 miles from home, we learned that to be true. And so did our children. The Lord might even double your blessings. We left six grandchildren at the airport that day and returned home to twelve. Maybe we should go again!

One day in our mission office, I noticed the shoes of one of our faithful, hardworking Elders. They were literally falling apart; I had never seen shoes quite like them before. I said, "You need a new pair of shoes." He said, "Sister Parkin, I haven't had time!" Then, I asked him for those shoes. Probably thinking that they didn't match my ensemble, he asked why I wanted them. I just said that I needed them. Someday I hope to send them to his sons and tell them what kind of a missionary their father was. He wore out his soles in the service of his God. Sisters, considering our own vast collections of shoes, couldn't we wear out at least one pair doing the same?

Ultimately, our testimony of Jesus filters through all that we do. Elder Henry B. Eyring taught, "If you want to know if I know that Jesus is the Christ, watch the way I live."[6] We can choose to live lives that bear record of him.

I bear record of the goodness and divinity of Jesus Christ. For three years I wore his name next to my own; not only was my identity never lost but it was enhanced by his. I know that he lives and that he loves us eternally—which he demonstrated through his obedience to our Father and through his atoning sacrifice. In sharing our testimonies of these extraordinary truths, I join with Elder Riebe in saying, "Nothing compares to it!"

Notes

1. Letter in author's possession.
2. In Sheri L. Dew, *Go Forward with Faith* (Salt Lake City: Deseret Book, 1996), 64.
3. Gordon B. Hinckley, "Feed the Lambs, Feed the Sheep," *Ensign*, May 1999, 110.
4. Neal A. Maxwell, "Jesus the Perfect Mentor," *Ensign*, February 2001, 16.
5. *The Words of Joseph Smith*, ed. Andrew F. Ehat and Lyndon W. Cook (Provo, Ut.: Religious Studies Center, 1980), 159.
6. Henry B. Eyring, leadership training session, England London South Mission, notes in author's possession.

"NO MORE STRANGERS AND FOREIGNERS"

James A. Toronto

This past year on a business trip, I found myself sitting on my hotel room balcony overlooking the teeming metropolis of Cairo, Egypt. Much had changed in my mind and heart in the nearly twenty-five years since my wife, Diane, and I first encountered this North African, Arab, Muslim city. Both of us had grown up in small, rural LDS communities—she in Declo, Idaho; I in Snowflake, Arizona. We had had little exposure to non-American, non-Christian peoples and cultures before we decided to seek adventure teaching school in Saudi Arabia.

After leaving the States, our first stop in the Middle East was Cairo, and our first impressions could not have been worse. The furnace blast of heat and humidity that greeted us as we stepped off the plane withered our Rocky Mountain souls. We found ourselves stranded in Cairo with no familiar system for making airline reservations to continue on. We were surrounded by masses of people who dressed in odd clothes, spoke a bizarre language, and seemingly possessed no notions of basic civility, such as waiting in lines and not staring at strangers. Our patience was pushed to the breaking point by hustlers and con men, and our senses were overpowered by unidentifiable foods, vile sanitary conditions, exotic sounds, and nauseating odors. Late one night, unable to sleep because of jet lag, stifling heat, kamikaze mosquitoes buzzing my ears, and a cacophony of frogs and

James A. Toronto received his Ph.D. in Islamic Studies from Harvard University and is an associate professor at Brigham Young University. He has lived with his family for ten years in the Middle East and currently serves as president of the Provo Utah Sharon East Stake. Jim and his wife, Diane Gillett Toronto, are the parents of Joseph, serving a mission in Italy, and Jenna, a junior in high school.

dogs outside our bedroom window, I said to Diane, "Tell me again why we decided to do this."

But we stuck it out; and the experience of living and working in Cairo, Amman, Khamis Mushait, Jubail, Boston, and Provo, among people of diverse religious, ethnic, racial, and political backgrounds has immensely enriched our lives. I realized that night as I sat on the balcony of the hotel, that what was exotic and repelling the first time in Cairo was now familiar and appealing. I had just eaten Egyptian foods for breakfast—*foul, ta'miya,* and mango juice—that I wouldn't have touched before but now not only liked, but craved because they are so healthy and delicious. I thought about how much I had learned to love the archeological and historical treasures of Cairo, the natural beauty of the Nile valley and the Sinai, and above all, the innate warmth, intelligence, resiliency, and good humor of the Egyptian people. How much of life and beauty, self-understanding and spiritual growth we would have missed had we avoided experiencing the world of other people, which seemed at first so alien and offensive.

Much may be gained by loving and learning from those who are different. This eternal truth is both fundamental in Christian spiritual life and vital to the well-being of the increasingly diverse communities in which we live. Though most Latter-day Saints understand the Savior's admonitions to reach out to "strangers and foreigners" among us, we must be aware of problems and challenges that still hinder our efforts to do so and to instill this principle in our young people. My comments will focus on interfaith issues, though the principles also apply to our relations with anyone whose political views and social status differ from ours.

"Entertaining Strangers": The Essence of Christian Discipleship

The need to love and learn from those outside our circles of experience is greater today than ever before. Studies, including the most recent U.S. census, show that our communities are becoming ever more diverse in terms of ethnicity, race, religion, and lifestyle. It is one of the ironies of our age that kindness, civility, and respect for differences seem to be at an all-time low just as our access to prosperity, creature comforts, and technology are at an all-time high. News reports of violence and bigotry rooted in racial, religious, and political distinctions assail us daily. We face challenges in the Church, too, as thousands of our Father's children from primarily non-North American, non-English speaking countries and cultures, many of them refugees fleeing political and economic hardship, join our congregations each year in need of refuge, support, and acceptance. Moreover, demographic trends in the Church show a large percentage of single adults—whether divorced, widowed, or never married—who often feel alienated in a community whose theology and activities center on the traditional nuclear family.

The vital need to understand and love those of differing religious, social, and philosophical backgrounds is rooted in fundamental gospel principles—humility, charity, respect for eternal truth, and recognition of God's love for all his children as taught by Jesus Christ and by ancient and modern prophets.

The Savior repeatedly affirmed Heavenly Father's concern for the well-being of each of his sons and daughters (see Luke 15) but warned his followers, in the parable of the good Samaritan, that true discipleship requires more than just a feeling of love for those around us. We must be willing to go out of our way, outside our comfort zone, to minister to those who, because of political, racial, or religious differences, we find difficult to love (see Luke 10). Jesus denounced intolerance and rivalry among religious groups and the tendency to extol one's own virtues and deprecate the spiritual status of others. Addressing a parable to those who "trusted in themselves, that they were righteous, and despised others," he condemned the prideful attitude of the Pharisee who prayed, "God, I thank thee, that I am not as other men are" and commended the humble demeanor of the publican who implored, "God be merciful to me a sinner" (Luke 18:9–14). In one of his most powerful teachings concerning the Last Judgment, Jesus explained that the ultimate test of Christian faith is our daily effort to bring healing, love, and nourishment to those among us who suffer physically, spiritually, or emotionally. He describes those individuals as hungering and thirsting, being strangers, prisoners, sick, and naked; in other words, those in society who don't fit in, who are scorned and rejected, whose needs may be difficult to see but are very real, who feel trapped, inadequate, and vulnerable (see Matthew 25).

The apostle Paul teaches eloquently that, motivated by the gift of God's grace in our lives, we should constantly watch for those who are far off and seek to bring them near. We should seek to help Christ break down the "wall of partition" that separates us from God and our fellow beings (Ephesians 2:14). By so doing, we discover the reciprocal nature of charity: in extending care to others—especially those outside our circle of experience—we find unexpected spiritual surprises and insights. In Paul's words: "Be not forgetful to entertain strangers: for thereby some have entertained angels unawares" (Hebrews 13:2).

Alma's missionary experience among the dissident Zoramites warns us against the spiritual danger of pridefully patting ourselves on the back. He records that the people would ascend a public pulpit, called Rameumpton, and pray: "Holy God, we believe that thou hast separated us from our brethren; . . . we believe that thou hast elected us to be thy holy children; . . . and thou hast elected us that we shall be saved, whilst all around us are elected to be cast by thy wrath down to hell; . . . And again we thank thee, O God, that we are a chosen and a holy people" (Alma 31:16–18). Later, referring to the pride of the Zoramites, Alma's counsel to his son Shiblon echoes the Savior's teachings about "despising others" and reminds Church members today of the need for humility in our relations with those of other faiths: "Do not say: O God, I thank thee that we are better than our brethren; but rather say: O Lord, forgive my unworthiness, and remember my brethren in mercy—yea, acknowledge your unworthiness before God at all times" (Alma 38:14).

The Book of Mormon is another witness that Heavenly Father "is mindful of every people, whatsoever land they may be in . . . and his bowels of mercy are over all the earth" (Alma 26:37; also 1 Nephi 1:14). His love and mercy extend to all people, regardless of race, social class, gender, or religion: "He inviteth them all to come unto him and partake of his goodness . . . black and white, bond and free, male and female; and he remembereth the heathen; and all are alike unto God, both Jew and Gentile" (2 Nephi 26:33). Because of this love for his children of all nations, the Savior has provided spiritual light to guide and enrich their lives in all times and places: "I bring forth my word unto the children of men, yea, even upon all the nations of the earth" (2 Nephi 29:7); "The Lord doth grant unto all nations, of their own nation and tongue, to teach his word, yea, in wisdom, all that he seeth fit that they should have" (Alma 29:8).

The Prophet Joseph Smith often expounded on this theme of the universality of God's love and the related need to remain open to all available sources of divine light and knowledge. "One of the grand fundamental principles of 'Mormonism,'" he said, "is to receive truth, let it come from whence it may."[1] The Prophet exhorted Church members to "gather all the good and true principles in the world and treasure them up, or we shall not come out true 'Mormons.'"[2] He incorporated these basic principles in the Articles of Faith, accepted now as official Church doctrine. The eleventh article articulates the Latter-day Saints' commitment to religious freedom and tolerance: all people should have the privilege to "worship how, where, or what they may." The thirteenth Article of Faith, on the other hand, goes beyond mere toleration to advocate respect for, even active searching after, all truth and virtue: it embodies our aspiration to do "good to all men" and to seek actively after "anything virtuous, lovely, or of good report or praiseworthy." In keeping with this theme, the Prophet Joseph cautioned against the ills of sectarian strife and urged Church members to set an example of charity and civility in their dealings with non-Mormons: "We ought always to be aware of those prejudices . . . against our friends, neighbors, and brethren of the world, who choose to differ from us in opinion and in matters of faith. . . .

"There is a love from God . . . which enables us to conduct ourselves with greater liberality towards all that are not of our faith, than what they exercise towards one another. . . .

" . . . Christians should cease wrangling and contending with each other, and cultivate the principles of union and friendship in their midst."[3]

Elder B. H. Roberts and apostle Orson F. Whitney, elaborating on this doctrine, concluded that philosophers, founders, and teachers of other religious traditions were inspired by the Lord to teach good and virtuous principles. Elder Roberts stated: "While the Church of Jesus Christ of Latter-day Saints is established for the instruction of men; and is one of God's instrumentalities for making known the truth; yet [God] is not limited to that institution for such purposes, neither in time nor place. God raises up wise men and prophets here and there among all the children of men, of their own tongue and nationality, speaking to them through means that they can comprehend; . . . Mormonism holds, then, that all the great teachers are servants of God, among all nations and in all ages. They are inspired men, appointed to instruct God's children according to the conditions in the midst of which he finds them."[4]

In the April 1921 general conference, Elder Whitney observed that God "is using not only his covenant people, but other peoples as well, to consummate a work, stupendous, magnificent, and altogether too arduous for this little handful of Saints to accomplish by and of themselves."[5]

LDS appreciation of the role of religious founders and philosophers can also be found in the 1978 First Presidency statement to the world regarding God's love for all mankind. This declaration states that "the great religious leaders of the world such as Mohammed, Confucius, and the Reformers, as well as philosophers including Socrates, Plato, and others, received a portion of God's light. Moral truths were given to them by God to enlighten whole nations and to bring a higher level of understanding to individuals."[6] During October 1991 general conference, Elder Howard W. Hunter summarized LDS views on religious respect and made this observation: "As members of the Church of Jesus Christ, we seek to bring all truth together. We seek to enlarge the circle of love and understanding among all the peoples of the earth. Thus we strive to establish peace and happiness, not only within Christianity but among all mankind."[7]

Other statements by Church leaders have continued to encourage members to foster amicable relations with people of other faiths by acknowledging the spiritual truth they possess, emphasizing the similarities in belief and lifestyle, and agreeing to disagree agreeably on the differences. For example, President George Albert Smith expressed this sentiment in a well-known quote: "We have come not to take away from you the truth and virtue you possess. We have come not to find fault with you nor criticize you. . . . Keep all the good that you have, and let us bring to you more good."[8]

A public statement issued by the First Presidency and the Twelve in October 1992 called upon "all people everywhere to recommit themselves to the time-honored ideals of tolerance and mutual respect. We sincerely believe that as we acknowledge one another with consideration and compassion we will discover that we can all peacefully coexist despite our deepest differences."[9]

In his speeches, writings, and interviews, President Gordon B. Hinckley has consistently advocated dialogue and mutual respect in interfaith relations. He was taught by his mother at a young age to respect those who are different, as recorded in a story from the *Friend*: "One day when President Hinckley was about five years old, he was sitting on his front porch with some friends. A family of another race walked down the street in front of the house. Young Gordon and his friends made some unkind remarks about the people. His mother heard what they said, and she took them inside to talk with them. She told them that all people are sons and daughters of God. That day he learned that we must respect and help one another, regardless of race, religion, wealth, or anything else."[10] President Hinckley has admonished members of the Church to cultivate "a spirit of affirmative gratitude" for those of differing religious, political, and philosophical persuasions, adding that "we do not in any way have to compromise our theology" in the process.[11] In response to a reporter's question during a TV interview, he gave this counsel: "Be respectful of the opinions and feelings of other people. Recognize their virtues; don't look for their faults. Look for their strengths and their virtues, and you will find strength and virtues that will be helpful in your own life."[12]

CHALLENGES TO ACCEPTING AND INCLUDING OTHERS

I am certain that the vast majority of Latter-day Saints understand these principles and are striving to be compassionate and inclusive in their relations with others. However, as my friend Reed Benson likes to say, "The biggest room in the world is the room for improvement." Experience has taught me that we as a community have a sizeable room to fill in this regard. Being aware of the problems and obstacles we face in living up to Christian ideals of interfaith respect, however, is the first step to dealing with them effectively.

As adviser to several non-LDS student groups on BYU campus and a teacher of world religions, I have had many opportunities to interact with those whose ethnicity, religion, politics, or lifestyle places them outside the BYU mainstream. We have discussed their experiences living as a minority in an LDS environment. Most of those I have known over the years expressed appreciation for our high standards and friendliness. Unfortunately, however, in too many instances, those of divergent backgrounds among us have felt excluded, demeaned, or diminished. Given the LDS ideals of acceptance and "affirmative gratitude" for those who are different, I have wondered what leads us to exhibit sometimes intolerant, unkind attitudes toward others. Why does society at large perceive us as a community characterized by insular attitudes toward outsiders? The following general observations about acceptance and inclusiveness might help us address these concerns.

1. I have observed that wherever one religion or philosophy of life dominates, it is easy, almost inevitable, for the majority to become insensitive to the minority. I do not say this to justify in any way the mistreatment that occurs, but only to observe that it seems to be a sad but universal reality. I base this on my experience living in LDS communities where those of other faiths sometimes have difficulty being accepted; on living as a Mormon minority among other Christians and

among non-Christians where I often felt the sting of prejudice, rejection, and suspicion because of my religion and nationality; and on having experienced social alienation as a religious person in a pervasively secular, even anti-religious graduate school environment and in my consulting work.

2. Factors related to our history as a church have contributed to attitudes and behaviors that sometimes contradict principles of tolerance and acceptance. For the first century or so after the Church's founding, the Saints established religious identity through differentiation rather than dialogue. They staked out a spot in the spiritual marketplace by drawing theological lines in the sand rather than seeking common ground with other religions. Now, with the Church more firmly established and successfully emerging "out of obscurity," the emphasis has shifted to interfaith respect and cooperation. But the old "us vs. them" attitudes still linger in the speech and actions of some members.

3. I have also observed that doctrinal misunderstandings often lie at the root of intolerant behavior and attitudes sometimes exhibited by Church members. Three prominent examples will illustrate.

First, sometimes Church members use a selective and therefore incomplete reading of scripture that misrepresents LDS doctrine concerning other religions. By referring only to the seemingly exclusivist language of certain scriptural passages while ignoring the scriptures' inclusivist dimensions, we unwittingly portray a sanctimonious, holier-than-thou stance that does not accurately reflect Church teachings and is offensive to nonmembers. In my comparative world religions course, I deal with this problem in the first minute of the first class period each semester. I begin the discussion by reading some scriptures familiar to all Latter-day Saints: The Church of Jesus Christ of Latter-day Saints is "the only true and living church upon the face of the whole earth" (D&C 1:30); the leaders of other faiths "draw near to me with their lips, but their hearts are far from me" and all their creeds are an "abomination" in God's sight (Joseph Smith–History 1:19); Jesus Christ is the only "way or means whereby man can be saved" (Alma 38:9).

Then I pose a question: Given this kind of language in our scriptures, why should we even bother studying other Christian and non-Christian religions at all? A lively discussion always ensues as students struggle to work through the ambiguity of two seemingly contradictory impulses in LDS doctrine: the uncompromising declaration of absolute truth restored in the latter days, and the compelling mandate to affirm and benefit from the light, virtue, and truth found in other religious traditions. Invariably, students reach the conclusion that, while we cannot compromise our testimony of restored truths, the attitude and language we choose to express that testimony make all the difference in our relations with those not of our faith. If we speak of "the only true and living Church" but ignore LDS teachings about "affirmative gratitude" for truth in all religions, we perpetuate an incomplete view of the restored gospel. We reinforce the erroneous idea that all other religions are completely false and dead and that our community does not value the spiritual experience of others.

A second source of misunderstanding that promotes division and strife is the perpetuation in the LDS community of popular myths masquerading as eternal doctrines. Among the most egregious examples of this are the speculative but widespread ideas about how premortal life affects the religious, social, and even racial status of people during mortal existence. While official LDS doctrine is unique in shedding much new light on pre-earth life and affirms a cause-effect relationship between the first and second estates (Abraham 3:24–26), we actually know very little about what that relationship is—exactly what it means from God's perspective to be "added upon." And yet, over the years, many books, articles, plays, and songs have been produced in the LDS community that flesh out the doctrinal skeleton with ideas that members often mistake as official Church teachings.

Often the most harmful forms of insensitivity and offense are innocent and unintentional. Some members have unfortunately drawn rather harmful conclusions from the pseudo-doctrines about premortality: for example, that faithful, valiant conduct in the first estate equates with being LDS, American, Caucasian, or prosperous in the second estate. The insidious inference drawn from this is that those who are born into another religion, race, nationality, or lower social class must have been less faithful and valiant in pre-earth life. You can imagine the psychological, emotional, and spiritual damage this false notion causes when someone, whether member or nonmember, from a diverse social or religious background encounters this idea. Unfortunate incidents of this type confirm that these attitudes still persist and problems still occur. In recent years, several minority LDS students have spoken publicly of their pain and disillusionment when told by well-meaning but misguided Church members that their racial status is a direct result of their lack of valor in premortality. One man wrote of being informed by his bishop that, according to "official" Church doctrine, his newly adopted, beautiful, dark-skinned daughter was born in Calcutta, India, because she was not valiant enough in her first estate to be born into more favorable physical circumstances.

Despite popular religious views on the subject, the truth is that the Church has never proffered an official statement about the complex issues related to our premortal choices and their consequences in earth life, about why some people are born into one race or religion and not another, or about how and why the Lord devises a timetable for providing the full blessings of the priesthood to his children of different racial, ethnic, and religious groups. In my opinion, Elder Bruce R. McConkie and Elder James E. Talmage articulated the most careful and satisfying statements of our doctrine on these issues: "When and where and under what circumstances are [God's children] sent to earth? . . . [T]here are no simple answers. Our finite limitations and our lack of knowledge of the innate capacities of all men do not let us envision the complexities of the Lord's system for sending his children to mortality" (McConkie).[13] "Our condition, position, situation upon the earth must be the result of causes operating before we came into possession of our mortal bodies. Now let it not be assumed that the man who counts himself most blessed in the things of the earth was, therefore, most deserving, for the things of the earth may not be, after all, the greatest blessings of God" (Talmage).[14]

My third and final example of how a skewed understanding of doctrine can lead to unkind attitudes and behavior is close to my heart and
own experience. For the past twenty-five years in my work in the
Middle East, many times I have read and heard the view that LDS
teachings about the gathering of Israel and the establishment of Zion
imply that the Church supports the Jews in their struggle with the
Palestinians and other Arabs in the Holy Land. There is not time or
space here to discuss adequately why this is an inaccurate interpreta-
tion of LDS doctrine and a misrepresentation of the Church's stance
on this extremely complex international political issue. Suffice it to say
for now that LDS authors, speakers, teachers, and celebrities who advocate and perpetuate these views are not official spokespersons for the
Church, even though they are often perceived and cited as such. Many
times over the years I have spoken with Arabs and Muslims, including
many students at BYU, who are friends of the Church but, having read
this popular LDS literature about the Middle East conflict, are deeply
troubled by what appears to be strong bias in favor of Israel. Some of
these unofficial and inflammatory LDS writings have even appeared in
Arab newspapers in the Middle East purporting to represent the
Mormon view on this issue. This problem is especially painful for members of the Church who are Arab (and they are numerous, active, committed, many having served missions and been endowed in the temple)
who love the gospel but are greatly perplexed and saddened when they
encounter attitudes among fellow members that reflect a pro-Israeli,
anti-Arab prejudice.

Those who do speak officially for the Church—the First Presidency
and the Twelve—have never expressed support for one side over
another. On the contrary, they have exhibited scrupulous impartiality
in all their utterances and actions dealing with the Middle East crisis
and have sought tirelessly to build strong relations with both Jews and
Arabs in an effort to bring about greater peace and stability in the
region. Elder Howard W. Hunter, who had in-depth understanding of
Middle Eastern issues, once addressed this concern in a talk at BYU:
"As members of the Lord's church, we need to lift our vision beyond

personal prejudices. We need to discover the supreme truth that indeed our Father is no respecter of persons. Sometimes we unduly offend brothers and sisters of other nations by assigning exclusiveness to one nationality of people over another. Let me cite, as an example of exclusiveness, the present problem in the Middle East—the conflict between the Arabs and the Jews. . . . Both the Jews and the Arabs are children of our Father. They are both children of promise, and as a church we do not take sides. We have love for and an interest in each."[15]

An unexpected but beneficial outcome of open-minded interaction with friends of other faiths is greater awareness of what is truly unique in one's own tradition. While Diane and I have learned to look for and appreciate the common ground of shared morals, ethics, and beliefs, we have also learned to appreciate how differences define us and help us understand more fully what it means to be a Latter-day Saint and what sets the restored gospel apart. Examining our similarities and differences with non-LDS friends has deepened our testimony of unique LDS doctrines—the nature of God, eternal progression, continuing revelation, temple work, and priesthood authority—that are problematic for nonmembers but form, we have concluded, the foundation of the gospel's power, beauty, and appeal throughout the world.

Notes

1. Joseph Smith, *Teachings of the Prophet Joseph Smith*, sel., Joseph Fielding Smith (Salt Lake City: Deseret Book, 1938), 313.
2. Ibid., 316.
3. Ibid., 146–47, 314.
4. B. H. Roberts, *Defense of the Faith and the Saints*, 2 vols. (Salt Lake City: Deseret News, 1907), 1:512.
5. Orson F. Whitney, Conference Report, April 1921, 32–33.
6. Quoted in Spencer J. Palmer, *The Expanding Church* (Salt Lake City: Deseret Book, 1978), v; also in Spencer J. Palmer, ed., *Mormons and Muslims: Spiritual Foundations and Modern Manifestations* (Provo: BYU Religious Studies Center, 1983), 208.
7. Howard W. Hunter, "The Gospel—A Global Faith," *Ensign*, November 1991, 18.

8. *Sharing the Gospel with Others: Excerpts from the Sermons of President George Albert Smith,* ed. Preston Nibley (Salt Lake City: Deseret Book, 1948), 12–13.

9. Quoted in Russell M. Nelson, "Teach Us Tolerance and Love," *Ensign,* May 1994, 71; see also *Church News,* 24 October 1992, 4.

10. Diane S. Nichols, "Heavenly Father Prepares the Prophet," *The Friend,* March 2001, 16.

11. Gordon B. Hinckley, "Out of Your Experience Here," *BYU Today,* March 1991, 37; also in Sheri L. Dew, *Go Forward with Faith: The Biography of Gordon B. Hinckley* (Salt Lake City: Deseret Book, 1996), 536.

12. Quoted in Sheri L. Dew, *Go Forward with Faith: The Biography of Gordon B. Hinckley* (Salt Lake City: Deseret Book, 1996), 576.

13. Bruce R. McConkie, *A New Witness for the Articles of Faith* (Salt Lake City: Deseret Book, 1985), 35.

14. James E. Talmage, "The Pre-Existence of Man," *Liahona, The Elder's Journal* 5 (29 February 1908), 990–95.

15. Howard W. Hunter, "All Are Alike Unto God," *BYU Speeches of the Year* (Provo: Brigham Young University Press, 1979), 35–36; see also Howard W. Hunter, *That We Might Have Joy* (Salt Lake City: Deseret Book, 1994), 74, 75.

Teaching Tolerance, Empathy, and Understanding

Diane Toronto

How do we teach our children to accept and include as friends those with different beliefs? What can our children learn from those of other faiths that strengthens their testimonies of the restored gospel? The real question, of course, is this: How do we adults first learn to do this? How can we—the mothers, fathers, teachers, and leaders—learn from the spiritual experience of others in a way that allows us to lead our children to have compassion and respect for those who differ from us?

When I was in fifth grade, I had to get glasses because I couldn't see the chalkboard at school and the world at large was fuzzy. I still remember coming out of the doctor's office sporting my new cat's-eye glasses and seeing for the first time details in buildings and faces, even the individual leaves on trees. I read every sign and billboard on the way home. I was amazed that a simple pair of glasses could clear my vision so dramatically. Suddenly I could see what had been beyond my normal range.

I grew up in a small but wonderful community in southern Idaho: Declo. I can remember only three teachers and a handful of kids at school that were not LDS. My exposure to significant people in my life who were not LDS was minimal. My exposure to non-Christians was limited to one. As I moved away to college, not much changed. I may have had what you could call "an inner near-sightedness." My vision was limited to the many good people in my community who were also

---

Diane Gillett Toronto has B.S. and M.Ed. degrees from Brigham Young University and has taught elementary school in Utah, Massachusetts, Saudi Arabia, Egypt, and Jordan. She serves in her ward Primary presidency. Diane and her husband, James A. Toronto, are the parents of Joseph, serving a mission in Italy, and Jenna, a junior in high school.

members of my church. This was not a bad thing; in fact, I believe it was the very reason that my parents sacrificed a very good job with the government and moved to Declo. They wanted a small town setting where they could raise their children in a safe environment, surrounded with good people, and have more time to spend with them.

After college, marriage, and a couple of years of teaching school, Jim and I moved to the Middle East. In this area of the world, Christians aren't allowed to proselyte, and so we shared our testimony of the gospel through example. Exposed for the first time to a variety of people from different Christian backgrounds, and to a whole multitude of people who weren't even Christians, my vision was again blurred. I needed an inner corrective lens. I remember my surprise at finding very good people in the world who were not LDS. It was like putting on those glasses again as a ten-year-old and realizing those individual faces that I could now see with such clarity were also Heavenly Father's much loved children. I could see inside them and knew that they valued many of the same things that I do.

As Jim and I came to know these wonderful people, my fears of associating with them left as did their fears of us. I was surprised to learn that they had feared me because of my "strange" religion!

To illustrate, I would like to share two experiences from that time in the Middle East. Jim was studying Arabic intensively at the American University in Cairo. In his group of students was a young Baptist minister named Randall. Randall and his wife, Nancy, lived only blocks from us. We had many things in common: income (or lack thereof), children, church duties (just different churches), husbands who were learning Arabic and coaching our children in soccer, and a Thursday night date routine that took us to find good, safe food. On many occasions we made that search together. As our friendship grew, barriers between us came down.

One night Jim and I were driving Nancy home through the back streets of our neighborhood when suddenly she said, "We really like you guys and we are worried that you won't be saved." I immediately responded, "We really like you guys, too, and have been praying for you." We told one another of our beliefs about what happens after this life and our hopes and fears for each other. We each left enlightened.

A few days later Nancy again broached the subject. This time she expanded on her new vision (which is what I had also been doing). She told us that knowing us had changed her view of people from our church. She had often heard negative things about our church. But once she got to know us she realized that we valued the same things. Most important, our conversations helped her to believe that people from our church were Christians after all. Our friendship helped both of us better understand each other's beliefs—and alleviate fears on both sides. By focusing on the common beliefs we shared, our vision of each other as children of Heavenly Father came into clearer focus.

The second experience took place while we were living and teaching school in Amman, Jordan. I had an aide, named Wafa, who was a Muslim. In the course of working together, we talked about our hopes and fears for our children growing up in today's world. One morning I was especially troubled over something that my children had done or said. Wafa simply said, "Have you prayed to God about your problem?" This advice came from a Muslim woman who had prayed for her own children. She was a woman of faith. Here I was supposed to be the example, but being so careful not to say anything about religion in this Muslim country, I had not communicated to her my own belief in God or in answers to my prayers. Instead she was taking the lead and was trying to help me by teaching me that God answers prayers. From then on, we often talked about our religious views and the common thread of a loving Heavenly Father who cares for all of his children. I had lost my fear of speaking about religion to her and discussed with her the beliefs we both shared. These experiences strengthened my testimony of a loving Heavenly Father who cares about all of his children— Christian, Muslim, Jew—all! (See 2 Nephi 26:33).

LEADING THE WAY

To teach children to accept and include those with different beliefs, we must be examples for them. Are you, as parents, teachers, and leaders, accepting of others? Do you include people of different beliefs in your life? I hope my two stories have conveyed the idea that we need to eliminate fears and preconceived ideas about other people and their beliefs. Other religions have truths. Focus on the truths that we have in common and invite conversation that can promote greater understanding. Doing these two things in a family setting can help teach our children by our example that we do care about people of other faiths.

We can also teach our children to be accepting and inclusive by helping them serve people—all people.

The fifth grade teacher at my school in Amman, Jordan, was the director of the Catholic congregation's music. At Christmastime she was in charge of the choir for the midnight mass at the monastery at Mt. Nebo. There weren't enough Catholics in the country to make a good choir, so she asked Jim and me to help her by singing in the choir. We recruited our children and many of our branch members. Soon the choir seats were full. We participated in their services and exposed our children to another religious service. Our children, in turn, saw their friends from school in their religious setting and gained an appreciation for the way they worshiped. The experience built bridges and made lasting memories for our family. We had so much fun singing that we volunteered again the following year.

Closer to home my sister and her family get to know their neighbors of diverse religions by doing little service projects for them: a plate of cookies, a lawn mowed, an early morning walk—killing them with kindness and then talking to them as friends—breaking down barriers.

LDS students and families from several local communities have given many hours of labor in helping build the Hare Krishna temple in Spanish Fork, Utah. The leader of the Hare Krishna temple speaks only in glowing terms of the help that has poured in from the community, including a $20,000 donation from the LDS Church. He loves his LDS neighbors. He even mentioned that some of his worshipers wearing turbans can hardly walk for any distance before someone pulls over and asks if they need a ride somewhere. He also says that he has received so many invitations to events from our church that he has to be selective in the ones he commits to. What a sterling example of an inclusive and accepting community.

A third point that I feel is important in teaching our children to be accepting and inclusive is communication. Talk to your families about what it means to be inclusive. Let them ask questions. Our children need to feel comfortable asking questions, knowing that we will listen to their concerns and experiences. In our family, Jim is especially good at this. If he heard the children talking about the weird way their friends prayed or commenting about their religious symbolism, he would use that as a teaching moment and tell the kids what their friends were doing and why. Sometimes he would even relate it to a similar form of worship in our own faith. Our children grew up respecting their friends for their religious beliefs.

A neighbor, Jennifer, told me that she has only one sister who is a member of the Church. When her children get together with their cousins who aren't members of the Church, they often learn something about their cousins' beliefs as they talk. One time the cousins said that the Godhead is one being. The children had questions that weren't immediately answered. Later during family scripture time, Jennifer's family read passages from the New Testament that answered those very questions. "This is so clear," they would say. "Why don't our cousins read the scriptures and find these answers for themselves?" Jennifer then explained that they have a modern translation of the Bible and other people have translated these passages to say that the Godhead is one being. Again, keeping the communication open and answering questions is critical.

Jennifer also told her children that differences will arise as they have these conversations with their cousins. They can have an attitude of learning and make it a positive experience, or they can be closed, intolerant, and angry during these discussions. Their attitudes will make all the difference. It will open doors or close doors.

Recently I asked many of my neighbors, family members, and friends how they would teach their children to be inclusive and respectful. My son, who is now nineteen, said, "Teach them while they are young." In my elementary school classroom, I use children's books to teach children about diversity. Together we read a story. Afterwards we list all of the ways that the child in the book is like the children in our classroom, and then we list the ways we are different. The children are always amazed at the many ways we are alike. There are many books that celebrate cultural and religious diversity. Use them as teaching tools.

Another friend, Pam, who joined the Church several years after associating with many good Latter-day Saints, gave this advice: "Be friends with people from all religions and don't ditch them when you find that they may not be interested in the gospel at a certain time in their lives." Others said, if you invite people to your church activities, be willing to accept invitations to their religious functions. It is not enough to tolerate; be open and accepting. Get to know and care about the people around you. If you sincerely care about them as people and children of God, it will show.

A friend mentioned that her children were occasionally invited to attend services of another denomination. She always encouraged them to go, feeling the contrast of different religious services was good for them. She helped them to see the truths in other religions while explaining that our church had additional truth. She had no fear that her children would leave the Church because they were and are well founded in their own beliefs. Her final comment was, "Truth stands on its own. The gospel can stand up to scrutiny." We seek truth wherever it is found. As we broaden our view of people around us, we receive a clearer vision of all the love Heavenly Father has for us and for all of his children.

BUILDING TESTIMONY THROUGH INTERFAITH RELATIONS

Based on our experience, Jim and I propose three ways to learn from those who differ from us socially, politically, and religiously. First, have empathy. Try to see things from their point of view, to understand their experience through their eyes and from their sources. If you want a friend or colleague to understand the depth, beauty, and appeal of the restored gospel and what it means to be LDS, you probably won't recommend they see *The Godmakers*. By the same token, don't see *Not without My Daughter* or read only newspaper accounts of terrorist activities to learn about the Islamic view of women's status and social change. Second, make fair comparisons. Don't compare the worst of theirs to the best of ours. Intellectual and spiritual integrity require that as we examine other belief systems, we hold up the mirror of self-scrutiny to our own community before we draw conclusions. For example, the eminent historian Jan Shipps, a specialist in Mormon history though she herself is not LDS, recently described in a lecture the reaction of her non-LDS students at the University of Illinois after their first reading of LDS history and theology. "How can intelligent, sane people believe anything that is so outrageous and irrational?" Her reply reflects the kind of honesty and fairness that we should aspire to as we interface with other religions: "The story of the First Vision and gold plates from an angel is not any crazier than the story of a dead man, Jesus, coming alive again and floating up to heaven. All religions believe things that can't be proved rationally." Third, have a humble heart and open mind. As admonished by the Savior and the prophets, be teachable, constantly seeking spiritual light and religious insight wherever it may be found.

Let me share some specific examples of how applying these three ground rules—empathy, fairness, and humility—in an interfaith setting has helped our family over the years learn much from our brothers and sisters of other faiths, while increasing our testimonies and understanding of gospel truths.

Jim's association with Eastern religions, particularly Buddhism, Hinduism, and Taoism, has reinforced to us the importance of finding quiet time for reflection, meditation, and pondering as a prerequisite for receiving spiritual peace, strength, and insight. A few years ago, with several BYU colleagues he visited Bodhgaya, India, the site of the Buddha's enlightenment, very early one morning. Underneath the Boddhi tree next to the main temple sat a Buddhist monk, cross-legged, perfectly still, intently focused on connecting with the Ultimate Reality for him: the Buddha nature within. Jim says that he has been inspired many times since then by the peace and serenity he felt in that spot and at that moment, a reminder of the many injunctions in LDS tradition to take time to be alone to refresh our spirits and renew our relationship with Heavenly Father. President Gordon B. Hinckley recently reminded church members of this eternal principle: "You need time to meditate and ponder, to think, to wonder at the great plan of happiness that the Lord has outlined for His children. . . .

"I heard President David O. McKay say to the members of the Twelve on one occasion, 'Brethren, we do not spend enough time meditating.'

"I believe that with all my heart. Our lives become extremely busy. We run from one thing to another. We wear ourselves out in thoughtless pursuit of goals which are highly ephemeral. We are entitled to spend some time with ourselves in introspection, in development."[1]

On many occasions, Jim and I have had the privilege of participating in Jewish rituals of worship, whether in homes for Sabbath eve and Passover services or in the synagogue for Torah reading and Bar Mitzvahs. We have observed with great interest the verbatim prayers and liturgy and the symbolic use of special clothing, objects, and actions. We have noted how comfortable and joyous the Jews are as they engage in these ancient rituals which provide a sense of perspective, meaning, and identity in their lives. By visiting synagogues, mosques, temples, and shrines and seeing how important ritual is in other religious communities, we have gained new insight and appreciation for the vital role of ritual in our own spiritual lives as we partake of the sacrament and attend the temple.

While living in Cairo, we were invited by a Muslim friend, Nabil, to participate in his family's evening "break-fast" meal during the month of fasting, Ramadan. As we entered their modest apartment in one of the most impoverished quarters of Cairo, we noticed in one room numerous peasant women (distinguishable by their black clothing) and their children all sitting on the floor with food spread out before them on a cloth, quietly waiting for the call to prayer that marks the end of fasting each day. When we asked if they were his relatives, he replied, "No, I don't know any of them. It is our habit to invite strangers off the street who cannot afford good food to share our Ramadan meal. We do this because it was one of the customs of our prophet, Muhammad." We were deeply moved by our Muslim friend's unselfishness and compassion for the poor. We were reminded of how many times friends and colleagues of other faiths have been exemplary in living principles of kindness, generosity, and charity for the outcasts in society. These evidences of truth and goodness in other religions do not weaken our testimonies; rather, they reinforce our gratitude for LDS teachings about a God of infinite love who reveals eternal truth to all of his children according to their readiness to accept it.

My final example is closer to home. Down the street from our home is the Rock Canyon Assembly of God, a protestant congregation located in the Edgemont area of Provo, one of the most intensely LDS areas on the planet. They are a religious minority if ever there was one. In mingling with them and talking with their leader, Reverend Dean Jackson, we became aware of a remarkable spirit of humility, forgiveness, and reaching out to others that is an inspiring example to all Christians. A few years ago, the congregants signed a petition expressing remorse and asking forgiveness for the ill-will they have felt at times towards their LDS neighbors. The petition, which was presented to a group of LDS church leaders and now hangs in the Joseph Smith building at Brigham Young University, reads in part: "In an effort to allow God's ministry of reconciliation to us to be evident in our lives, we the undersigned do hereby declare that in times past our attitudes and actions toward members of The Church of Jesus Christ of Latter-day Saints have been completely unlike that which was demonstrated through the example of our Lord and Savior Jesus Christ. We therefore join . . . in humble and sincere repentance for this behavior. Having received forgiveness from God, we now ask for forgiveness from the members of [the LDS Church]." Reverend Jackson reports that this effort at interfaith reconciliation has brought about "a whole deeper level" in his congregation as members have begun to overcome their suspicion and fears of Mormons and even to attend LDS ward parties![2] We find their actions to be humbling and motivating: humbling because of the profound example of Christlike love exhibited by a religious minority in our own backyard, and motivating because of the desire it stirs in us to seek to alleviate the sense of alienation—of being "strangers and foreigners"—that they and others like them have felt over the years living in the LDS heartland.

That experience has confirmed the truthfulness of Paul's admonition to "entertain strangers," for thereby we have indeed entertained "angels" who have blessed us with righteous example and spiritual light. Jim and I add our testimony to President Hinckley's that if we "look for [the strength and virtues of others, we] will find strength and virtues that will be helpful in [our] own life."

In conclusion, Jim and I have found that the only way to teach our children to accept and learn from those who are different is to first learn to do so ourselves. To set an example of respect and tolerance, we must correctly understand LDS doctrines about our Heavenly Father's love for all his children and about the truths he has revealed throughout history to bless their lives. Latter-day Saints believe that it is vital to acknowledge and benefit from the spiritual light found in other religions, while seeking humbly to share the additional measure of eternal truth provided by latter-day revelation.

The Prophet Joseph Smith, in one of his most eloquent pronouncements on respect and compassion, taught that Heavenly Father will take complex circumstances into account and judge the lives of all his children based on a divine, merciful perspective that surpasses our limited human understanding: "While one portion of the human race is judging and condemning the other without mercy, the Great Parent of the universe looks upon the whole of the human family with a fatherly care and paternal regard; He views them as His offspring, and without any of those contracted feelings that influence the children of men. . . . He holds the reins of judgment in His hands; He is a wise Lawgiver, and will judge all men, not according to the narrow, contracted notions of men . . . [and] 'not according to what they have not, but according to what they have.' . . . Those who have a law, will be judged by that law."[3]

May we have such vision and testimony of God's love for his children of all walks of life that we willingly "treasure up" divine light wherever it has been revealed and "entertain strangers" among us, thus discovering "angels" who teach and inspire us. May we "bear record of . . . Christ" in our lives by dismantling "walls of partition"—intolerance, pride, suspicion, and rivalry—and by teaching our children to love and learn from our brothers and sisters of different backgrounds, viewing them no more as "strangers and foreigners."

Notes

1. Gordon B. Hinckley, "Life's Obligations," *Ensign*, February 1999, 5.
2. Dean Merrill, "A Peacemaker in Provo: How One Pentecostal Pastor Taught His Congregation to Love Mormons," *Christianity Today* (7 February 2000): 66–72.
3. Joseph Smith, *Teachings of the Prophet Joseph Smith*, sel. Joseph Fielding Smith (Salt Lake City: Deseret Book, 1938), 218.

BEARING RECORD OF CHRIST

Merrill J. Bateman

The theme of this year's women's conference volume is taken from Doctrine and Covenants 68:6: "Wherefore, be of good cheer, and do not fear, for I the Lord am with you, and will stand by you; and ye shall bear record of me, even Jesus Christ, that I am the Son of the living God, that I was, that I am, and that I am to come." The scripture reminds us of our responsibility to be ardent witnesses for the Savior, who is the Son of the living God. The Savior said in his intercessory prayer that it is "life eternal, [to] know thee the only true God, and Jesus Christ, whom thou hast sent" (John 17:3). Through the restored gospel, we know more about the Father and Son and our relationship with them than any other people. Thus, we carry a major responsibility to share that knowledge with the world.

TO WHOM SHALL WE BEAR RECORD?

All of us understand that every nation, kindred, tongue, and people must hear the gospel. But are there priorities? Our first responsibility in bearing witness of Christ and his gospel is to our own families. The family is a divine institution designed to build faith in each succeeding generation, to link families in an unbroken chain from Adam to the last faithful child born. Children can live on borrowed light for a limited time only. They must be taught and encouraged to obtain their own witness so they may choose to be obedient to gospel

Merrill J. Bateman, a member of the First Quorum of the Seventy, serves as president of Brigham Young University. He has served as presiding bishop of the Church and as dean of the College of Business and School of Management at BYU. He and his wife, Marilyn, are the parents of seven children and grandparents of twenty.

truths. From Adam to the present day, the building of intergenerational families of faith has been the hallmark of Zion (Moses 5:12; Deuteronomy 6:6–7; D&C 68:25, 28). The plan of happiness depends on linking parents to children and children to parents—in faith and by covenant. Moroni warned Joseph Smith that "the whole earth would be utterly wasted" if the "hearts of the children" were not turned to their parents and the parents to the children (D&C 2:3, 2).

The Proclamation on the Family reconfirms the importance of home and family in the Lord's plan. In part it states: "By divine design, fathers are to preside over their families in love and righteousness and are responsible to provide the necessities of life and protection for their families. Mothers are primarily responsible for the nurture of their children. In these sacred responsibilities, fathers and mothers are obligated to help one another as equal partners."[1]

Although both parents are responsible for teaching the young, women—mothers, grandmothers, sisters, and aunts—are equipped with a special spiritual gift of nurturing which creates a bond with children and makes women effective teachers. I am reminded of the stripling warriors of Helaman, who were taught the gospel by their mothers. Helaman describes these young men as follows: "They were men who were true at all times in whatsoever thing they were entrusted. . . . they had been taught by their mothers, that if they did not doubt, God would deliver them. And they rehearsed unto me the words of their mothers, saying: We do not doubt our mothers knew it" (Alma 53:20; 56:47–48). The influence of a mother is profound.

Doctrine and Covenants 68 states clearly the Lord's instructions to parents in Zion. They are to teach their children "the doctrine of repentance, faith in Christ the Son of the living God, and of baptism and the gift of the Holy Ghost . . . [and] to pray, and . . . walk uprightly before the Lord" (D&C 68:25, 28). The first responsibility of parents is to bear record of Christ to their family, to help each member put on the shield of faith (D&C 27:15–17).[2] The Church can assist, but most of the work must be done in the home. It is critical that each faithful generation be linked with the next so men and women may receive a fulness of joy and the earth not "be utterly wasted" but fulfill its purpose and destiny.

When we have taken care of our families, our second responsibility is to our neighbor. Unless we have a formal mission call, most of our work will be across the street or around the corner among acquaintances within the communities in which we live.

In proclaiming the gospel, love is the key that opens doors. Jesus said that his disciples would be known by the love they have for one another (John 13:35). I believe that missionaries in the field receive a special gift of love for the people they are called to serve. Newly returned missionaries often say that they served in the greatest mission and among the best people on earth. These feelings frequently come early in their mission as a gift from the Holy Ghost to help them become effective teachers and witnesses. Love is a gift of the Spirit for which we should pray, asking the Lord to bless us with special feelings for those whom we may influence.

The parable of the good Samaritan teaches us how to build strong relationships with our neighbor. It is through acts of service. The Levite and the priest, not wanting to be involved with the injured traveler, passed by on the other side of the road. Sometimes, we, like the two priests, pass by opportunities to share the gospel. Generally, we worry that we will offend our neighbor. If this is the case, why not follow the example of the good Samaritan? He did not ask the man his religion or try to convert him while he was lying on the ground. He simply bound up the man's wounds, set him on his animal, took him to the nearest inn, and paid for his care (Luke 10:30–37).

As members of the Church, we can serve our neighbors with quiet acts of kindness and pray that they will ask us questions that will allow us to bear record of Christ. Once a relationship of trust is established, opportunities to share emerge. Over time, neighbors will experience significant events that will open doors to teach fundamental truths. Events such as births, deaths, and marriages, trials and disappointments in life will often open doors to teach precious, fundamental truths.

A Unique Message Concerning Christ

The unique truths of the restored gospel concerning Christ can best be explained by following the format outlined in Doctrine and Covenants 68:6. There the Lord tells Joseph Smith how we should bear record of him—that he is the "Son of the living God, that I was, that I am, and that I am to come." The statement emphasizes the relationship Christ has with the Father in the context of his premortal life, his life on earth, and his future return.

Christ is the literal Son of the living God. This is the most important fact to know about him. Most Christian creeds acknowledge that Christ is the Son, but they do not know what that means. The Athanasian creed teaches that "the Father, Son, and Holy Ghost form a Trinity, but they are unified in One Substance. Each of them is Incomprehensible, but there is only One Incomprehensible. Each is eternal, but there is only One Eternal."[3] The major Protestant churches teach that God is "without body, parts, or passions."[4] Elder James E. Talmage commented on these statements as follows: "It would be difficult to conceive of a greater number of inconsistencies and contradictions, expressed in words as few. . . . The immateriality of God as asserted in these declarations of sectarian faith is entirely at variance with the scriptures, and absolutely contradicted by the revelations of God's person and attributes."[5]

Fortunately for us, the First Vision clearly establishes the individuality of the Father and the Son—each has an immortalized, glorified body of flesh and bones. Revelation also teaches that the Holy Ghost is a separate personage but one of spirit (Joseph Smith–History 1:16–17; D&C 130:22). A review of the Savior's premortality, his time on earth, and his future return will put in perspective the important relationship that Christ has with the Father. It also helps us understand our relationship to them.

The Premortal World—I Was

Through modern-day revelation we learn that Christ had a conscious, intelligent existence as a personage of spirit before coming to this earth (Abraham 3:27–28). We believe that Christ was the first-born spirit son of Heavenly Parents, with God as his father (Colossians 1:15; D&C 110:4). Modern revelation also teaches that "spirit is matter, but it is more refined or pure, and can only be discerned by purer eyes" (D&C 131:7). Thus a spirit person is not an ethereal wisp of nothingness. A spirit person consists of matter that resembles a person in the flesh. We further believe that every person born on this earth lived in that same premortal world of spirits and was an intelligent offspring of that same Father, with Jesus as our eldest brother (Numbers 16:22; Colossians 1:15; Hebrews 2:17; Abraham 3:27–28).

In the premortal world Jesus was known as Jehovah, the God of the Old Testament (1 Nephi 21:26; Moses 3:5–8). Through his seniority as the oldest and because of the light and truth within him, he was a god before coming to earth (John 1:1). We also know that he was the Creator of the worlds under the direction of the Father (Moses 1:32–33).

A Grand Council took place in the world of spirits, and Father presented a plan for the progression of his children. We know of Satan's opposition, that he was cast out and he drew many spirits with him. The Father's plan granted us agency, the right to choose good or evil, and the Father knew that all of us would sin. The only way to reach our ultimate goal was through a Savior, someone who would voluntarily atone for and redeem the repentant sinner. Jesus, or Jehovah, was called and foreordained to be the sacrificial lamb—the mediator of the covenant made between the Father and his children (1 Peter 1:19–20; Abraham 3:22–28).

Our doctrines concerning the premortal world are unique. Few people on earth understand that we lived before coming to earth and that mortality is the second act in a multi-act drama.

The spirit personage passes through four stages. The first is the unembodied state in the spirit world, of which we have been speaking. The second is an embodied state, which is earth life, or mortality. The third is a disembodied state—the time between death and resurrection. A re-embodied, or resurrected, state is the final stage. Every spirit person passes through these stages. Individuals still wait in the spirit world for their turn in mortality. At the present time, six billion people are living on earth "to see if they will do all things whatsoever the Lord their God shall command them" (Abraham 3:25). And billions have passed on to the postmortal sphere to await the resurrection. The Savior and the righteous who lived prior to his time on earth plus a few others have reached the fourth or final stage, that of re-embodiment (Matthew 27:52–53; Joseph Smith–History 1:33). In every phase or estate we are dependent on Christ and his atonement, even in the premortal world (D&C 93:38; John 15:1–8; D&C 138; Moroni 10:32–33).[6]

Mortality—I Am

The second stage of the Savior's life was mortality, or life on earth. The Savior's unique earthly heritage received from a mortal mother and an immortal Father is critical to understanding his mission and atonement. From Mary he received the seeds of mortality, which gave him the capacity to die. As the Only Begotten in the flesh, he obtained immortal seeds from his Father, which meant that he could live forever (John 1:14). He is not only the Son of the living God in the world of spirits but also the Son of the living God in mortality. Jesus told his listeners on one occasion, "For as the Father hath life in himself; so hath he given to the Son to have life in himself" (John 5:26).

Later Jesus told the Jews: "Therefore doth my Father love me, because I lay down my life, that I might take it again. No man taketh it from me, but I lay it down of myself. I have power to lay it down, and I have power to take it again. This commandment have I received of my Father" (John 10:17–18).

Jesus had the power to live forever. Death for him was a choice. He did not have to die. The Atonement was a voluntary sacrifice by an infinite and eternal being (Alma 34:10, 14). Because of his immortal heritage, he had the capacity to suffer the consequences of sin for all mankind. The Savior revealed to the Prophet Joseph the awfulness of that experience. He said: "For behold, I, God, have suffered these things for all, that they might not suffer if they would repent; . . .

Which suffering caused myself, even God, the greatest of all, to tremble because of pain, and to bleed at every pore, and to suffer both body and spirit—and would that I might not drink the bitter cup, and shrink" (D&C 19:16, 18).

In addition to sin, he experienced the pains, sufferings, sicknesses, temptations, and weaknesses of each person who has ever lived on the earth or who ever will live on it, in order to "know according to the flesh how to succor his people according to their infirmities" (Alma 7:12). The Atonement was not only infinite and eternal in its consequences but also intimate. Jesus came to know each of us in a way that allows him to support us in times of need, to heal the broken heart, to perfect us and to pull us under his wings (Moroni 10:32–33). It is important that we share this knowledge about Christ, his mission, his atoning sacrifice, and his power with others and bring them to Christ.

We also have a clearer view of the resurrection and its importance because we understand the role played by the physical body in the eternities. In contrast to much of Christianity, which believes that the body shackles the spirit, we recognize the body as one of the grand prizes of mortality. We look forward to the day when our bodies and spirits are inseparably connected through the resurrection, bringing us a fulness of joy (D&C 93:33–34). In that day, the body will be incorruptible, resistant to disease, decay, and death. And it will have the power of eternal life if we prove worthy (D&C 131:4).

HE WILL COME AGAIN

Prophets from the beginning of time have prophesied not only of Jesus' first coming but also of his second. The first time he came as a newborn babe in humble circumstances. His second coming will be in power and great glory (Matthew 25:31). He will come unexpectedly "as a thief in the night" (2 Peter 3:10). His first visit will be to one of his homes—the temple (Malachi 3:1).

He will also visit the Mount of Olives, the scene of his discussion with the Twelve regarding his second coming. The prophet Zechariah prophesied that Jesus would stand on the Mount and show those there the marks of the crucifixion. In turn, the people will ask, "What are these wounds in thine hands? Then he shall answer, Those with which I was wounded in the house of my friends" (Zechariah 13:6). Zechariah indicates that there will be great mourning in Jerusalem as they look upon him whom they pierced, "and they shall mourn for him, as one mourneth for his only son, and shall be in bitterness for him, as one that is in bitterness for his firstborn" (Zechariah 12:10). Zechariah understood the relationship of the Savior to the Father both in the premortal sphere as well as in mortality.

As Zechariah notes, Jesus will return with the identifying marks in his hands, feet, and side, evidence of his crucifixion and atonement. Just as the Nephites "fell to the earth" in reverence, so the Jews will in that future day recognize the great sacrifice he made for them and all mankind. I suspect he will invite them, as he did the Nephites, to come one by one to "thrust their hands into his side, and [to] feel the prints of the nails in his hands and in his feet" that they may "know of a surety and . . . bear record, that it [is] he, of whom it was written by the prophets, that should come" (3 Nephi 11:15).

One of the signs of the Second Coming is that the gospel will be "preached in all the world for a witness unto all nations" (Matthew 24:14). Within eighteen months of the establishment of the Church, the Lord told Joseph Smith that the restored gospel should be taken to "every nation, and kindred, and tongue, and people" (D&C 133:37). The Lord's directive remains in force. The opportunity is ours to share the singular message of the restored gospel with our family and our neighbors.

I bear witness that Jesus is the Son of the living God, our eldest Brother in the spirit world. He was foreordained before the foundations of this earth to be the Savior of all mankind. This earth was his footstool. This is the earth chosen from among all the earths he created to be the place of his birth, ministry, and atonement. I know that the day will come when you and I will kneel at his feet and express our profound love for him and deep gratitude that he did not shrink in partaking of the bitter cup. It is my prayer that we will prove faithful.

Notes

1. First Presidency and Council of the Twelve Apostles of The Church of Jesus Christ of Latter-day Saints, "The Family: A Proclamation to the World," *Ensign*, November 1995, 102.

2. See, for example, Boyd K. Packer, "The Shield of Faith," *Ensign*, May 1995, 8.

3. Bruce R. McConkie, *Mormon Doctrine*, 2d ed. (Salt Lake City: Bookcraft, 1966), 55–56; s.v. "Athanasian Creed."

4. James E. Talmage, *Articles of Faith*, 12th ed. (Salt Lake City: The Church of Jesus Christ of Latter-day Saints, 1955), 48.

5. Ibid., 48.

6. See Robert J. Matthews, *Behold the Messiah* (Salt Lake City: Bookcraft, 1994), 3–4.

IN GIVING ALL WE HAVE

⋊⃝⋉

Gail Miller

I was born of goodly parents who taught me to love the Savior and the truths of his gospel. My favorite bedtime stories came from a wonderful Bible storybook with captivating illustrations on every other page that made the stories come alive for me. I learned to be secure in the knowledge that I am a child of God and that my Heavenly Father loves me. I had a happy, carefree childhood. During my teenage years, our ward had great competitive teams, and I loved playing softball, volleyball, and basketball. When I turned eighteen and was no longer eligible to play ball with the young women, I felt out of place at church. Besides, my job as a telephone operator required me to work on Sunday, and it was easy to lose my connection to my ward. Soon I was working full time, dating in my spare time, and found myself almost entirely inactive in the Church.

In 1965 I married my high school sweetheart who was also from a strong LDS family. Larry and I had good jobs, lived in a nice apartment, and felt that life was good. Our first son was born the following year. We felt happy and self-sufficient—so much so that neither of us gave much thought to involving ourselves in church activity, prayer, scripture reading, or any kind of church service.

During those early married years, Larry played competitive softball at a world class level. His Salt Lake City team was struggling, and in 1970 he was recruited to pitch for a team in Denver. We moved our

---

Gail Miller is the founder of a nonprofit organization to help women and children in jeopardy. She is active in civic service and has served in two stake and several ward Relief Society presidencies. She and her husband, Larry, are the parents of five children and grandparents of nineteen.

small family, which now included two sons, from Salt Lake City to Littleton, Colorado. Because we had not been attending church in Salt Lake, our records did not follow us. One morning when we had been in Littleton for about a year, our oldest son, who was then about five, asked, "Mommy, where does God live?" I knew instantly that I had been neglecting core truths deeply imbedded in my soul. I had failed to feed my spirit, and now I was neglecting to feed the souls of my children. The boys were loved, well fed and well dressed, lived in a comfortable home with plenty of toys, open space for exploring, a swing set, and a huge sandbox in the backyard. I had thought that was everything they needed. Until my five-year-old asked that question, I had not realized that I had failed to provide them nourishment from our Heavenly Father and our Savior.

I knew immediately what I had to do. I started calling the wards listed in our area until I found the right one. As luck would have it, the Primary president answered. This was in the days when Primary was held every Wednesday at 4 o'clock, and it just happened to be Wednesday. Dear Sister Steel treated me like I was a long lost friend. She invited me to bring the boys and "come right over." When we arrived, she made sure I felt welcome, introduced me to the other women at Primary, saw to it that the boys were happy in their classes, and gave me some information about the "Penny Parade" going on that week. Soon we had home teachers and visiting teachers assigned to fellowship us back into activity. It was easy. Each meeting I attended touched my spirit as I connected with truths planted in my heart long ago. I knew that I was home again.

It took Larry longer to feel comfortable with our new ward family. Not only was he working ninety hours a week in a new job to support his little family (which was soon to increase by one more), but his "world caliber" softball took most of his time on weekends. Softball was serious business to him, and he wasn't sure he had time for anything that would interfere with his determination to win a world softball championship.

During our years in Colorado, 1970 to 1979, our family increased from two children to five. Larry advanced up the job ladder to a secure position in a growing company, and the bishop and home teachers did a masterful job fellowshipping us. In the latter part of 1978, the bishop challenged Larry to work toward ordination into the Melchizedek Priesthood. The biggest obstacle was tithing. We did not pay tithing. Larry came home after talking to the bishop and said (because I was the one who paid the bills), "Starting January first, pay tithing on my full paycheck and don't ever ask me again—just do it!" (He didn't want the chance to be tempted to change his mind.)

We didn't realize it at the time, but our obedience to the law of tithing was the beginning of a new life for us. Looking back, we are sure that our Father in Heaven was preparing us for a lifelong stewardship. That same month, January 1979, Larry's boss, whom he admired greatly and expected to work for forever, told Larry the business needed to be rearranged. His eight sons, some of whom were now old enough to come into the business, were ready to start taking on responsibility for the company. He asked Larry to give up his position as operations manager over five car dealerships and go back (with no cut in pay) to being general manager of a single Toyota dealership in order to train his oldest son. Although complimented that Mr. Stevinson wanted him to teach his son, Larry saw this as a personal and professional blow to his career and before long was very unhappy with the change. During this same period, we had planned a family trip to Utah, ending in Salt Lake to visit relatives.

In Salt Lake, Larry had lunch with a friend who owned a Toyota dealership. Often, whenever they talked business, Larry would ask in jest, "When are you going to sell me your store?" The answer was always the same, "Why would I want to do that?" However, on this particular day when Larry asked, his friend answered, "How about today?" Truly surprised but ready for the challenge, they wrote up a contract on a napkin, shook hands, and Larry became the owner of his first business. Within a week, he had moved back to Salt Lake to set up shop as Larry H. Miller Toyota on South State Street.

After the children finished their "year-round" school year on

August 9, the rest of us followed Larry. We found a comfortable home in Sandy, and the children started school again on August 27, much to their dismay. They had no summer vacation that year!

In May of the following year, our "Colorado" bishop, Brother Lowell Madsen, and our diligent home teachers, Brother Steve Carpenter and Brother Larry Hunter, with their wives came to Salt Lake to witness our family's sealing in the Salt Lake Temple. Before the ceremony, the officiator, President L. Ray Christiansen, talked to us of things to come in our lives and of the impact that we would have on thousands of people, perhaps even hundreds of thousands of people, in Salt Lake City and beyond. Taken completely off guard, we had no way of knowing what he was talking about and even wondered if he knew what he was talking about. We could not imagine such a thing happening to us.

We did not set out in the business world with any grand scheme. We just wanted security. We paid our tithing and tried to be honest, do what was right, and serve the Lord by being good stewards over what he had given us. Along with these efforts came abundant opportunities to touch other people's lives in meaningful ways.

In 1985, after engaging in a variety of mostly successful business opportunities, we were approached about investing in the Utah Jazz, Salt Lake's professional basketball team. The Jazz were hoping to pay off their debt this way and stay in Utah, rather than be sold into another market. Larry, who had now learned some things about shoring up a struggling new business during the economic downturn of the early 80's, was willing to talk. After much soul searching and discussion between the two of us, Larry sought advice from a local priesthood leader. This admired leader advised Larry to make the decision based on the merits of our ability to (1) handle it financially and (2) deal with life in the public eye. He then expressed some of his own opinions on the topic, explaining that if we understood what would be involved and felt that we could handle both the financial and public ramifications of that choice, then we should also recognize the benefits to the Church if the Jazz were to stay in Utah. Quite surprised,

Larry asked why. The answer: "All over the world when the word *Utah* is heard, people relate it to Mormons. NBA game results are published worldwide. When people see or hear about the Utah Jazz, they think of Utah and right behind that they think of the Mormons. The truth is that, in the future, you will be able to rehearse many reasons why it is important to keep the Jazz here."

With that advice, we purchased the Utah Jazz, half in 1985 and half in 1986. Since that decision, in spite of what some may think, things have not always been easy. Many trials have come into our lives to test and refine us. Some doors have been opened and others have been closed. Our children have been tested. We have had deep joys and deep sorrows. We have been given much—and where much is given, much is required.

That priesthood leader's words have come true. People from around the world, as well as from Salt Lake, have written, telling us ways they have been touched to seek out the Church after hearing about it through the Utah Jazz. Let me share a recent letter.

Dear Brother Miller,

About one year ago, I did not know anything about The Church of Jesus Christ of Latter-day Saints, but I loved the Utah Jazz! Many people mocked me for liking and admiring your team since I have lived in southern California my whole life. However, I explained to people that the Jazz had a certain appeal that runs deeper than just basketball. . . . The way the Jazz players as a whole conduct themselves in interviews and their no-nonsense, businesslike approach to the game . . . along with their sense of morals off the court is what put them over the top for me. . . .

The time came where I had to see in person the team that overcame the odds through unselfish play and feeding off each other's energy. . . . [O]n April 1, I believe, I flew to Salt Lake City. I wanted the best seat possible against the Houston Rockets, then with Pippen, Barkley, and Hakeem. The ticket broker said he had a third row seat along the rail behind the Jazz bench. . . . He said, "Come on, man, with this seat anything is possible. Karl Malone will hit the game winner and give you a high five on the way out!" I thought to myself, *Nice pitch, but this guy does not know who he is talking to. All he had to say was, 'I have a ticket left,' and that would have been enough for me!*

The atmosphere was great, not like the Hollywood scene in L. A. that I was accustomed to. The usher even directed me to feel free to use the bathroom down the tunnel near the team's locker room where I accidentally walked out for the second half near some of my favorite players. But the Jazz were down by about 15 with five and a half minutes left to play, and I turned to a friendly face next to me and said, "Gosh, they will have to make almost all the rest of their shots and deny the red hot Rockets any points." It looked dismal at best. But the Jazz did almost exactly that and went on a 17–0 run to end the game! Karl Malone hit the game winner and he gave me a high-five as the streamers came down and the team exited!! The silly ticket broker called the game to a tee, and I felt that such a moment for me would take a long time to be matched.

The next day, however, I visited the Temple grounds and . . . the reverence of it all, including the tour and the visitors center, topped even the game. I was touched by the Holy Ghost and I had an overwhelming desire to pray and my communication with Heavenly Father was never so clear! My heart ached with joy! . . . my life changed forever. . . . I became a Latter-day Saint on January 14, 2001. . . . I know this church is true and I wanted to show my appreciation to you and your team and share with you how God works in mysterious and joyful ways at times and how the Utah Jazz brought me to the Church of Jesus Christ of Latter-day Saints.[1]

In such ways, our lives have been blessed because of this stewardship. We have been able to provide thousands of quality jobs for families, build an entrepreneurship facility for Salt Lake Community College, contribute to church facilities and programs that provide wholesome competition for young athletes, form a scholarship fund for qualified children of our employees, organize a nonprofit charity that helps women and children in jeopardy in the community, and many other worthwhile endeavors. We feel a very strong responsibility to do good things with what we have been given.

In Leviticus 19:9–10 we are told, "And when ye reap the harvest of your land, thou shalt not wholly reap the corners of thy field, neither shalt thou gather the gleanings of thy harvest. And thou shalt not glean thy vineyard, neither shalt thou gather every grape of thy vine-yard; thou shalt leave them for the poor and stranger: I am the Lord your god." There is great need all around us. We can all reach out to others who need our help, no matter what our place is along this earthly journey.

The "spirit" of service is often planted in the hearts of those we help, and they, feeling the love of our Savior through our service to them, gain a desire to help others. In this way the army of the Lord's servants grows.

A few years ago, before the breakup of the Soviet Union, Larry and I met a man from the Ukraine named Peter, who had been sent to the United States by the Soviet government to learn more about the American way of doing business. He lived with a host family in the Provo area and wanted, among other things, to see how an automobile business was run. He was referred to us. We were immediately impressed with his gentle spirit and became friends. He later told us this story:

"As a young boy about twelve, living in Siberia, I had a recurring dream, in which I found myself in a very pleasant place but one unfa-miliar to me. It was very beautiful. I could see the colors of the trees and the flowers and hear the songs of the birds and feel the warmth of the air. I could see the majesty of the snowcapped mountains on one side, and when I turned around and looked to the opposite side, I could see a mountain with a great scar on it. I had no idea where this place was and didn't understand why the dream kept coming back to me . . . until years later when on this trip to Utah, my host family took me on a sightseeing trip to the This Is the Place Monument in Salt Lake City. As I was standing near the monument, it occurred to me that it was as if I was back in my dream. I was hearing the same sounds and seeing the same sights. I knew that as I turned around to the west I would see the mountain with the scar on it [the Bingham Copper Mine]. I real-ized instantly that this really was the place—the place in my dream."

Peter soon began making arrangements to try to stay in the United States. Government permission to leave was unheard of at the time.

The Soviets always kept at least one member of the family in the USSR to assure the return of a traveler. After many unsuccessful attempts to get his wife and son to Utah, he finally made a deal with God: "If you will help me get my family here, I will join the LDS church." Not long afterward, the Soviets changed their minds and allowed his family to join him. He kept his promise and joined the Church. On Easter weekend of the following year, he went to the temple. About a year later, the breakup of the Soviet Union was set in motion. Peter was happily settled in his new "home" and living a good life. We were amazed, then, when one day he told us he was going back to the Ukraine. Why would he leave the security and opportunity of a free country and return to a land of oppression and uncertainty? His answer was simple: "I cannot stay here with the knowledge I now have about how to do things to help my people and not share it with them."

He and his family faced many trials and tribulations back in the Ukraine. Corruption was rampant, and government leadership was weak. The mafia was taking over wherever they could, and Peter could see that his efforts were in vain. He was not being paid for working as a professor of languages at a university and neither was his wife, who was a professor of physics. Inflation was 3,000 percent a year, and food was scarce. The family survived by trading what they had with friends and doing odd jobs when they could find them. Soon Peter's wife became very ill. Local hospitals had no medicine or medical supplies. Patients had to find and bring their own. All the good doctors had left the country, and his wife was getting sicker by the day. In desperation, Peter called us. Some very good people came to their aid, and we were able to get her to the United States for treatment. By the time she reached Utah, she was in late stage three of four stages of breast cancer, and hope of survival was very slim. She underwent treatment for about a year, staying by herself in a small downtown Salt Lake apartment. Peter was allowed to leave the country only to bring her here and take her home. Volunteers from her apartment building and from the American Cancer Society took her to her appointments and helped her during chemotherapy, T-cell harvest, and transplant

therapy. She was declared cured at the end of her treatment, and prepared to go home. Deeply moved by her experience, she said, "I want
to go back to my country and be of service like I have seen here. They
don't have that in my country."

This woman had seen a precious truth in action. She had learned
the secret of happiness.

President Gordon B. Hinckley said: "Do you want to be happy?
Forget yourself and get lost in this great cause. Lend your efforts to
helping people. . . . Work to lift and serve His sons and daughters. You
will come to know a happiness that you have never known before. . . .
Let's get the cankering, selfish attitude out of our lives . . . and stand a
little taller . . . in the service of others."[2]

I have a strong testimony of service. Service is love. The Savior
loved us so much that he gave his life for us. We are here to do his
work; we are his hands and his feet. We can put our arms around those
who are hurting and soothe their pain. We can lift the oppressed. We
can calm a troubled child. We can clothe the naked and heal the sick
and feed the hungry. We can say a kind word where one is needed or
be a listening ear to those who need to talk. Virtuous women can be
an ever-growing force of righteousness. Our compassion can fill our
homes and neighborhoods and spill across our borders to fill the world.

Notes

1. Letter in possession of author.
2. *Teachings of Gordon B. Hinckley* (Salt Lake City: Deseret Book, 1997),
   597.

"Ye Are My Friends"

Elizabeth A. Clark

As I was growing up in the Washington, D.C., area, being the only girl my age at church was the bane of my existence. At that point in my life, the ten boys my age just didn't make up for having no girl-friends at church. Worse yet, I never had another member of the Church—with the exception of my sister—in any of my school classes. Making friends with people of other faiths was therefore natural and necessary.

My friends were good people, we had much in common, and we enjoyed each other. We did not, however, discuss religion. In one memorable high school U.S. history class, however, that all changed. Our teacher was lecturing about nineteenth century westward expansion and suddenly moved to the topic of the Mormon pioneer trek west. Somehow she knew I was a Mormon and asked if I had anything to add. I'm ashamed to admit now that I just sat there, speechless and embarrassed. If I could have slid any lower in my chair, I would have.

At that moment, I was experiencing in the flesh the great lurking fear of all teenagers—I seemed strange, foreign, different. A friend sitting behind me that day whispered a question to me about what the teacher had been saying. Again I'm ashamed to admit that I couldn't even turn to face her. I whispered back some cursory answer and hoped that would be the end of it.

Looking back now, I'm not sure which surprised me more at the

Elizabeth A. Clark, associate director of the BYU International Center for Law and Religion Studies, works with government leaders and scholars throughout the world to help promote religious freedom. She received a juris doctor from Brigham Young University and practiced Supreme Court and appellate litigation in a law firm in Washington, D. C.

time: being found out as a Church member or discovering soon after how little that seemed to bother my friend. I had somehow imagined that if she found out, she would hate me forever, or at least ignore me for a day or two out of embarrassment—which, for a teenager, is just as bad. Instead, she actually seemed interested in my beliefs.

That day I started to learn what I only truly realized years later—that you don't have to give up your beliefs to have friends, even friends of other faiths. In fact, hiding my beliefs meant hiding a part of myself, which made it difficult to have real friends of any background.

I currently work at the Brigham Young University International Center for Law and Religion Studies, a group designed to promote religious liberty throughout the world. In that effort, we work with good people of many denominations—Catholics, Protestants, Muslims, Eastern Orthodox, Jews, Jehovah's Witnesses, Bahá'ís, Seventh-day Adventists, and many, many others. I am continually inspired by their dedication and faithfulness to their beliefs. One woman we worked with, Karen Lord, passed away earlier this year. A colleague wrote the following lines of tribute to her: "[Karen] had a passion for religious liberty that was more than professional, rooted in a deep Christian faith. I was always impressed by her frequent reference to prayer as an important tool in political and diplomatic struggles. . . .

" . . . Those who knew her witnessed her passionate advocacy of the rights of Muslims, Orthodox Christians, Buddhists, and many of the new and smaller religious groups that suffer discrimination at the hands of prejudice . . . , [groups] whose beliefs she could never have shared personally."[1]

The goodness and dedication exhibited by people of other faiths should not come as a surprise to us. President Howard W. Hunter taught that "God operates among his children in all nations, and those who seek God are entitled to further light and knowledge, regardless of their race, nationality, or cultural traditions."[2] Elder Orson F. Whitney, in a conference address, taught that many great leaders of other religious traditions were inspired: "[God] is using not only his covenant people, but other peoples as well, to consummate a work, stupendous, magnificent, and altogether too arduous for this little handful of Saints to accomplish by and of themselves." In addition to sending men bearing the authority of the holy priesthood, God has sent "other good and great men, not bearing the Priesthood, but possessing profundity of thought, great wisdom, and a desire to uplift their fellows . . . [to give nations] that portion of truth that they were able to receive and wisely use."[3]

Other Church leaders have also taught this principle. President Spencer W. Kimball affirmed that "great religious leaders of the world" received "a portion of God's light" and that "moral truths were given to [these leaders] by God to enlighten whole nations and to bring a higher level of understanding to individuals."[4] B. H. Roberts noted: "Mormonism holds, then, that all the great teachers are servants of God; among all nations and in all ages. They are inspired men, appointed to instruct God's children according to the conditions in the midst of which he finds them."[5] Joseph Smith, addressing a congregation of Saints in Nauvoo, said: "Have the Presbyterians any truth? Yes. Have the Baptists, Methodists, etc., any truth? Yes. They all have a little truth mixed with error. We should gather all of the good and true principles in the world and treasure them up, or we will not come out true 'Mormons.'"[6]

If our attitude towards others is, as President Hinckley has put it, to "bring all the good that you have and let us see if we can add to it,"[7] we must first recognize the good that others do have. If we want to be good neighbors and friends to people of other faiths, it is not enough to merely tolerate them. Joseph Smith understood this as well. He explained, "When we see virtuous qualities in men, we should always acknowledge them, let their understanding be what it may in relation to creeds and doctrine."[8] Withholding praise or thinking we are better than others is prideful and hurtful. As President Hunter taught, "There is no underlying excuse for smugness, arrogance or pride."[9] Trying to build ourselves up by tearing others down is simply not the Lord's way.

I reflect with gratitude on the examples of friends of all faiths who have refused to poke fun at or ridicule other people's beliefs, no matter how strange they may seem. And I'm sure my beliefs have seemed plenty strange to many of them. Their conscious decisions to avoid criticism have made them quiet but powerful witnesses of Christ in my life. It has been said that a friend is a guardian of one's soul. We should never abuse the trust inherent in our friendships with people of other faiths by disparaging something that they may hold sacred.

This said, I want to make it clear that recognizing divine influence in the beliefs, lives, and work of people of other faiths does not make us relativists. We do not need to sympathize with, endorse, or uphold incorrect doctrine.[10] It does not mean that we need to compromise our testimony of the restored gospel.

Some Church members see a contradiction or paradox between, on the one hand, espousing the ideas of God's light and truth given to all and, on the other hand, holding to a testimony of a restored authority to speak and act for God. This perceived tension manifests itself in several ways. Some may feel uncomfortable and exclusionary accepting the Lord's proclamation that this is his only true and living church. At the other extreme, some may be uncomfortable in recognizing the great goodness and truths among our brothers and sisters of other faiths, feeling that this somehow diminishes the miracle of the Restoration. Can an understanding that God loves and works in the lives of all his children be reconciled with a claim of divinely restored authority? Are we forced to choose between the two?

It is my testimony that the choice is not either-or. The real choice here is not between anything-goes relativism and smug superiority, nor recognizing the tangible goodness and inspiration in others' lives and maintaining an equally sure testimony of the Restoration. The real choice is simply to have faith in Jesus Christ and to more completely understand his gospel of love. Joseph Smith described this divine love: "Love is one of the chief characteristics of Deity, and ought to be manifested by those who aspire to be the sons [and daughters] of God. A man filled with the love of God is not content with blessing his family alone, but ranges through the whole world, anxious to bless the whole human race."[11] Surely, if we want to emulate our Heavenly Parents, we must see all their children with the same love, concern, and respect that they do.[12]

Accepting the restored gospel does not limit our ability to love and admire others. To the contrary, the more we come to know Christ, the deeper our conviction grows that he restored his priesthood and his Church to the earth through Joseph Smith so that through temple ordinances all his children in all countries and throughout all generations might have the blessings of the priesthood and eternal families. All truth everywhere is from God. "God has revealed all the truth that is now in . . . the world," asserted Brigham Young, "whether it be scientific or religious."[13] There is no paradox when love and truth are brought together in Christ.[14]

Let me return for a moment to my high school years. That traumatic day in my U.S. history class was a turning point for me. In the following years as I continued to strengthen my faith by reading the Book of Mormon, praying, and attending church, I learned to actually enjoy discussing my beliefs. At that point, I still couldn't answer my friends' questions to my satisfaction nor, I'm sure, to theirs, but my testimony grew as I shared what I knew.

In time I encountered a second tension, or paradox, one that many of us struggle with: Can we be both friends and missionaries? Over the years, I have gradually learned the wisdom of what I learned in the Missionary Training Center—the importance of building on common beliefs rather than jumping headfirst into a doctrinal fray. The basis of any religious discussion should be an appreciation and respect for the sincerity of other people's beliefs and the many truths they hold dear.[15] We need to realize that we can learn from them, just as they can learn from us. Over the years, my friends of other faiths have been patient with me as I have found my way in the gospel. I trust that they have forgiven me and continue to forgive me for being too pushy, too slow to listen to them, or too scared to be honest about who I am.

In time I finally learned how to bridge the gap I had perceived between being a missionary and being a friend. Missionary work is not so much about memorizing scriptures or presenting organized discussions

as it is about simply being daily living witnesses of Jesus Christ and following the promptings of the Holy Ghost. That's true whether we are
talking with someone from Argentina or Arizona, from the other side
of the world, or from just next door. To me this truth is crystallized in
two short statements. Elder Holland has said: "Asking every member to
be a missionary is not nearly as crucial as asking every member to be a
member!"[16] And President Hinckley concludes: "Our kindness may be
the most persuasive argument for that which we believe."[17] Surely, we
can combine showing kindness and living our beliefs with being a friend
to people of other faiths.

In my work, I see the quiet power of righteous and joyful lives all
the time. For example, each year BYU hosts a major international conference on religious liberty that brings together sixty to seventy scholars, judges, and government officials from over thirty-five countries
who deal with religious policy. Recognizing the sensitivity of their positions and the fact that they are coming for an academic conference, we
specifically ask host students not to actively proselyte. But the students
and other members the delegates meet can't hide the joy and peace
that they find in the gospel. And the delegates can't miss it.

They comment on how our students "radiate goodness" or how
they can "feel [their] goodness and see it in [their] eyes." After a few
days among members, one delegate asked me: "Now why is it that
people don't like your church?" Another government leader noted,
"Many negative things" are said about the Church in his country, "and
I believed them." However, he added, associating with members for a
few days "has completely reversed my view." Whether or not they can
verbalize it, I have found that members of other faiths exposed to faithful, cheerful Saints can't help but feel the Holy Spirit.

Even though our students try not to initiate conversations about
the Church with delegates, conference participants often bring up the
topic themselves. If we are approachable and friendly, they usually ask
question after question about our beliefs and practices. I've been asked
about everything from missionary life to my views on women and the
priesthood to the meaning of the word *Zion* in "Zion's Bank." In my

experience, the Lord places in our way opportunities to explain our views and bear testimony if we are willing to respond with humility and quiet faith.

Despite our love and testimony, some people will not agree with our beliefs. That should not affect our love for them. We must also respect their rights to worship according to the dictates of their own consciences. President Hinckley has repeatedly quoted a wonderful statement of Joseph Smith, one which he refers to as his personal standard: "If it has been demonstrated that I have been willing to die for a 'Mormon,' I am bold to declare before heaven that I am just as ready to die in defending the rights of a Presbyterian, a Baptist, or a good man of any denomination; for the same principle which would trample upon the rights of the Latter-day Saints would trample upon the rights of the Roman Catholics, or of any other denomination who may be unpopular and too weak to defend themselves."[18]

What can we do when people disagree, besides allowing them to do so? President Hinckley explained, "We can disagree with people without being disagreeable. We can disagree without raising our voices and becoming angry and vindictive in our ways. We must learn to do so. We as a Christian community must practice a greater spirit of Christ in our lives, of love one for another, and extend that to all people regardless of whom they worship or how they worship."[19] We must allow all men and women the privilege of worshiping how, where, or what they may, not just because we want them to respect our right to worship, but because it is the right thing to do.[20]

It is also what Christ would do. Indeed, Brigham Young taught that during Christ's millennial reign, "when the Kingdom of God is fully set up and established on the face of the earth, and takes the preeminence over all other nations and kingdoms, it will protect the people in the enjoyment of their rights, no matter what they believe, what they profess, or what they worship."[21] Joseph Smith similarly taught the power of principle over pride and love over simply wanting to be right: "If I esteem mankind to be in error, shall I bear down on them? No. I will lift them up, and in their own way too, if I cannot persuade them my way is better."[22]

Being a friend with someone of another faith can be as richly rewarding as being a friend to someone of our own faith. As with all commandments, our prophet's exhortation to reach out and be friends with people of other faiths is a blessing, not a burden. The Lord loves them as much as he loves us. He not only uses us to bless their lives, but so very often also uses them to bless our lives.

Let me share one last personal experience. A year ago, I was living in Washington, D.C., working at a law firm. I began having a series of health problems that left me lying on my sofa sapped of strength for three months straight. For one reason or another, probably because of my own stubbornness, no one at church realized how sick I was. However, a friend from work wouldn't leave me in peace. Sharon ignored my protests of "I'm fine," and came to visit, bearing groceries. She washed my stacks of dirty dishes and came back again and again, with books and more food. She did all of this after working sixty-plus hours a week as an attorney. Her example was a powerful witness of Christ's love at a time when I desperately needed it. During the course of our friendship I had hoped and still hope to be an instrument to bless her life, but in the meantime she has certainly been an instrument to bless mine.

Jesus taught, "As I have loved you, . . . love one another. By this shall all men know that ye are my disciples, if ye have love one to another" (John 13:34–35). Our Savior asks us as his disciples to bear record of Christ through our love and lives. I cannot deny the many witnesses I have been given of Jesus Christ. I know that he lives. I know that this is his restored Church. I know that he loves all his Father's children with a love that we can only begin to understand and appreciate.

Notes

1. T. Jeremy Gunn, *In Memoriam: Karen S. Lord, 1976–2001* (available on-line at http://www.cesnur.org/2001/karenlord.htm).

2. Howard W. Hunter, *That We Might Have Joy* (Salt Lake City: Deseret Book, 1994), 60.

3. Orson F. Whitney, Conference Report, April 1921, 32–33; in Hunter, *That We Might have Joy*, 60–61.

4. First Presidency Statement, "God's Love for All Mankind," 15 February 1978, as quoted in R. Lanier Britsch, "I Have a Question," *Ensign*, January 1988, 48.

5. B. H. Roberts, *Defense of the Faith and the Saints*, 2 vols. (Salt Lake City: Deseret News, 1907), 1:512.

6. Joseph Smith, *History of the Church of Jesus Christ of Latter-day Saints*, 7 vols., 2d ed. rev. (Salt Lake City: The Church of Jesus Christ of Latter-day Saints, 1932–51), 5:517.

7. Gordon B. Hinckley, "The BYU Experience," in *Brigham Young University 1997–98 Speeches* (Provo: Brigham Young University Press, 1998). This thought has also been expressed by Presidents Howard W. Hunter and George Albert Smith. See Hunter, *That We Might Have Joy*, 62; and George Albert Smith, *Sharing the Gospel with Others: Excerpts from the Sermons of President Smith*, comp. Preston Nibley (Salt Lake City: Deseret News Press, 1948), 12–13.

8. Smith, *History of the Church*, 5:156. President Hinckley has similarly explained: "We can be appreciative [of other religions] in a very sincere way. We must not only be tolerant, but we must cultivate a spirit of affirmative gratitude for those who do not see things quite as we see them. . . . The strength of our position as we understand it will become clearer and more precious as we allow others the same privilege of conscience that we so highly prize. We must learn to accord appreciation and respect for others who are as sincere in their beliefs and practices as are we" (Gordon B. Hinckley, "Out of Your Experience Here," in *1990–91 Devotional & Fireside Speeches* [Provo: Brigham Young University Press, 1991], 25, 30).

9. Hunter, *That We Might Have Joy*, 60.

10. Elder Dallin H. Oaks described the contours of tolerance: "The gospel message is a continuing constructive criticism of all that is wretched or sordid in society. But Christians, who are commanded to be charitable, should be 'speaking the truth in love' and shunning personal attacks and shrill denunciations. Our public communications—even those that are protesting deficiencies—should be reasoned in content and positive in spirit" (*The Lord's Way* [Salt Lake City: Deseret Book, 1991], 194).

11. Smith, *History of the Church*, 4:227.

12. Joseph Smith perhaps put this best: "While one portion of the human race is judging and condemning the other without mercy, the Great

Parent of the universe looks upon the whole of the human family with a fatherly care and paternal regard; He views them as His offspring, and without any of those contracted feelings that influence the children of men" (*History of the Church*, 4:595).

13. Brigham Young, *Discourses of Brigham Young*, sel. John A. Widtsoe (1925; reprint, Salt Lake City: Bookcraft, 1998), 2.

14. See Hunter, *That We Might Have Joy*, 58–59.

15. Elder M. Russell Ballard noted in this regard that "all of our interpersonal relationships should be built on a foundation of mutual respect, trust, and appreciation. But that shouldn't prevent us from sharing deeply held religious feelings with each other. Indeed, we may find that our [religious and] philosophical differences add flavor and perspective to our relationships, especially if those relationships are built on true values, openness, respect, trust and understanding. *Especially* understanding" (*Our Search for Happiness* [Salt Lake City: Deseret Book, 1993], 5; emphasis in original).

16. Jeffrey R. Holland, "Witnesses Unto Me," *Ensign*, May 2001, 14–15.

17. Gordon B. Hinckley, "We Bear Witness of Him," *Ensign*, May 1998, 5.

18. Joseph Smith, *History of the Church*, 5:498; as quoted in *Teachings of Gordon B. Hinckley* (Salt Lake City: Deseret Book, 1997), 665.

19. *Teachings of Gordon B. Hinckley*, 667.

20. John Taylor commented: "All religious classes . . . have the right to worship God as they please, they have the right to either receive or reject the Gospel of Jesus Christ. If we had power to force it upon them we would not do it; freedom of the mind, and the free exercise of the rights of men is part of our religious belief; therefore, we would not coerce them if we could" (*Journal of Discourses*, 26 vols. [London: Latter-day Saints' Book Depot, 1854–86], 26:96–97).

21. *Teachings of Presidents of the Church: Brigham Young* (Salt Lake City: The Church of Jesus Christ of Latter-day Saints, 1997), 324. See also on page 268: "Whoever lives to see the Kingdom of God fully established upon the earth will see a government that will protect every person in his rights. If that government was now reigning . . . you would see the Roman Catholic, the Greek Catholic, the Episcopalian, the Presbyterian, the Methodist, the Baptist, the Quaker, the Shaker, the [Hindi], the [Muslim], and every class of worshipers most strictly protected in all their municipal rights and in the privileges of worshiping who, what, and when they pleased, not infringing upon the rights of others."

22. Joseph Smith, as quoted in John Henry Evans, *Joseph Smith: An American Prophet* (Salt Lake City: Deseret Book, 1989), 228.

I Had to Look
a Little Further

Barbara Naatjes

I am a convert. I grew up in another faith and participated in all its meetings and activities. I loved my church and I loved the people who attended it.

I was one of those unusual little children who actually listened in church. And because I listened, I had questions—ones that I sometimes couldn't get answered. Some of them weren't particularly significant; others were more serious. For example, no one could tell me what the unforgivable sin was, so I worried a lot that I had already committed it.

As I got older, some of my questions became more serious, particularly as I tied together various pieces of doctrine. One summer I attended a camp with the theme: "To God alone the glory." We were taught very carefully that the reason God had created us was to give him glory. I have to admit that seemed a bit self-centered to me, especially when I started to think about some of the other doctrine I'd been taught. I was particularly troubled by the teaching that to avoid eternal agony and torment a person had to come to believe in Jesus Christ and be baptized in this lifetime. I knew that of all the billions of people who would be born on the earth, only a very small percentage would be taught about Jesus Christ, let alone accept him and be baptized. I also had been taught and believed that God was omniscient, that he knew everything that had happened, was happening, and would happen in

---

Barbara Skie Naatjes is a former stake Relief Society president, ward and stake Young Women president, and early morning seminary teacher. She currently serves as the stake public affairs director. She and her husband, Robert W. Naatjes, who is the bishop of their ward, are converts to the Church. They are the parents of five children and grandparents of twelve.

the future. In other words, he knew before he created the world and its peoples that only a small percent of those peoples would meet the requirement necessary to avoid eternal agony, an agony equivalent to being on fire forever and ever. If God was also omnipotent, or all powerful, it seemed he could have arranged things any way he wanted. This was my dilemma: it was possible for me not to kill, commit adultery, or steal. But the greatest of all commandments—to love the Lord my God with all my heart, soul, and mind (Matthew 22:37)—I couldn't do, not if God deliberately let all those people suffer eternal agony. Even as weak and mortal as I was, I would not have done that.

Of course, I asked people about this. During my university years, I even asked the president of the Lutheran Church when he came to Augustana College. I had the opportunity to talk with him privately after a meeting with a small group of student body officers. As I told him my dilemma about not being able to love God and why, he looked at me and was absolutely silent. He said nothing. After a long minute, he finally said, "I invite you to join me in praying for the salvation of the world." Then he turned and walked away. I knew from that point on that I had to look a little further.

I continued to talk to people of other religions about this and never got a good answer. Most answers shifted the blame. "Well, see, it's our fault. We're just not good enough missionaries." That didn't help. Over the years I kept trying to push the dilemma to the back of my mind but I couldn't forget it.

One Christmas after I was married, some friends sent my husband, Bob, and me a Book of Mormon. At one time Bob had expressed an interest in knowing about their church, and our friends asked if we'd be willing to have the missionary discussions. We were. When the missionaries came, I invited them to sit on the couch across from where Bob and I were sitting, and then without further ado I presented my persistent dilemma. To my surprise, their faces lit up. "Yes, we can answer your question," they said, "but we like to teach things in a particular order, and, if you wouldn't mind, we'd like to follow that order."

I said, "That's fine. I've waited a long time. I can wait a little bit longer."

I want you to imagine what it was like for me to receive the discussion on the plan of life, to know that we all lived as spirit children of our Father in Heaven before we came to earth, and that there was a plan in place that *everyone* who had ever lived on earth would be taught the gospel of Jesus Christ and have a chance to accept it, whether in this life or the next. That night, the missionaries asked if my husband and I would kneel down and pray with them to know if what we had been taught was true. They asked me to be the voice for that prayer. As I asked Heavenly Father to tell me if these things were true, I was absolutely filled with the witness of the Holy Spirit.

Imagine how I felt when I read in 2 Nephi 2:25: "Adam fell that man might be; and men are, that they might have joy." To know this about Heavenly Father, that his purpose is for us to have joy, was what I had been searching to know. He wants us to have what he has, to know what he knows, and to live the life that he lives. We are his *children*. We are not his creation, like an oak tree; you and I are each his *child*.

These teachings changed my life. Bob and I joyfully joined the Church. I still had questions to ponder, but now I had the tools to find answers. May I share some of the truths I have discovered during my life as a Latter-day Saint?

I was struck when I found this wonderful truth from Ezra Taft Benson, "When obedience ceases to be an irritant and becomes our quest, at that moment God will endow us with power."[1] I absolutely know that to be true! When our desires are simply to be obedient and we just want to know how, when our goal is to be like Heavenly Father and we just want to know how, then knowledge can come to us. At this stage we become receptive to the answers and ideas that we receive. I'm convinced that obedience is the key to spiritual power. It is the key to peace and happiness in this life. It is the key to a fulness of joy in the life to come. It is the price we pay to be apprentices to Jesus Christ himself.

So why do we sometimes struggle to be obedient? I believe the main reason we do is that we don't know and trust the Savior enough. If we really knew him and trusted him fully, how hard would it be to be obedient? One of my daughters is teaching the Laurels in her ward. As she began working with these young women, sixteen to eighteen years of age, she found it surprisingly difficult to convince them that God's ways were better than the ways of the world. She was shocked at how resistant the girls could be to that idea. She pondered about this and discussed it with me. One day she called and said, "Mom, I've finally figured out what the problem is. They think they're smarter than God!" Truly, isn't that what we're all thinking when we decide to be disobedient? Aren't we saying, *Generally he's smarter, but in this case, I've got a little extra insight. My way's going to be better.* Isn't that what we're doing?

We need to remind ourselves who the Savior is. We need to remember not only his sinlessness, but also his love and mercy. We need to remember his intelligence and his wisdom and his power. Remember that he has created worlds without number. He has seen billions upon billions of lives lived. He knows the behavior, the thoughts, the feelings, the intents of the heart; and he's seen the consequences. If we had that kind of insight and wisdom, think of what we would know. Instead, what we know comes from our own very limited life experience.

The Lord says, "And worlds without number have I created . . . and innumerable are they unto man" (Moses 1:33, 35). In Moses 7:30, Enoch says, after having been shown all of the Savior's creations, "And were it possible that man could number the particles of the earth, yea, millions of earths like this, it would not be a beginning to the number of thy creations." These are not just poetic expressions.

The Hubble telescope and other scientific marvels now show these verses of scripture to be accurate statements of what the Lord has created. Our own solar system is 7.3 billion miles across. That seems really vast. Mars, Jupiter, the earth, the sun. That solar system is a speck, a tiny speck, in the Milky Way, our galaxy, which is 480,000 trillion miles across, or 80,000 light years. A light year is the distance light can travel in a year. In a second light travels almost eight times around the world. How far would we go in 80,000 years traveling that fast? That's the size of the Milky Way. And the Milky Way is but an insignificant speck in the known universe. That's what scientists now know about how vast creation is. The Savior created all of that. Think of what he knows that we don't know.

In reality, every time we don't do what the Lord says, we're running our own experiment in human relations. Scientists run experiments by keeping all but one variable constant. For example, they might specify one chemical as the variable and then run an experiment multiple times with that chemical in place, noting the consistency of the results. Then they take out the chemical and run the experiment again. Scientists then have a pretty good idea about what that chemical does under particular conditions.

But does this work in human relations? How can we say, "All right, everybody. Do everything over again exactly as you did this past week. I'm going to make a few changes and see what happens"? I think we would all like to "re-roll" the tape and give something another try, to see if we could change an outcome we didn't like. And wouldn't it be great if in the meantime, everybody else did things exactly as they had during the past week so we could be sure that the difference in results was due to our actions? Unfortunately, life isn't an experiment. We can't put our lives on rewind. We have to take somebody's word for what works and what doesn't. We don't have time to figure out everything by ourselves. We won't live long enough.

Consider this question, How many people do you know who are wise enough, bright enough, kind enough, unselfish enough, and powerful enough that you would turn your life over to them? How many people would you trust with your eternal life? How many people would you trust with the eternal life of everyone who has ever lived or ever will live? That's how much we trusted the Savior when we walked and talked with him and knew him personally. We know we did because we are here, and that means we chose to follow a plan of life in which he was the central, pivotal person. The plan would fail unless he was willing and able to do everything he said he would do—descend from the kind of power he used to create worlds, come to this earth to live a sinless life, take upon himself the sins of everybody who had ever lived and ever would live, settle the demands of justice that we might not suffer if we repent, and then conquer death for each one of us. That's what he had to get done. If we knew him before we were born and we trusted him to do all of that, why not take his word now about what brings happiness and what doesn't?

I have a son who was assigned, while in law school, to write one side of a case in great depth. His professor collected all the papers and said, "All right. Your next assignment is to write the opposite side of the case." Scott told a friend, "I can't do this. I believe every argument I made in that first paper. There's no way I can write the other side." His friend, who was a year ahead in law school, said, "Just put your mind to it. Something will come to you." Within half an hour, Scott had refuted all of his own arguments. I'm convinced that without the scriptures, without living apostles and prophets, we could convince ourselves of any self-serving idea. We could rationalize and persuade ourselves to believe almost anything.

What's wrong with relying principally on the advice of experts around us—the family therapists, psychologists, and so forth? Can they tell us what brings happiness and what doesn't? Let's compare some of the "expert" advice from the past two decades with what the Lord has said to us.

For a number of years, experts told us that if we were not happy in our marriages, our children would be better off if we got a divorce because unhappy couples don't make good role models or good parents. A lot of people bought into that argument. A book that psychiatrists actually passed out to people in counseling said if you were sticking it out in an unhappy marriage, you were addicted to your spouse. To be happy you needed to get over that addiction! How do you think Heavenly Father and the Savior feel about our decisions when we base them only on the words of a celebrity guest on the talk-show circuit instead of on what he has told us in the scriptures? Does the word *short-sighted* come to mind? At the same time we were hearing some of this advice, the Lord was telling us to marry in the temple, apply the principles of the gospel to our relationships, forgive one another, work out our differences, and go forward. In a recent review of the book, *The Unexpected Legacy of Divorce*,[2] Alan J. Hawkins wrote, "Wallerstein and her co-authors claim that the effects [of divorce] are deeper, long-term, and more troubling than most social scientists have suggested. Divorce rips apart a child's world and irrevocably changes its direction. Its most harmful and profound effects are not visible until early adulthood, when children of divorce are trying to form intimate relationships. When faced with the question of whether children are better off if their unhappy parents stick it out for the sake of the children, the authors offer an unflinching politically incorrect 'yes' (with appropriate asterisks for situations of violence, abuse, addiction, and serious pathology)."[3]

In preparing to write *The Case for Marriage*,[4] co-author Linda J. Waite observed, "Some of the research I did . . . shows that in many cases, staying together is the best solution if the marriage becomes unhappy. I used data from the National Survey of Families and Households to address this issue. Thirteen thousand adults were interviewed in the late 1980s and again five years later. At the first interview, one of the questions asked was how they would rate their marriage on a scale of 1 to 7, 1 being 'just awful' and 7 being 'fabulous.' I looked at those who said . . . my marriage is a 'one.' . . . Of those who said in 1987 that their marriages were awful, 87 percent said five years later that their marriages were either pretty good or very good, either a 'six' or a 'seven.'"[5] I think that in a lot of cases when marriages are unhappy, that unhappiness is temporary. It doesn't last. We are, however, more willing to leave than we used to be if we hit a rough patch. We are less likely to work it through, despite the evidence that dramatic turnarounds are commonplace. They are, in fact, the *typical* experience.

Let's also look at parenting advice. For years it was hard to find many pediatricians or other experts who felt that long-term daycare was harmful in any way. In fact, they seemed to think it might be an advantage. No one appeared to worry at all if parents weren't at home when children were teenagers. That wasn't even an issue. My Minneapolis newspaper ran an article about a recent study reported in the media that showed an increase in negative behavior in children who spent time in daycare. "The child care findings come from a continuing federal study that tracked 1,300 youngsters who had been in daycare from infancy to kindergarten. 'These most recent results show that the more time youngsters spend in [day]care, the more likely they are to have behavior problems when they reach kindergarten,' said Jay Belski, an investigator for the National Institute of Child and Human Development study. 'They're more aggressive and noncompliant and get in lots of fights,' Belski said, 'as well as talking too much, arguing a lot, and demanding a lot of attention.' He cautioned that 'the differences in comparison with other youngsters are small, however, and it is impossible to know if they'll last. . . . The effects on the children, however, show up no matter the quality of child care or mothering at home, for both boys and girls, for both richer and poorer families." Another researcher, Sarah Freedman, said, "This study also showed that good child care does improve school readiness," but she added by comparison, "the influence of good parenting on school readiness was almost four times as strong as the difference a daycare makes."[6]

Even more stunning was this finding by the American Medical Association: "Latch-key kids who spend time home alone are more likely to engage in unhealthy, risky behavior than children who have adult supervision. A study of nearly 5,000 children indicates that children who spend eleven or more hours a week in self-care as opposed to those with adults at home are twice as likely to use alcohol, twice as likely to smoke, almost twice as likely to use marijuana. These figures persist for every grade and every economic group, are consistent with whether the child is active or not in church, school, sports, or other activities."[7]

Sometimes I wonder when we are going to get the message. How long will it take us to put our faith in Heavenly Father, in the scriptures, in the teachings of living apostles and prophets? How long can we run our own personal experiments? And at what cost to ourselves and to our families?

Sometimes we just have to hold fast to what we already know. Often we hear quoted the scripture that talks about growing in faith and knowledge "line upon line, and precept upon precept" (D&C 98:12). That can't happen, though, unless we stay firm with what we already know. We can't keep going back and revisiting our first decisions over and over. If we do, we remain in the same place, never moving up or on. Joseph Smith didn't have to have the First Vision more than once. Brigham Young didn't say, "This is the place," and go home and revisit his decision. But don't we sometimes do that? We're sure something is true, we feel good about it, we feel impressed by the Spirit about it, and then rather than taking action we delay or we waffle, and the power leaves us. We climb only when we can finally, absolutely decide, once and for all, that certain things are true—that we believe in them and we will live according to them. Only then do we have a foundation on which to build.

I testify that two things are necessary to our spiritual growth. First and foremost, when we have a bedrock, spiritual experience, we must stay true to the witness of that moment. We must remember it, acknowledge it, and build on it. Second, whenever we are in a meeting or are reading something and feel impressed by the Spirit to make a change in our behavior or take action, we should do so immediately. I am convinced that immediate obedience generates tremendous power and energy.

When Bob and I were taking the missionary discussions, for example, we were given the Word of Wisdom lesson. After the lesson, the missionaries left, almost casually, assuming we were living it. Well, both of us smoked. The missionaries had no idea because Bob smoked at work and I hardly smoked at all, so there was no tobacco smell in our house. We closed the door after the elders left, and Bob started to pull out a cigarette and I said, "Are you sure you want to do that?" He answered, "You know, I guess I don't." I said, "What if we just get rid of all this stuff?" So we got rid of the tobacco. For the first time in our lives, we had a bottle of alcohol in our house. We got rid of that, too. The coffee went. The Savior fought that battle for us. I've read that overcoming tobacco can be harder than overcoming cocaine, but we had not one problem. Zip, it was done. Now and then as we've visited with people who are being taught the Word of Wisdom, I've told them my story and said, "Now, please start living it right now. The Lord will fight your battle for you." But they think, *Well, let's see. I'm not going to be baptized for another six weeks and I've got a little time.* Then the battle's on. I'm convinced that the first time we know something is true, the first time the Spirit tells us to do something, if we act upon it, we will receive power to do it.

Heavenly Father loves us. We are his children. There is a place in his heart and in the celestial kingdom for each one of us. He is doing all he can to help us choose him and to accept the Atonement in our lives. He wants us to understand that with "faith unto repentance" the Atonement will cover us and make us whole and worthy to be back in his presence. Our Heavenly Father and the Savior live and love us. They want us to know what they know, live as they live, and feel the fulness of joy that they feel. Their power is available to help us be all that they would have us be.

Notes

1. Quoted in Donald L. Staheli, "Obedience—Life's Great Challenge," *Ensign*, May 1998, 81.
2. Judith Wallerstein, Julia Lewis, and Sandy Blakeslee, *The Unexpected Legacy of Divorce: A 25 Year Landmark Study*, 1st ed. (New York: Hyperion, 2000).
3. Alan J. Hawkins, "1 Divorce Book, 2 Marriage Books," *Marriage & Families*, April 2001:26.
4. Linda J. Waite and Maggie Gallagher, *The Case for Marriage: Why Married People Are Happier, Healthier, and Better Off Financially* (New York: Doubleday, 2000).
5. Linda J. Waite, "5 Marriage Myths, 6 Marriage Benefits," *Marriage & Families*, April 2001:20–21.

6. H. J. Cummins, "Researchers Link Lifestyle to Problems of Childhood," *Star Tribune*, 19 April 2001, A4.

7. *Journal of the American Medical Association*, vol. 268, no. 1993, quoted in Aviation Medical Bulletin January 2000.

RUN AND NOT BE WEARY

Carol Wilkinson

One freezing winter day in Devon, England, my missionary companion and I were working hard to meet the statistical expectations of our zone leaders. We were in poor shape, statistically and physically. After a healthy first missionary year, I had succumbed to the long working hours, cold apartments, and winter weather and had contracted a bad bronchial infection. Determined to keep working, I was only slowly recovering from the infection. Not to be outdone, my elderly companion had a chronic bladder problem. What a couple of crocks we were! The bitter wind blowing off the Atlantic Ocean seemed to go straight through my ribs as it made its way up onto the moors. It was a Friday afternoon, and we were still supposed to teach four more first discussions and hand out several copies of the Book of Mormon before the end of the day. As the senior companion, I felt anxious as we knocked on door after door without success. Finally, a woman listened to us on her doorstep. As I spoke to her of Joseph Smith, I realized my speech was wooden and devoid of the Spirit. She wasn't interested in our message, and I couldn't blame her. As we walked away, I told my companion how stressed and physically worn out I felt, that there was no way we could meet our goal for the week, and that the elders would just have to lump it.

Several times since my mission I've felt that same kind of numbing weariness that hinders my ability to feel the Spirit and bear record

Carol Wilkinson, originally from England, is an assistant professor of physical education at Brigham Young University, where she teaches pedagogy and philosophy/ethics. She is currently serving in her ward as the Young Women president.

of the Savior. I know I'm not alone. Mental and physical weariness is the plague of women of our time. What can we do to stave it off and optimize our effectiveness as witnesses of our Lord? To minimize physical fatigue, we should get enough rest, exercise regularly, eat a balanced diet, and not run faster than we have strength. These things will entitle us to the promise in D&C 89:20—the ability to "run and not be weary." What else can we do to relieve the stress in our lives?

Western culture describes stress as a loss of control. In contrast, Eastern philosophies consider it an absence of inner peace. Let's explore several avenues that tap into our spiritual selves and can help restore inner peace.

The first avenue is writing in a journal. At the turn of the twentieth century, British East Africa, as Kenya was then known, was a land for the adventurous that spread from Mount Kilimanjaro to the Serengeti Plain. Many Europeans were lured by the challenge of this land. Dane Karen Blixen was one of these hopeful new residents who settled down to forge a new life in the hills just outside Nairobi. During the seventeen years Karen lived in Africa, she contracted syphilis from an unfaithful husband, broke off her relationship with him, lost her farm in a fire and her land to bankruptcy.

Writer and lecturer Brian Seaward describes how Karen coped during this time: "Throughout her life in Africa, Karen wrote. Writing and storytelling became a release, almost an escape, but in every case, a means to cope with the changes she encountered. Upon what she called 'an ungraceful return' to her home in Denmark, Karen began to organize and compose the memories of her African adventures. The result: a wonderful collection of personal experiences intertwining the sad with the sublime (written under the pen name Isak Dinesen) that became the classic memoir *Out of Africa.*" Seaward concludes from Karen's writing: "While not everyone is a novelist, we all have life adventures that merit, often necessitate, expression; expression that helps to ease the pain of the soul. In the words of Karen Blixen, 'All sorrows can be borne, if you put them in a story.'"[1]

Journals originally functioned as a record to guide adventurers on long trips and orient them for a safe trip home. I think they can still serve the same purpose in a different dimension; they can help provide a safe return passage to our eternal home.

President Spencer W. Kimball ardently encouraged us to keep journals, promising us that they will be great inspiration to our families. In addition, journal writing helps synthesize personal thoughts, feelings, and insights that can lead to spiritual growth.

It's important to include in our journals more than just the spiritual and positive aspects of our lives. There is something about writing down difficult personal thoughts, not with the purpose of dwelling on them, but with the desire to move forward, that gives us permission to let them go. President Kimball said, "Your journal should contain your true self rather than a picture of you when you are 'made up' for a public performance. There is a temptation to paint one's virtues in rich color and whitewash the vices, but there is also the opposite pitfall of accentuating the negative. Personally, I have little respect for anyone who delves into the ugly phases of the life he is portraying. . . . The truth should be told, but we should not emphasize the negative."[2]

On a daily basis it might be hard to see changes in our perceptions of stressful events. But by objectively rereading previous journal entries, we may discover attitude patterns that can help us deal more effectively with stressful issues.

A second avenue to inner peace is self-acceptance and its related trait, the ability to forgive. Feelings of low self-worth can drain us. Lao Tzu, the ancient Chinese philosopher and father of Taoism, said, "The way of inner peace begins with self-acceptance, to seek peace outside is to leave it behind."[3] Increased self-awareness, realizing that we really are daughters of our Father in Heaven, helps us accept and love ourselves. Understanding the love our Father in Heaven has for us boosts that self-acceptance. Elder Neal A. Maxwell states, "God loves us all—saint and sinner alike—with a perfect and everlasting love. We have His love, if not His approval. It is our love for Him that remains to be developed."[4]

Taking offense easily is a symptom of low self-esteem. But none of us is exempt. We've all been offended by others and sometimes we feel resentful towards them. There's a saying that holding a grudge is like drinking poison and hoping the other person will die. Resentments can sour our own view of life, and bitter feelings toward others create defensiveness and vulnerability to stress. By forgiving others and asking our Father for forgiveness for our bitter feelings, the power of the Atonement can sweep away these feelings and bring peace.

Meditation is a third avenue to spiritual strength. The word *meditation* brings to mind images of Tibetan monks with shaved heads. But Latter-day Saints are asked to do this on a regular basis. (Meditate, that is, not shave our heads!) President Gordon B. Hinckley often asks the First Presidency and the Quorum of the Twelve to take time for pondering, for introspection, and for meditation.[5] As he does so, our prophet often refers to a statement from David O. McKay: "Meditation is the language of the soul. It is defined as 'a form of private devotion, or spiritual exercise, consisting in deep, continued reflection on some religious theme.'"[6]

How often do we meditate? How do we learn to meditate and focus so that we can be edified from the experience? Before our Father can commune with us, we must create the proper learning environment. The Savior set the pattern. How many times did he remove himself from his very busy ministry to go to a mountain apart and be alone to commune with his Father? Sister Patricia T. Holland says, "The price to be paid for this kind of communion is time and your best powers of concentration. . . . This communing with God has to be . . . when things are still, when the house is quiet and [your] mind is calm."[7] This can happen in your house, in the temple, or in some outdoor setting. Then, as expressed in an ancient Chinese proverb, when the student is ready, the teacher will come.

Here are some steps that have helped me ponder and meditate:

Step 1. Focusing. Recognize that you are going to stop thinking about worldly things and try to focus your mind on things of an eternal nature.

Step 2. Emptying. Emptying is a cleansing of your consciousness so that spiritual growth can continue. A Buddhist monk was visited by an American professor. The professor held out his cup, and the monk poured in tea until the cup was overflowing. Still he continued to pour. The amazed professor asked why he kept pouring. The monk replied, "Your mind is like this cup. It is so full of concepts, that there is no room for new wisdom."[8] We need to empty our minds of thoughts of the world—ill feelings towards others, what you need to do at work tomorrow, how to juggle running three children to three different places at the same time. If you're like me, you have encountered this problem already when entering the temple. Those distracting thoughts must be left behind if you are to have a meaningful experience. The same is true in meditating. The emptying process is a cleansing of the spirit. Connecting with God and being filled requires a settled, calm mind.

Step 3. Centering. In this phase, I reflect on who I am and what my purpose is in life. I ask myself, Am I on track to fulfilling my life's mission? If not, what must I do? What can I do to help build the kingdom? I also think of other gospel issues that I am seeking further light and knowledge about. During this uninterrupted time, I address those questions that can be answered only in the midst of deep solitude. I try to reach out and feel connected to my Father in Heaven. When I have done this, I can follow the advice of Brigham Young, who said, "All I have to do is . . . keep my spirit, feelings and conscience like a sheet of blank paper, and let the Spirit and power of God write upon it what he pleases."[9]

Step 4. Grounding. Once I feel connected to my Father in Heaven, I am filled with new knowledge and insight, which grounds me. Communication occurs with the divine during this phase, and I can sense the influence of the Holy Ghost. I feel peaceful yet energized.

Sister Holland states, "We need to simplify and spiritualize and celestialize. If most of what we are doing doesn't fit these categories, if at least some portion of our day is not turned to heaven, then we have a wrenching, rending emptiness awaiting us—isolation of the first order—and we will find no cloak of charity with which to protect ourselves or our sisters. . . . I am not being Pollyannish about this. I have already said that I know very well the demands upon a woman's time. It is because I know them so well that I am speaking as I am. I am speaking not only out of the depths of my heart but also out of the depths of my experience. You can say, 'It can't be done. There is too much to do. It takes too much energy.' Yes, you can say that—but you may miss forever the divine knock at the door."[10]

A *fourth avenue is prayer*. We have never been required to run faster than we have strength, but we are required to be diligent and pray always. "Where Can I Turn for Peace?"[11] we ask in a well-loved Latter-day Saint hymn. The answer: There is only one, our Savior, who can really give us the peace we are searching for.

As we pray to our Father in Heaven, we need to learn to *commune* with him, and not just talk to him. As another hymn requests: "Oh, may my soul commune with thee And find thy holy peace."[12] As we know from latter-day revelations, "The spirit and the body are the soul of man" (D&C 88:15). So how does our soul commune with him? Once I was praying and found that words simply weren't enough to express what I felt. In my frustration as I knelt there, I reached out to my Father with the feelings of my heart, with my whole soul yearning and pleading, and something quite remarkable happened: I was answered back in the same way. A feeling of love, peace, and strength filled me. In that moment, I experienced the words of the hymn, "He answers privately, reaches my reaching."[13] My most meaningful two-way communication with my Father has been when I use words to communicate and also engage my heart and soul, my whole being, to project the deep feeling that lies within. In response, God reveals himself through thoughts to my mind and quite amazing feelings in my heart. In fact, it is through our hearts that we go beyond knowing about the qualities of God and really come to know and commune with him. God's love is the supreme quality that we seek to feel—and become. Love is a boundless, divine energy. When love is pure, it becomes a tremendous source of healing energy, for ourselves and for others.

When we consciously shift from the motivation of fear to the motivation of love, great things are possible.

In weary moments, remember that God loves you. Oh, how he loves you. Isaiah, speaking Messianically, attests to this love: "For the mountains shall depart, and the hills be removed; but my kindness shall not depart from thee, neither shall the covenant of my peace be removed, saith the Lord that hath mercy on thee" (Isaiah 54:10).

When you're feeling stressed, do what you can to change your perception of the situation, make temporal changes to simplify your life and decrease the stress, and fill your inner well by communicating with the divine. Plead for the Savior's help. He is right there beside you, though you may not feel him when you're weary. He *is* there and waits for you to knock. As you do, you will find revealed an oasis of love, peace, strength, and knowledge to renew and refresh you—making it possible to run and not be weary in the journey through life.

Notes

1. Brian Seaward, *Managing Stress* (Boston: Jones and Bartlett Publishers, Inc., 1994), 164–65.
2. Spencer W. Kimball, "President Kimball Speaks out on Personal Journals," *Ensign*, December 1980, 60.
3. Lao Tzu, *Tao Te Ching*, trans. J. C. H. Wu (Boston, 1990).
4. Neal A. Maxwell, *All These Things Shall Give Thee Experience* (Salt Lake City: Deseret Book, 1979), 3.
5. As noted in Patricia T. Holland, *A Quiet Heart* (Salt Lake City: Bookcraft, 2000), 8–9.
6. David O. McKay, Conference Report, April 1946, 113.
7. Patricia T. Holland, *A Quiet Heart* (Salt Lake City: Bookcraft, 2000), 7–8.
8. In Seaward, *Managing Stress*, 127.
9. Brigham Young, *Deseret News Weekly*, 19 April 1871, 125; see also Preston Nibley, *Brigham Young: The Man and the Work*, 4th ed. (Salt Lake City: Deseret Book, 1960), 469.
10. Holland, *A Quiet Heart*, 10.
11. Emma Lou Thayne, "Where Can I Turn for Peace," *Hymns of The Church of Jesus Christ of Latter-day Saints* (Salt Lake City: The Church of Jesus Christ of Latter-day Saints, 1985), no. 129.

12. Lorin F. Wheelwright, "Oh, May My Soul Commune with Thee," *Hymns*, no. 123.
13. Thayne, "Where Can I Turn for Peace," *Hymns*, no. 129.

CONNECTING THE DOTS

✺⟨⦁⟩✺

Heidi S. Swinton

Thirty years ago I was attending graduate school in our nation's capital. I lived right downtown, just blocks from the White House and Lafayette Park. When I needed to be alone, Lafayette Park was where I went. I was in a special journalism program then with an illustrious writing career before me. But somehow it didn't feel right.

On a December day in 1971, I sat for five hours in that park, eyes closed, arms folded, with just an occasional glance to make sure the hordes of war protestors were keeping their distance. And I prayed. I prayed for direction and answers; I prayed for resolution to a question I had been asking for almost a year. Should I stay and pursue the job opportunities calling my name? Or should I go home and marry that straight-arrow law student?

It's a no-brainer now, but at the time I was confused. I was asking the Lord to tell me what to do. Today, I have a better grasp of how faith and agency work together. The Lord doesn't decide for us any more than he simply fixes what is broken or changes the rules so we can always win. That is not the eternal plan of happiness. At that time, I just wanted to resolve my five-year courtship and get on with life—either married or not married. But no "Do this" or "Do that" came to me that afternoon. Finally, a thought settled in my mind: *As soon as you see Jeff, you'll know what to do.* It was the still, small voice—"Hearken to the voice of the Lord your God" (D&C 33:1).

Heidi S. Swinton is an award-winning documentary writer and author. She has written several documentaries on Church subjects, including "American Prophet: The Story of Joseph Smith" and "Trail of Hope: The Story of the Mormon Trail." Heidi serves as a member of one of the Church's curriculum writing committees and as a member of the advisory board for BYU–TV.

Within hours, my roommate and I had piled into her car and begun hearkening home across the heartland of America with more speed than the pioneers but with about the same eagerness to reach Zion. We drove straight through the first night, then straight through the next, arriving home early on a Sunday morning. A few hours later, Jeff rang the bell. The answer to my future stood a doorknob away.

I remember opening that door and feeling peace. "Let not your heart be troubled," said the Lord. "My peace I give unto you" (John 14:1, 27). As it turned out, Jeff had been petitioning the Lord that Friday afternoon as well, and his answer was similar to mine: "As soon as you see Heidi, you will know what to do." I share my life today with that dear friend, wise confidant, and eternal companion.

That scene could be cast as a love story's "Happily ever after" moment. But what was more significant to us about it was the realization that "I the Lord am with you, and will stand by you; and ye shall bear record of me, . . . that I am the Son of . . . God, that I was, that I am, and that I am to come" (D&C 68:6). Looking back, I can see a host of other experiences in my growing-up years that led to that understanding, but this was the point at which the dots began to connect.

Perhaps this is the essence of faith, to draw together the many times that the Lord has been with us, the many ways that he has helped us, the many gifts that we have been given. And for what purpose? That we "might know thee the only true God, and Jesus Christ, whom thou hast sent" (John 17:3).

Years later I put another scripture to that time: "Remember that it is upon the rock of our Redeemer, who is Christ, the Son of God, that ye must build your foundation; . . . a sure foundation . . . whereon if men build they cannot fall" (Helaman 5:12).

Though we cannot see the end from the beginning from where we stand, or see the resolution to the host of difficulties that surround us, we can feel the presence of one who was "lifted up upon the cross . . . , that [he] might draw all men unto [him]" (3 Nephi 27:14).

Jeff and I bear witness that building upon such a foundation is the essence of a faithful family. It begins in the temple with "what . . . God hath joined together" (Matthew 19:6). Five children, three apartments, three houses, one snake, and six dogs later, faith in Jesus Christ is the center of our relationship, the driving and sustaining force in our lives.

Faith is so often described by events—like me sitting on the park bench. Those events illustrate and give place and time to the moment we received the testimony that Jesus is the Savior. Usually they are singular, and we count our growth by enumerating them. But faith is also constructed of the small lines that connect those dots. Faith is made up of the little things that are rarely written down, but become evidence that the Lord is there in between as well as on the spot. In fact, the journey is what gives faith its resonance and strength.

So how do we connect the dots when we wonder if we can even keep going? Most of our days are made up of the stuff in between. That's where faith is shaped and toughened. Prayer is a connector; so are patience, humility, diligence, and charity. Confidence in the Lord, that he knows us and knows "the way" back home, helps connect the dots, as does his promise, "not as the world giveth, give I unto you" (John 14:27).

There is no question that the adversary is chipping away at the edges of our sensitivity, our civility, and our standards. He is compromising our trust one with another. He attacks everything that speaks of righteousness, duty, spirituality, or priesthood blessings. The world is contentious and greedy, saturated with sex, and full of itself. Self-confidence, self-esteem, and self-expression have replaced the fullness of faith we find in Mary, "My soul doth magnify the Lord, and my spirit hath rejoiced in God my Saviour" (Luke 1:46–47).

What does Christ call us to do? "Lay aside the things of this world, and seek for the things of a better," the Lord said to Emma Smith (D&C 25:10). How did she do it at a time when she had to pump water from a well and grow her own food? How do you do it in a world that measures value by dress size and paychecks?

Today, I wouldn't trade the cover of *Time* magazine or a *New York Times* best-seller that once called my name for notes like this one from our missionary son Jonathan in England: "I received Mom's letter today, which said that she and Dad put my name in the temple. I know that is why I have had such a great week. I have felt the Lord this week with his hands on my shoulders letting me know that he cares for me and leads me. I am striving to do my best, to do all that he asks."[1]

Sometimes we struggle to fit our connecting dots into the pattern. We may be serving a mission "in the [lowliest] part of [the] vineyard" (Jacob 5:13) or being asked essentially to "sell all that thou hast, and . . . follow me" (Luke 18:22). Sometimes such hearkening means being childless or single. A single mother raised me; she did double duty as a parent. I remember always watching the door when I was in a school concert or a production. She would make it just in time; she'd stand beaming at me from the back, over her arm the green plaid coat she wore for ten years. While so much in our lives seemed outside the pattern, her assurance gave me faith in little things.

Sarah Rich, a Nauvoo refugee turned plains pioneer, is a great example of that kind of faith. She and nearly six thousand other Saints left behind the temple they had so valiantly constructed against all attacks of the adversary. She wrote: "If it had not been for the faith and knowledge that was bestowed upon us in that temple by the influence and help of the Spirit of the Lord our journey would have been like one taking a leap in the dark."[2]

Faith is found in living our covenants made in the temple: the deliberate and daily practice of sacrifice, service, and complete commitment to what Joseph Smith called "the cause of Christ."[3] The Savior said, "I came into the world to do the will of my Father" (3 Nephi 27:13). So did we. His pattern should be our pattern. Do we have faith for the journey?

My great-great-great-grandmother Bathsheba Bigler Smith has been an example to me of such faith. She was a young wife and mother in Nauvoo in its fast-start years. Married to George A. Smith, the youngest member of the Quorum of the Twelve Apostles, she was no stranger to the work of the Lord. She cared for her family with whole-souled devotion; she roofed their home when her husband was serving a mission; at age nineteen, she was in attendance at the organization of the Female Relief Society; she received her endowment in the Red Brick Store when the Prophet Joseph accelerated giving the temple ordinances; she worked tirelessly in the Nauvoo Temple those six critical weeks when Saints lined up to make holy covenants with the Lord.

And then, in the midst of the stormy persecutions and in the company of her husband, family, and fellow Saints, she abandoned her home in Nauvoo. She wrote: "We left a comfortable home, the accumulations of four years of labor and thrift and took away with us only a few much needed articles such as clothing, bedding and provisions. We left everything else behind us for our enemies.

"My last act in that precious spot was to tidy the rooms, sweep up the floor, and set the broom in its accustomed place behind the door. Then with emotions in my heart which I could not now pen and which I then strove with success to conceal, I gently closed the door and faced an unknown future, faced a new life, a greater destiny as I well knew, but I faced it with faith in God."[4]

There was no shaking her fist at the sky, no crying out, "How could you let this happen to me?" She may have closed the door on her home, but in the wagon she took with her the foundation for another—her faith. Where does such faith come from?

"Now I was going into the wilderness," she said, "but I was going with the man I loved dearer than my life. I had my little children. I had heard [the voice of the Lord], so I stepped into the wagon with a certain degree of serenity."[5]

That serenity was born of a testimony that Jesus is the Christ, the Son of God. Her faith in him was the core of her existence. I've closed many doors in my life and, with faith in God, moved on. Faith gets you through a very bad day or a series of them. I've buried a child—his name is Christian—wondering how I would go forward, then found that my faith carried me. This year our last child, Ian, leaves home. Our eldest child, Cameron, and his wife, Kristin, go to medical school in the East. Our son Daniel is getting married next week. Doors are closing all around me. Ahead is a new leg of the journey. It will take faith in God.

How is it for you? Do you recognize that the Lord has felt pain beyond our understanding? And because of his atonement, we have the capacity to connect the dots, to journey forward. It's a matter of faith.

One of my favorite poems, written in 1947 by Vilate Raile, pays tribute to that unfailing faith. Talking about pioneers, she says:

> *They cut desire into short lengths*
> *And fed it to the hungry fires of courage.*
> *Long after—when the flames had died—*
> *Molten Gold gleamed in the ashes.*
> *They gathered it into bruised palms*
> *And handed it to their children*
> *And their children's children. Forever.*[6]

"They cut desire into short lengths." It's a way of measuring faith. We progress line upon line, the Lord says. "In short lengths." In our journey of stops and starts, we must feed "the hungry fires of courage" along the way. And at the end, molten gold will gleam in the ashes. I love the image of gold emerging from the charred embers, as if to say, "Thou shalt be lifted up at the last day" (D&C 5:35). I think of bruised palms—not pierced, as were the Savior's—bruised by our lives of work and trial. It is the hand of the Lord that reached out to Peter when, losing courage, he began to slip into the water. That same hand reaches out to us. We hand down that faith to our children and our children's children. Faith is what ties families together, forever.

By faith we connect the dots to those who have gone before. I never imagined myself a family history buff. For the most part I saw my faith being played out in different Church arenas. But something happened to me inside, where faith resides. I started to research the Swinton line. This line of research seems logical, except Jeff isn't really a Swinton; he's a Miller. The name Swinton was adopted from his stepfather.

The first day I walked into the Family History Library, the books and aisles of microfilm made even grocery stores look malnourished. I started to work and struggled through weeks and months ahead. It was hard work. I was starting at the grandfather, which wasn't that far back. I prayed; I pawed through books; I couldn't find anything to open that line. No names, no dates, no places.

One Saturday morning, the phone rang. A friend who had recently moved from my ward said, "I was just looking on the Internet and saw a picture of Linton J. Swinton. Are you related to him?" I gasped. Linton was the name of the grandfather. "There's a picture of him on the Internet for sale for ten dollars," she said. "Let me give you the site." I bought the photograph, and when it came, I found a clue. On the back was written, "Linton, 16½ months old." On the front was the photographer's name and the words Brooklyn, New York. Linton J. Swinton was not from Washington State, as family tradition suggested, but from the other side of the country! I went to Brooklyn records from 1893; there he was—a birth date and parents. There was hope, but I wasn't home free yet.

For months I searched for names and found nothing. I prayed and went to the temple, thinking that the names might drop down from the sky. Nothing. Yet, I loved the work. I had to set a timer so that I would get to what was pressing, or I would have looked for dead Swintons all day long. They were always in the back of my mind. They had the faith I would find them.

In desperation, I posted a note on a bulletin board on a genealogy site. Can anyone connect the dots from Kenneth to Linton to the next generations? Months and months I waited. Then last October, I did my routine check of the message board, and found an e-mail from Australia with information that fit the sequence. I sent money for copies and for more information. In February stacks of material came in the mail. I had found the Swintons from East Lothian, Scotland. William and his oldest son, David, had emigrated in 1839 to the United States. After a brief stop in Birmingham, Alabama, they had settled in Warsaw, Illinois. Connect the dots!

Warsaw is forty miles south of Nauvoo. Warsaw, the hotbed of anti-

Mormon hostility. I am in the midst of writing a documentary on the Nauvoo Temple; I am steeped in Nauvoo, 1839 to 1846. Both Jeff's and my lines stream west through Nauvoo. It was no fluke that I was impressed to work on that line. I found the Swintons—seven generations so far—and now I have their names ready for temple work. This is faith on both sides of the veil.

Faith also asks us to set aside our fears. "Be strong and of a good courage," God told Joshua as he faced giants in the promised land (Joshua 1:6). To the early Saints he spoke of faith this way: "Fear not, little flock" (D&C 6:34; 35:27). Fear—it's the opposite of faith. That's why the Lord is always cautioning, "Be of good cheer, and do not fear" (D&C 68:6). Fear, like the mists of darkness, is Satan's way of trying to cloud our vision. What the adversary does not understand is that those who have eyes to see, who are not looking around them, are looking ahead where the sky is illuminated with the Savior's promise, "Where I am [there] ye shall be also" (D&C 27:18).

Faith is the overriding theme of book after book in the scriptures. I love the faith of Isaiah: "And the Lord shall guide thee continually, and satisfy thy soul in drought, and make fat thy bones: and thou shalt be like a watered garden, and like a spring of water, whose waters fail not" (Isaiah 58:11). And the strength of Hannah: "For this child I prayed; and the Lord hath given me my petition which I asked of him" (1 Samuel 1:27).

Some people can open the scriptures and point to a verse at random for answers, but reading every day connects the dots for me. When I need strength, a witness, or personal inspiration, it's right there on the page where I have read that morning or the day before, underlined with a date; the Lord knew just what I would need, what counsel, what teaching.

Let me quickly dispel the idea that I have always been an avid scripture reader. Years ago, I was preparing to teach a Relief Society lesson. My scriptures were brand new, the kind a perfectionist like me would like—the pages were crisp, pristine, no underlining or writing in the margins. The morning of my lesson, I decided I would read to the

class the suggested passage right from my new set of scriptures instead
of from the manual. "Behold my Spirit is upon you, . . . and the mountains shall flee before you, and the rivers shall turn from their course;
and thou shalt abide in me, and I in you; therefore walk with me"
(Moses 6:34).

I pulled out my scriptures to mark the verse, Moses 6:34, and
turned to the Bible. *Let's see, Moses ought to be somewhere near the front,*
I thought as I scrolled down those tabs. *Hmm. Nothing looks like Moses.*
I began leafing through the pages. No Moses. I turned to the table of
contents at the front of the Bible—no Moses. I was stunned and called
my mother. With great consternation I said, "You will not believe this.
They left the book of Moses out of my Bible." After a long pause she
gently suggested, "Maybe that's because it's in the Pearl of Great Price."

It's all a matter of faith. Faith in Jesus Christ is the first principle
of the gospel, the essence of our earthly experience. We exercise faith
in Jesus Christ or we don't. It's that simple.

When visiting New York in 1832, Joseph Smith wrote home to
Emma: "O how long, O Lord, shall this order of things exist and darkness cover the Earth and gross darkness cover the people." He continued, "I pray that God will give you [Emma] strength that you may not
faint. I pray God to soften the hearts of those around you to be kind to
you and take the burden off your shoulders as much as possible . . . but
you must comfort yourself knowing that God is your friend in heaven
and that you have one true and living friend on Earth, your husband."[7]

I know that counsel to be true.

The Lord also says to Emma through Joseph, "Hearken unto the
voice of the Lord your God, while I speak unto you, . . . my daughter"
(D&C 25:1). I have heard that voice in my own home.

Last Sunday I sat in the special blue chair in our living room; Jeff
and three of our five sons circled around me, their hands on my head.
It was a singular spiritual experience; our youngest son, Ian, ordained
an elder earlier that day, was giving his first priesthood blessing—to his
mom.

I know that my Redeemer lives. I love him; I love his work; I love his gospel. My sweetest moments are those described so beautifully by Isaiah, "Seek ye the Lord while he may be found, call ye upon him while he is near" (Isaiah 55:6). With such faith, may we connect the dots from here to eternity.

Notes

1. Letter in author's possession.
2. Sarah Rich, as quoted in Carol Cornwall Madsen, *Journey to Zion: Voices from the Mormon Trail* (Salt Lake City: Deseret Book, 1997), 173.
3. Joseph Smith, *The Personal Writings of Joseph Smith*, ed. Dean C. Jessee (Salt Lake City: Deseret Book, 1984), 246.
4. Bathsheba Bigler Smith, as quoted in Carol Cornwall Madsen, ed., *In Their Own Words: Women and the Story of Nauvoo* (Salt Lake City: Deseret Book, 1994), 213; also in Heidi S. Swinton, "On Your Right Hand and on Your Left," *Every Good Thing: Talks from the 1997 BYU Women's Conference*, ed. Dawn Anderson, Dlora Dalton, and Susette Green (Salt Lake City: Deseret Book, 1998), 322.
5. Ibid.
6. Vilate Raile, in Asahel D. Woodruff, *Parent and Youth* (Salt Lake City: Deseret Sunday School Union Board, 1952), 124; also in *Selected Writings of Gerald N. Lund*, Gospel Scholars Series (Salt Lake City: Deseret Book, 1999), 402–3.
7. Joseph Smith, *Personal Writings of Joseph Smith*, 252–53; spelling and punctuation standardized.

"Go Ye Out to Meet Him"

Jeffrey C. Swinton

Last month my scripture reading led me to Doctrine and Covenants 133. The headnote read, "Prefacing this revelation the Prophet wrote: 'At this time there were many things which the Elders desired to know relative to preaching the Gospel to the inhabitants of the earth, and concerning the gathering; and in order to walk by the true light, and be instructed from on high.'"

That caught my attention, particularly the words "in order to walk by the true light, and be instructed from on high." Always anxious to know more about how to walk in the light and receive instructions from the Lord, I read on.

Verse 10, which speaks of Jesus Christ as the Bridegroom, opened a window in my mind. It says, "Awake and arise and go forth to meet the Bridegroom; behold and lo, the Bridegroom cometh; go ye out to meet him." For some reason the proactive phrasing—"awake and arise and go forth" and "go ye out to meet him"—energized me. I reflected whether in my own life I am really going out to meet him, or if I am waiting for him to come to me.

Our willingness to go out to meet him is, in large part, predicated on our testimony of who he really is and why his life is so important in ours. My testimony of Jesus Christ is an ever-evolving story. It did not come all at once. I don't recall waking up one morning and knowing every aspect of our Church was true. Some may have that experience;

Jeffrey C. Swinton, a Salt Lake City attorney, is the executive director of the Salt Lake Inner City Project. He and his wife, Heidi, are the parents of four sons. He is serving as a stake president.

however, my testimony has grown more "line upon line, [and] precept upon precept" (D&C 98:12).

It began in high school while I was singing with the seminary choir. I still remember the feeling—not because of a good memory but because the experience has been replicated hundreds if not thousands of times since. I have come to recognize the feeling as a spiritual confirmation. The Lord counseled Oliver Cowdery that in his case, the Lord would "cause that your bosom shall burn within you" (D&C 9:8). We each have our own way of describing how we feel. I have occasionally called it "the shivers"—not that it is cold but that it is spine tingling, like something cutting diagonally down and across my back.

I recall having that feeling while singing "Come, Come, Ye Saints"[1] to conclude our seminary choir performances, but most memorable was what I felt at the end of that year in a choir testimony meeting. The feeling then was dramatic and unmistakable, even though I could not then articulate what it really meant.

As the years have progressed, I have come to realize that the feeling of "the shivers" is the Lord's way of telling me yes: yes, that story is true; yes, that is the right solution; yes, that is the right person.

In that same revelation, Oliver was told, "You must study it out in your mind; then you must ask me if it be right" (D&C 9:8). From that I learned not to expect an answer to come in full sentences without any effort on my part. I read that passage as the Lord saying, "Don't expect me to answer the question without giving me your choices."

There have been times when an answer has come to me with an entire concept laid out in my head. More typical, however, are the occasions when I have asked the Lord *yes* or *no* questions. The Lord is not restricted to answering in a single word, of course, but I have found it easier for me to recognize a simple answer. All I have to do is know when the Lord is saying yes. Each time that has happened, my testimony has been strengthened.

I picture my testimony as a brick wall. At first, the wall looked a bit like a checkerboard, a brick here and a brick there with spaces in between, covering a broad area but with many holes. Many yes answers were among those bricks:

Yes, I should go on a mission.

Yes, I should marry Heidi.

Yes, our firstborn son, who had died, actually lives on the other side of the veil.

For many of these bricks, I can recall the circumstances and the place. The answer about the mission? It came on a freeway off-ramp while driving Heidi home from a date. Imagine how excited she was. That wasn't in the script. The confirmation that I should marry Heidi? I knew on first sight after she returned home from graduate school— four and a half years after we had begun dating. And of our firstborn son? While standing at his graveside. Heidi and I stood among weeping friends and family, yet we were cloaked with a spirit that spoke peace to our hearts and to our minds. In each case that same feeling paused to touch me as if it were a familiar friend, always showing up just at the right moment.

Over time, what I had been taught became undeniable—the Spirit works within the Church. But what about all those stories? An angel? Gold plates? The truthfulness of the Book of Mormon? One at a time, over the years, those questions have been answered, and with each answer, another brick has been inserted in the wall of my testimony.

About twenty years ago, I sat near the rear of the congregation at the unveiling of a historic painting of Moroni delivering the gold plates to Joseph Smith on the Hill Cumorah. I was one of two bishops serving in the building where the painting, once painted on a brick wall, had now been restored and was being unveiled at the front of the chapel. I had seen it dozens of times as we arranged for its placement, but that night the painting was undraped as its history was told and the mood set, and without forethought or even anticipation, "the shivers" began, saying, "Yes, what is depicted in this painting actually occurred just as Joseph Smith said it did." Another brick had been cemented in, a specific spiritual confirmation that I knew meant yes.

My confirmation of the truthfulness of the Book of Mormon is another story. I had read it a number of times and borne testimony of it, but had never felt that I had had a specific confirmation of its truthfulness as described in Moroni 10:4. Then one morning, while on my exercycle with the Book of Mormon on the reading stand, I once again concluded the entire Book of Mormon. I had come to the tenth chapter of Moroni, not for the first time, but *prepared* this time. I had received it, pondered it in my heart, asked God the Eternal Father in the name of Christ if it were true, with a sincere heart and with real intent and with faith in Christ. And then, as promised, it happened. Just as clear and distinct as confirmations in the past, "the shivers" coursed through me as I read the words: "He will manifest the truth of it unto you, by the power of the Holy Ghost" (v. 4).

I have learned that a *yes* can come in many places: On the freeway or in the congregation, on an exercycle or at the side of a grave. As I think about it, I find myself humming the tune to "Count Your Blessings" and substituting the words, "Count the yesses, name them one by one."[2]

The wall of my testimony was filling in beautifully. I knew that the Book of Mormon is the word of God and that Joseph Smith was the prophet of God who received the gold plates from an angel. I knew there is life after death. But I was lacking the most significant brick of all.

I recall when my seminary teacher bore his testimony to our class by reading Doctrine and Covenants 46:13. "To some it is given by the Holy Ghost to know that Jesus Christ is the Son of God, and that he was crucified for the sins of the world." He told us he was one who could so witness. He had been given to know by the Holy Ghost. He had felt a yes.

He then read verse 14: "To others it is given to believe on their words, that they also might have eternal life if they continue faithful." He invited us to believe on his words if we did not yet have a testimony of our own. I remember accepting that invitation and thinking of myself as a verse 14 guy, one to whom it is given to believe on the words of another. I wondered then, and often thereafter, what it would feel like to be a verse 13 guy, to know for myself through a confirmation of the Holy Ghost.

Years passed and the wall of my testimony continued to strengthen. Then twelve years ago, Heidi received the assignment from Deseret Book to research and compile the testimonies of each of the latter-day prophets concerning his testimony of and reverence for Jesus Christ. She was both excited and overwhelmed. She was to read everything that every man who became the president of the Church in this dispensation ever wrote or said at any time in his life concerning his testimony of Jesus Christ and then compile those testimonies into one book. (This was before general availability of computer-assisted research.) Heidi would be searching through original records, published books and articles, and microfilm in the Church Archives. Because she was under a short deadline, she asked me to help. With great enthusiasm I accepted the assignment, and the work became a team effort—like so many other things in our marriage.

This was not the first time we had worked together for a common spiritual purpose. As with other Latter-day Saint couples, most major decisions in our life have been based upon joint spiritual confirmations, and somehow gospel-related topics have regularly woven their way into most of our conversations. Throughout our marriage, Heidi and I have taken turns strengthening one another's testimony. Heidi's book on the prophets was another singular opportunity. It was a bit of a quest: Heidi and Jeff in search of testimonies of the Savior—not just for a book but also and perhaps most important, for themselves. I was anxious to participate, honestly believing that this might open the door for me to step into the realm of verse 13.

Heidi began with President Harold B. Lee. President Lee had been a neighbor of mine in my youth and had sealed our marriage in the temple. We each felt close to him. When she had completed a chapter containing many quotations from his talks and writings, she set it aside, believing that his testimony had been well covered. One day while she was sitting at home in a closet we had outfitted as a tiny office, she felt a prompting to go to the Church Archives and do further research on Harold B. Lee. Three times she discounted the prompting, rationalizing that it was too late in the day, it would take too long, she had sufficient material for the chapter, and she would not know where to start when she got there.

After the third prompting, she gave up resisting and drove to the archives an hour and a half before it closed. She parked her car and walked right past the desk. "Heidi, you must be in a hurry," said one of the staff members, noting that Heidi had forgotten to check in her purse. "What can I help you with?" Heidi asked for the Harold B. Lee microfilm. When the cart came, the staff member said, "Which roll do you want?" I recall Heidi telling me how she mustered a dramatic posture and said, "I don't know."

Not knowing why she had been sent and still certain it was a waste of time, she looked aimlessly through microfilm rolls of President Lee's talks and writings, which had become very familiar to her. Tape after tape rolled by, and then she was prompted to stop when she read in the index of a roll the name of a 1971 speech given by President Lee to seminary and institute instructors. It was entitled "Objectives of Church Education."

You wouldn't think that title would stop someone who was looking for a talk that spoke of his testimony of Jesus Christ. Nevertheless, she felt prompted to read and found a dramatic paragraph she had never seen before. Was that the purpose of her errand? The peaceful answer was yes. She copied the paragraph and inserted it into the Harold B. Lee chapter. She told me of the experience that evening but didn't share with me what she had found.

Some time later Heidi asked me to review the completed chapters to see how they flowed and whether the material was appropriate and not duplicated. I can still remember sitting in my office downtown and reading the Harold B. Lee chapter. One paragraph caught me off guard, and the shivers began. It was clear. It was dramatic. It said yes.

I wrote about my spiritual confirmation in the margin and later returned the chapter to Heidi without sharing the experience. Several days later she called me at my office: "I was just reading your comments in the Harold B. Lee chapter." You know the rest of the story. The paragraph that touched me so profoundly was the very paragraph she had found that day in the archives. It may be that no one else on earth has ever been touched spiritually by that paragraph. But what was important for me was that I had been. In a joint effort between husband and wife to fulfill an assignment, Heidi had been directed by the Spirit to find and then include the very words that would resonate with my spirit. I am so grateful to her for responding to the prompting the third time it came.

We both learned a great deal as we compiled material for the book. We naively expected to come across stories of face-to-face communications between latter-day prophets and Jesus Christ. If those encounters occurred, the Church presidents didn't speak publicly about them. But what they did say was even more significant. To a man, in one way or another, each of them said that his testimony of Jesus Christ was built upon a confirmation from the Holy Ghost. We learned that we don't have to see him to know him.

Let me share with you the paragraph that touched my soul and prompted my own spiritual confirmation. President Lee said, "When I came to this position as a member of the Quorum of the Twelve, I was told that my chief responsibility now was to bear testimony of the divine mission of the Lord and Savior of the world. That was almost a crushing realization of what it meant to be a member of the Quorum of the Twelve Apostles. I was assigned to give the Easter talk the Sunday night following the general conference. As I locked myself in one of the rooms of the Church office building, I took out my Bible and read from the four Gospels the life of the Master, particularly leading down to his crucifixion and resurrection. And as I read, I became aware that something different was happening. It no longer was just a story of the doings of the Master, but I realized that I was having an awareness of something I had not had before. It seemed that I was reliving. I was feeling intently the actual experiences about which I was reading. And when I stood that Sunday night, after expressing myself as to the divine mission of the Lord, I said, 'And now, as one of the least among you, I declare with all my soul that I know . . . ' I knew with a certainty that [which] I had never known before. Whether that was the more sure word of prophecy I had received, I don't know. But it was with such conviction!"

And then these words, which gave me the shivers: "More powerful than sight is the witness of the Holy Spirit which bears testimony to your spirit that God lives, that Jesus is the Christ, that this is indeed the work of God. I knew it because I had felt it, and there had been a testimony borne to my soul that I could not deny."[3] When I read that paragraph, the witness about which he was talking was happening to me. I couldn't doubt it, and I will never forget it.

That was a big brick and a big yes. The most critical of all. And it is still there—carefully mortared into place as the centerpiece of the wall of my testimony. Like so many times in our marriage, Heidi was the catalyst. No longer did I have to believe on the testimonies of others about Jesus Christ. A testimony had come to me by the power of the Holy Ghost as had been promised.

I don't believe I am unique.

President Gordon B. Hinckley, at the 2000 First Presidency Christmas devotional, spoke of the Prophet Joseph Smith as Christ's "great testator." He cited, as an example, the unequivocal testimony from the Johnson Farm in Hiram, Ohio, found in Doctrine and Covenants 76: "And now, after the many testimonies which have been given of him, this is the testimony, last of all, which we give of him: That he lives! For we saw him, even on the right hand of God; and we heard the voice bearing record that he is the Only Begotten of the Father" (D&C 76:22–23).

President Hinckley affirmed that each of us can also know. He said: "The testimony of the great Prophet of this dispensation has been repeated and confirmed by generations of Latter-day Saints who have received a certain knowledge by the power of the Holy Ghost."[4]

Are you one of them? I read President Hinckley's statement as an invitation to each of us to join the generations of Latter-day Saints who have received that certain knowledge by the power of the Holy Ghost.

President Ezra Taft Benson said: "A most priceless blessing available to every member of the Church is a testimony of the divinity of Jesus Christ and His church."[5] In the process and as a means of gaining that testimony, and thereafter, we would all do well to abide by the counsel of Alma to his son Helaman, found in Alma 37:36–37. "Yea, and cry unto God for all thy support; yea, let all thy doings be unto the Lord, and whithersoever thou goest let it be in the Lord; yea, let all thy thoughts be directed unto the Lord; yea, let the affections of thy heart be placed upon the Lord forever.

"Counsel with the Lord in all thy doings, and he will direct thee for good; yea, when thou liest down at night lie down unto the Lord, that he may watch over you in your sleep; and when thou risest in the morning let thy heart be full of thanks unto God." He ends then with the promise: "And if ye do these things, ye shall be lifted up at the last day."

How important is it to gain a testimony of Jesus Christ? Ask yourself this question: How important is it that you be lifted up at the last day? My advice? "Go ye out to meet him." If you are married, make it a joint effort. Be proactive in the things you do that will refine and cleanse your receptors so when the Holy Ghost testifies to you, you will be worthy to receive it. Then in that day when you do meet Jesus Christ, you will recognize him because you will already know who he is by the power of the Holy Ghost.

My life is different now that verse 13 is mine. I conclude with part of verse 13 in my own testimony. I testify that I now "know that Jesus Christ is the Son of God, and that he was crucified for the sins of the world."

Notes

1. William Clayton, "Come, Come, Ye Saints," *Hymns of The Church of Jesus Christ of Latter-day Saints* (Salt Lake City: The Church of Jesus Christ of Latter-day Saints, 1985), no. 30.
2. "Count Your Blessings," *Hymns*, no. 241.

3. Harold B. Lee, "Objectives of Church Education," address to seminary and institute personnel, 17 June 1970, Brigham Young University, 7–8, LDS Church Archives; see also *I Know That My Redeemer Lives: Latter-day Prophets Testify of the Savior* (Salt Lake City: Deseret Book, 1990), 170.

4. Gordon B. Hinckley, "First Presidency Christmas Devotional 3 December 2000: My Redeemer Lives," *Ensign*, February 2001, 72.

5. Ezra Taft Benson, *Come unto Christ* (Salt Lake City: Deseret Book, 1993), 11.

TRIALS TO PASS THROUGH, TRIALS TO LIVE WITH

S. Brent Scharman

"What a wonderful time it is to be alive, here at the turn of a milestone century!" wrote President Gordon B. Hinckley. "[M]y plea is that we stop seeking out the storms and enjoy more fully the sunlight. I am suggesting that as we go through life, we 'accentuate the positive.'"[1] Good advice, but as President Hinckley and many other authorities also acknowledge, life is difficult. Compare these words, also President Hinckley's, from his biography: "I have felt a sense of sadness and depression the last few days," he admitted privately. "It has almost overwhelmed me."[2] In addition, "I have put on a veneer of smiles," he confided in his journal on another occasion, "but I feel under a deep cloud of depression. I suppose it is the spirit of the adversary, but it is real indeed."[3]

These sobering words of President Hinckley, in sharp contrast to his usual sunny good cheer, make clear that discouraging times, even depressing times, can be part of life for any of us—even the most optimistic and spiritual. For some, depression is brief, circumstantial, and passes. For others, it can be more serious and consuming.

In 1976, when I was hired by LDS Family Services, it was my first full-time professional job since graduation and a quick descent from the academic world of theory and role-plays to the sometimes harsh world of reality. It wasn't shocking to me—I was thirty-two and had seen my share of earthly challenges—but it was humbling to see that the

S. Brent Scharman, a licensed psychologist, manages the Evaluation and Training Department of LDS Family Services and is chair of the Church's Missionary Mental Health Committee. He and his wife, Jan, have a combined family of ten children. Brent currently serves on a stake high council.

streams of Latter-day Saints coming for help were good people who had been working hard to improve their lives and their relationships, but without finding the happiness and contentment for which they were searching.

One of my most powerful memories is of a small weekly meeting of women who were all experiencing the same problem—depression. Each of these women was intelligent, sincere, and clearly doing her best to live the gospel. Nevertheless, a common thread emerged in their reports. Each felt inadequate and somehow unworthy. As a young and rather inexperienced practitioner, I was hard pressed not to fall into the trap of just giving them pep talks and pointing out how capable they were and how wonderful their lives seemed to be. On the few occasions when I attempted that approach, they surprised me by reassuring me that I was wrong and discounting my observations of them. Eventually the group ended and we each went our separate ways. Nothing dramatic had happened, but we had all learned some things and grown from taking risks and sharing. We all, including myself, went back to our worlds with a better acceptance of our imperfections and, I hope, with a clearer understanding of our individual worth and value.

After twenty-five years working as a clinician with LDS Family Services in the Salt Lake agency, I have observed that women experience significant amounts of depression.[4] I have also observed that women have tremendous resiliency, are not content to remain unhappy, and, through facing their feelings and learning to solve problems, are generally able to find the peace they seek. Men, of course, experience depression as well, but are less inclined to request help.

In a Family Services devotional, a colleague of mine recently told a touching story of a client he had not seen for five years. At the time of their last contact the client had been struggling with a host of feelings and behaviors, all frustrating and disappointing. Depression and discouragement were the end result of his lengthy battle. For a variety of reasons, my friend and this individual could no longer continue meeting. They had had good therapy sessions, medications had been prescribed, but neither had helped significantly. As they met for the last time, my friend encouraged the client to "just keep doing the basics," which he described as attending church meetings, hanging onto his church calling, keeping the commandments, and serving others.

My friend related the experience because he had just heard from the client, who was now doing remarkably well. He was active in the church, attending the temple, and happy, experiencing none of the old depressed feelings. My friend considered the events a fulfillment of the direction Alma gave his son in Alma 38:5—"And now my son, Shiblon, I would that ye should remember, that as much as ye shall put your trust in God even so much ye shall be delivered out of your trials, and your troubles, and your afflictions, and ye shall be lifted up at the last day."

As I heard the story, I felt I was hearing about a miracle just as real as the New Testament miracles that seem so dramatic when we read them. I don't know why life got better for this man who prayed and showed faith, when life doesn't get better for everyone who follows that formula. I can only offer this comment by Elder Neal A. Maxwell: "Some of the most important prayers we have offered are those that were not answered as we hoped they might have been."[5]

Membership and activity in the Church do not exempt us from unpleasant feelings, though the meaning and purpose they give to life help us cope. In addition, they regularly bring us in contact with a nurturing support group. Above all, they help us understand how the atonement of Jesus Christ can have personal relevance in our lives.

Do people have more problems today than they used to? I believe they do, and, what's more, the problems seem to be more complex. Why? I find a number of reasons, including the following:

- Unhealthy, excessive competition in school and on the job
- Unreasonably long work hours to gain financial independence
- Inadequate sleep, which reduces the ability to cope
- Increased efforts to meet personal needs in selfish ways, i.e., bigger homes, status purchases, "keeping up with the Joneses"
- A harsh media, which not only overloads us with immediate,

matter-of-fact reporting of terrible tragedies, but bombards us with examples of physical attacks, verbal confrontation, shocking revelations, excessive debates on every subject, belittling of any opponents, criticism, negativism, broken relationships, and selfish decisions

- Erosion of trust in accepted traditions and history
- Decisions at every level prompted by fear of legal recrimination rather than honest intent
- Divorce, with accompanying financial and emotional insecurity
- Single parenting, which burdens the adult and disadvantages the child
- Challenges of one parent working two jobs or both parents working
- Hectic lifestyles that limit personal rejuvenation and family connections
- Overindulged children who don't learn to work or face life's challenges
- An increase in unhealthy and addictive influences such as drugs, alcohol, pornography, gambling

Any or all of these can lead to significant anxiety and depression. In addition, personal observations, combined with feedback from coworkers,[6] have pointed to several factors that are more common among LDS women who are experiencing depression or anxiety. Perfectionism inevitably causes disappointment with self, fear of failure, or low self-esteem. Feelings of powerlessness and futility come from disappointment over critical eternal issues such as infertility, divorce, singleness, or wayward family members. Many women feel frustrated trying to resolve some women's issues, such as working outside the home or trying to combine careers and motherhood. Some have difficulty accepting a biological predisposition (to anxiety, addiction, depressions, and so on). Biological predispositions can be particularly frustrating in the environment of strong LDS belief in the doctrine of agency and self-determination.

In spite of the reality of these problems and more serious mental health problems, I find reason for hope. I love the words of President

Hinckley: "We must walk with hope and faith. We must speak affir-matively and cultivate an attitude of confidence. We all have the capacity to do so."[7]

Hope, beneficial in and of itself, motivates us to get the help that we need. Hope competes with our worries, and the stronger of the two emotions wins an important battle. Daniel Goleman, author of *Emotional Intelligence*, notes: "Our worries become self-fulfilling prophecies, propelling us toward the very disaster they predict. . . . People who are hopeful evidence less depression than others . . . , are less anxious in general, and have fewer emotional distresses. . . . Optimism and hope, like helplessness and despair, can be learned."[8]

Elder Boyd K. Packer once remarked: "Teach our members that if they have a good, miserable day once in a while, or several in a row, to stand steady and face them. Things will straighten out. There is great purpose in our struggle in life."[9] How do we know when our anxiety or depression is one that will pass after a few "good, miserable days" or one that won't? Further, how do we know when we're experiencing thoughts and feelings which we can resolve ourselves or when we need revelation, or divine intervention, or medical help?

Overcoming anxiety, depression, and other emotional conditions generally takes both personal revelation and personal effort along with all the resources at our disposal. "Through Christ and his church, those who struggle can obtain help," counseled Elder Dallin H. Oaks. "This help comes through fasting and prayer, through the truths of the gospel, through church attendance and service, through the counsel of inspired leaders, and, where necessary, through professional assis-tance."[10] One of the benefits of living today is the multitude of helps we have at our immediate disposal. To overlook them is to unnecessar-ily delay our healing.

Let me make four observations from my experiences with Church members who have sought counseling at LDS Family Services or BYU. First, these individuals were experiencing distress severe enough to make them take action and request outside help. Second, most had already spent time on their own praying and pondering about their

condition and were still suffering. Third, most of these individuals felt
that counseling was helpful and that their condition improved. Fourth,
in each case counseling combined the efforts of a values-based therapist, a nonjudgmental ecclesiastical leader who provided gospel-based
direction, and, when needed, a physician to prescribe medication.

When an emotional state has some biological roots, medication
can help. It's beyond the scope of this article to clarify how you can tell
the difference, but four important observations would be:

1. The more physical symptoms you have, such as sleep disturbance, appetite disturbance, memory problems, difficulties with concentration, and inability to feel pleasure, the more likely that there's a
biological component to your condition.

2. The less control you have of the feelings and the more they seem
to come and go at will with no logical explanation, the more likely
they are to have a biological base.

3. The more your feelings are deteriorating progressively and pre-
venting you from carrying out daily tasks, the more likely it is a biological source.

4. A family pattern of similar problems among blood relatives
makes a biological base likely.

Distressing moods generally pass in time, sometimes because we
actively intervene and problem solve, and sometimes because they just
seem to lose their power. In fact, our moods are most often neutral,
with periodic highs and lows. Feelings that are intense, controlling, and
do not pass in a matter of weeks, however, require some type of intervention. Research suggests that most depression will respond adequately to treatment within a period of months. Medication usually
helps a little quicker than talk therapy, but talk therapy provides long-
term insight and behavior change. The best professional treatment
generally combines both approaches.

Occasionally people do not fully recover from behavioral or emotional conditions. Life for them can become a discouraging series of
emotional ups and downs that may feel cruel and unfair. "Some
undergo searing developments that cut suddenly into mortality's status

quo," commented Elder Neal A. Maxwell. "Some have trials to pass *through*, while still others have allotments they are to live *with*."[11] Though disappointing, having to live without being healed may be little different from enduring other unwanted challenges, like diabetes, asthma, or arthritis.

On November 18, 1995, violinist Itzhak Perlman came on stage to give a concert at Avery Fisher Hall at Lincoln Center in New York City. Getting on stage is no small achievement for Perlman, who was stricken with polio as a child, has braces on both legs, and walks with the aid of two crutches. At this particular concert, Mr. Perlman finally got to his chair, released the braces, and adjusted his legs prior to performing. "Just as he finished the first few bars," reported newspaper editorialist Jack Reimer, "one of the strings on his violin broke. You could hear it snap—it went off like gunfire across the room." The audience assumed he would leave the stage to either replace the string or exchange violins.

"But he didn't. Instead, he waited a moment, closed his eyes and then signaled the conductor to begin again. The orchestra began, and he played from where he had left off. And he played with such passion and such power and such purity as they had never heard before.

"Of course, anyone knows that it is impossible to play a symphonic work with just three strings. I know that, and you know that. You could see him modulating, changing, recomposing the piece in his head. At one point, it sounded like he was de-tuning the strings to get new sounds from them that they had never made before.

"When he finished, there was an awesome silence in the room. And then people rose and cheered. There was an extraordinary outburst of applause from every corner of the auditorium. We were all on our feet, screaming and cheering, doing everything we could to show how much we appreciated what he had done.

"He smiled, wiped the sweat from his brow, raised his bow to quiet us, and then he said, not boastfully, but in a quiet, pensive, reverent tone, 'You know sometimes it is the artist's task to find out how much music you can still make with what you have left.'"[12]

Some who struggle with anxiety or depression are periodically called upon to live their lives as though they were playing with three strings. It's miraculous when the outcome is supernal, as was the performance of Itzhak Perlman. Sometimes it's also miraculous when the outcome is merely to keep going one more day.

The ultimate solution to life's challenges lies in understanding how the Savior's atonement applies in our lives. "The Savior's Atonement is stunningly inclusive," Sheri Dew explained. "His Atonement makes available all of the power, peace, light, and strength that we need to deal with life's challenges—those ranging from our own mistakes and sins to trials over which we have no control but we still feel pain.

" . . . Our responsibility is to learn to draw upon the power of the Atonement. Otherwise, we walk through mortality relying solely on our own strength."[13]

Life is worthwhile in spite of its struggles. Some of our most important learning can evolve from suffering and coping with anxiety, depression, fears, and worries. It is within our ability to shape the thoughts and feelings we have and learn to control our behavior.

This personal revelation of President James E. Faust touches me: "At times I have stumbled and been less than I should have been. All of us experience those wrenching, defining, difficult decisions that move us to a higher level of spirituality. They are the Gethsemanes of our lives that bring with them great pain and anguish. Sometimes they are too sacred to be shared publicly. They are the watershed experiences that help purge us of our unrighteous desires for the things of the world. As the scales of worldliness are taken from our eyes, we see more clearly who we are and what our responsibilities are concerning our divine destiny."[14]

Whatever degree of depression, anxiety, or other worldly pain you may be experiencing, I pray that it may be made more bearable by a clear understanding of who you are, from whence you came, and your ultimate eternal potential. No one, from the least to the greatest, is exempt from the pain. Yet after the trial comes the promised joy and peace. You may depend on that.

Notes

1. Gordon B. Hinckley, *Standing for Something: Ten Neglected Virtues That Will Heal Our Hearts and Homes* (New York: Times Books, 2000), 101.

2. Gordon B. Hinckley, in Sheri L. Dew, *Go Forward With Faith: The Biography of Gordon B. Hinckley* (Salt Lake City: Deseret Book Co. 1996), 382.

3. Ibid., 384.

4. Studies have consistently shown that members of the Church are no more likely to experience depression than nonmembers.

5. Neal A. Maxwell, "Jesus, the Perfect Mentor," *Ensign*, February 2001, 12.

6. Last year approximately 130,000 hours of clinical counseling were conducted at the offices of LDS Family Services. Approximately 21,000 hours were conducted at the counseling center at BYU.

7. Hinckley, *Standing for Something*, 104.

8. Daniel Goleman, *Emotional Intelligence* (New York: Bantam Books, 1995), 84, 87, 89.

9. Boyd K. Packer, *That All May Be Edified* (Salt Lake City: Bookcraft, 1982), 94.

10. Dallin H.Oaks, "Same-Gender Attraction," *Ensign*, October 1995, 13–14.

11. Neal A. Maxwell, "Content with the Things Allotted Unto Us," *Ensign*, May 2000, 72; emphasis in original.

12. Jack Riemer, "To Do with What We Have," *Houston Chronicle*, 10 February 2001.

13. Sheri L. Dew, "Our Only Chance," *Ensign*, May 1999, 66–67.

14. James E. Faust, "A Growing Testimony," *Ensign*, November, 2000, 59.

WHEN HEARTS FAIL THEM

Dana Templeman

A man once tried to reach one of his workers at home. The employee's little boy answered the phone and whispered, "Hello." The man asked, "Is your daddy home?" "Yes," came the reply. "Can I talk to him?" the man persisted. "No," the little boy said, continuing to whisper. The man then asked, "Is your mother home?" "Yes," the little boy said. "Can I talk to her?" "No." Feeling a little irritated by now, the man asked if anyone else was there. "Yes," the boy replied, "the policemen." Now the employer was becoming concerned and asked if he could talk to one of the policemen. "No," replied the little boy, "they are busy talking to the firemen." Alarmed, the employer quickly asked, "What is going on?" The boy fell silent for a moment, then responded, "They're looking for me."

This story illustrates an important truth: There are times family members and friends don't respond to our attempts to help them. Even though their hearts may be filled with righteous desires, feelings of anxiety, depression, inadequacy, or other adversities may be holding them back.

According to the 1999 surgeon general's report on mental health, nearly one in five Americans suffers from a mental or behavioral disorder in a given year. These disorders affect males and females of all ages, ethnic groups, religious backgrounds, races, and socio-economic classes. Causes may include environmental, biological, genetic, and

Dana Brewer Templeman is a licensed therapist with a master's degree in social work. She is currently assigned as Director of International Adoption Development for LDS Family Services. Dana is the mother of four sons. She serves as a teacher in her ward Relief Society.

psychological factors. Treatment varies. There is no "one size fits all" solution. Medication, psychotherapy, support, and education can help, but it takes courage and faith for individuals, like the little boy in the story, to come out of hiding, to be found, to ask for help—and to receive it. With these thoughts in mind, what can we do when we see someone we care about struggling?

First, don't assume that an individual who is mentally ill just lacks the willpower to get better. If we are angry or ashamed of people with mental illness, then we are perpetuating the stigma, shame, and guilt that are associated with any mental disorder.

In a recent talk, Elder Alexander B. Morrison addressed some of the concerns caused by mental distress and illness: "[There are some] who, in their lack of understanding and empathy, mistakenly believe that the mentally ill just need to 'snap out of it, show a little backbone and get on with life.' Those who believe that way display a grievous lack of knowledge and compassion. The facts are that seriously mentally ill persons simply cannot, through an exercise of will, get out of the predicament they are in. They need help, encouragement, understanding and love. Anyone who has ever witnessed the incredible, well-nigh unbearable pain of a severe panic attack, knows full well that nobody would suffer that way if all that was needed was to show a little willpower. No one who has witnessed the almost indescribable sadness of a severely depressed person, who perhaps can't even get out of bed, who cries all day or retreats into hopeless apathy, or tries to kill himself, would ever think for a moment that mental illness is just a problem of willpower. We don't say to persons with heart disease or cancer, 'just grow up and get over it.' Neither should we treat the mentally ill in such an uncompassionate and unhelpful way."[1]

Elder Morrison also noted: "We are learning that many mental illnesses result from chemical disorders in the brain, just as diabetes results from a chemical disorder in the pancreas." He concluded his talk by saying that he hoped we could "rid ourselves of the stigma and bias about this important problem. With knowledge and understanding comes love, acceptance, empathy and enfoldment."[2]

Second, don't blame the individual or yourself. Name-calling, label-ing, and judging are not productive and often leave unnecessary emo-tional wounds that create lasting barriers in relationships. For example, several years ago a friend of mine was under a great deal of stress from his employment. The stress continued to intensify, and he eventually became depressed. He wanted to be a good provider and meet the growing needs of his family, but he soon realized he needed help. He finally shared his feelings of despair and hopelessness with his wife, even admitting that he had experienced some suicidal thoughts. All he wanted was her understanding, sympathy, and perhaps an offer of sup-port. To his deep disappointment, she remained silent. When he fin-ished pouring out his heart to her, she told him his feelings were his own fault and his problem. Fortunately, this man found help and recov-ered from his depression, but the hurt remains to this day. He continues to feel that his wife sees him as weak and really does not care about him.

"Most often, in their lack of understanding about the causes of mental illness, victims blame themselves," says Elder Morrison, "and many seem unable to rid themselves of terrible, though undefined, feel-ings that somehow, some way, they are the cause of their own pain—even when they're not. Parents, spouses, or other family members too often harrow up their minds trying futilely to determine where they went wrong. They pray over and over again for forgiveness, when there is no objective evidence they have anything of note to be forgiven of. . . . Of course, in the vast majority of instances none of this works, for the simple reason that the victim's thoughts and behavior result from disease processes which are not caused by the actions of others, includ-ing God.

"Ascribing blame for mental illness causes unnecessary suffering for all concerned and takes time and energy which would better be used to increase understanding of what actually is happening—to get a com-plete assessment and proper diagnosis of the illness involved."[3]

Third, try to understand the person who is suffering. Remember he or she is a beloved child of God. Symptoms or adversities are elements of our human experience and do not reflect our individual worth. To help someone, take the time to learn about that person. What is important to them? What are their fears? How do they cope? What things upset or irritate them? Learn about their illness, or struggles, and then listen to what they say so you can gain a sense of what they are experiencing and how it affects them. By understanding them, you can take a more active role in their recovery.

My friend's brother suffers from schizophrenia. On one visit, she and other family members were irritated that he kept turning up the volume on the television. When my friend took the time to ask him about it, she was surprised to learn that he turned up the volume to drown out the voices in his head. What seemed logical to him was seen as irrational to observers. Once my friend learned the reason for his behavior, she was able to help him find alternatives that were more socially acceptable.

When trying to help, be considerate of the individual's agency. Force may only compound the problem. Ask how you can help meet needs and goals, and don't assume that the way you would handle things is the best way. For instance, you may enjoy running and the sense of well-being it gives you. A depressed person who is experiencing fatigue and low motivation might find this same activity stressful and unrewarding. In fact, not being able to meet your expectations could add to their guilt and feeling of worthlessness.

It is always good to stress that you want to help, that you care, and that you will be there for them. Encourage them to stick to their treatment plan and to take recommended medication. Remind them how valuable they are to you and to others. Often people who are suffering think there is nowhere to turn. Yet help is available and recovery is possible. Offer to help them locate whatever resources and assistance they may need to follow through with a treatment plan.

Fourth, develop coping skills for yourself as a caregiver. Be aware of your own feelings, embarrassment, and limitations. Find someone you can talk to. Keep a journal. Putting your feelings into words can often help you organize your thoughts and envision constructive solutions.

Work on developing patience. It is hard to watch those we love struggle with illnesses, trials, and disappointments, and only natural to hope that they will be healed through fasting and prayer. Yet, most often, people who are mentally ill do not get well overnight. It can take weeks or months for medication or therapy to take effect, or even make a noticeable difference. It can be frustrating when initial treatment fails, and the suffering person must try new medications and approaches. They may get well only to relapse. Patience is vital.

You may start to feel that their struggles are becoming *your* adversity in life. Anger can result from fear and frustration. Find appropriate ways to express your feelings. If emotions escalate, take a "time-out." Sometimes adults need them too.

In a conference address, Elder Richard G. Scott counseled: "Don't let the workings of adversity totally absorb your life. Try to understand what you can. Act where you are able; then let the matter rest with the Lord for a period while you give to others in worthy ways before you take on appropriate concern again."[4]

Be patient and kind to yourself. You cannot do everything. In the scriptures we are instructed not to "run faster" than we "have strength" (D&C 10:4). Draw on the strength from others when needed and remember to take care of yourself in the process. Even the Savior took forty days to refill his cup

At one time or another, we all may find ourselves in emotional turmoil. In 1 Kings 18–19, we read about Elijah, who found himself in a state of mental and emotional stress. Here was a man, one of the greatest, most dedicated prophets of all time, who had become so effective in his ministry in Israel that the Queen, Jezebel, wanted him killed. Elijah "went a day's journey into the wilderness, and came and sat down under a juniper tree: and he requested for himself that he might die; and said, It is enough; now, O Lord, take away my life" (19:4). The Lord responded to his mental anxiety by touching him (physical contact), providing him with food (physical comfort), sending a friend (social comfort), and having his friend administer to him (spiritual comfort). What a perfect example of the kind of compassion we should emulate.

Though we are more comfortable surrounded by people who are just like us, the Lord encourages us as church members to reach out to those who are struggling. Your contact and service may be the only way someone in emotional turmoil will be able to feel the Spirit. The Lord's work is accomplished with our hearts and our hands. By learning to be understanding, patient, and supportive of others, we can assist the Lord in bringing them the promised peace they long for.

Notes

1. Alexander B. Morrison, "Some Myths and Misconceptions about Mental Illness," presentation to Pioneer Welfare Region Leaders, Salt Lake City, 21 April 2001, 4.
2. Ibid., 2, 5.
3. Ibid., 3.
4. Richard G. Scott, "Trust in the Lord," *Ensign*, November 1995, 17.

FOR HEAVEN'S SAKE

Helen Monson

Despite my angelic appearance, I was a mischievous child. As the second of three girls, I was either fighting with one sister or bullying the other. When my sisters were not around, I tried to get attention in other ways—usually by getting into trouble.

One day I plugged up the bathroom sink just to see how full it could get. Only when the water verged on overflowing did I attempt to pull the plug. Unfortunately, my three-year-old arms were no match for the tightly stuck plug, and my slippery, wet hands could not shut off the tap. Soon water was dripping all down the sides of the sink and onto the floor, and as I watched helplessly, I wondered what type of punishment fit this type of crime.

Downstairs, Mother, who was talking on the phone, felt a drip on her forehead. Looking up, she saw water seeping through the ceiling. She rushed upstairs into the bathroom, saw me at the sink, and exclaimed, "What on earth are you doing, for heaven's sake?"

Her words have stayed with me through the years, and have gradually taken on a new meaning. As each of us passes through life, we ought to pause on a regular basis and ask ourselves, "What on *earth* am I doing for *heaven's* sake?"

When I asked myself that question two years ago, I wasn't pleased with my reply. I determined right then that I would not have to answer the same way in the future, that somehow I was going to make a difference. I prayed for direction. Even though I am a full-time student at

Helen Monson, a convert to the Church from Wales, is a graduate of Brigham Young University in human development. She has done genealogy research for more than five thousand family names. She is married to Michael Monson, a law student at Brigham Young University.

Brigham Young University with a full-time job, church callings, and a full social life, the unexpected answer came to me that I should pursue my family history research. Because I am a convert to the Church, no research had been done on either side of my family. One grandparent had tried to help me by giving me a few names and dates, but most of them turned out to be inaccurate. Nevertheless, it was a start, and I began what has become one of my greatest passions and an incredible blessing in my life.

In his book, *The Holy Temple*, Boyd K. Packer points out, "Temple and genealogical work constitutes a living testimony of the ministry of the Lord Jesus Christ. He wrought the Atonement; He set in operation the resurrection. . . .

"Every thought or word or act we direct at this sacred work is pleasing to the Lord. Every hour spent on genealogical research, however unproductive it appears, is worthwhile. It is pleasing to the Lord. It is our testimony to Him that we accept the doctrine of the resurrection and the plan of salvation."[1] Elder Dallin H. Oaks has counseled, "Our effort is not to compel *everyone* to do *everything*, but to encourage *everyone* to do *something*."[2] For me, starting genealogy was simply a matter of trial and error, until I understood what I should be looking for and where to find it. Although it can become tedious at times, the process of research is not hard; it just requires perseverance and dedication.

I first began tracing my ancestry at the Utah Valley Family History Library on campus at BYU, looking through old census records, church records, and books. Once a young man in my ward, who had shown quite an interest in me of late, asked me if he could accompany me to the library. He was taking a family history class at BYU and thought he might need my "expertise"! We were at that awkward stage of dating, still trying to impress each other, but also watching out for signs of weirdness.

At the library, I helped him find the records that he needed to look through and left him working while I went to the microfilm room to look for my own family names. I placed my roll of film onto the spindle, attached it to the empty reel, and then turned the handle to wind the reel forward or backward as I looked for information.

I was trying to find a certain section of the microfilm and adjust the focus before I sat down to make myself comfortable for close-up work. With one arm pumping the handle vigorously and both eyes glued to the screen, I had no idea that my head was so close to the reel until it was too late. I had completely wound my hair into the empty reel. Pull as hard as I could, there was no escaping and no one nearby to help. I considered shouting out across the library, "Help, I'm stuck in the genealogy machine!" and began laughing hysterically. Luckily my friend heard me and came to see what was so funny. Chuckling, he kindly set me free; but needless to say, our relationship did not last very long beyond that point.

I do not tell you this story to terrify you of the demon machines they keep hidden down in the library, but merely to point out that if I can recover from such an embarrassing genealogical ordeal and still continue to love this work, it must be very significant and rewarding. I bear testimony that this service brings an increase of love to our lives. My heart has become full of love in *all* aspects of my life, and my relationships with family and friends have improved dramatically.

President Joseph Fielding Smith said, "There is no work equal to that in the temple for the dead in teaching a man to love his neighbor as himself."[3] President Hinckley has stated, "This work, unselfishly given in behalf of those on the other side, comes nearer to the unparalleled vicarious work of the Savior than any other of which I know."[4]

A passage in *House of Glory*, by S. Michael Wilcox, illuminates the very essence of how we serve our brothers and sisters in the temple. "Here are my eyes; together we will look upon the beauty of the Lord's house. Here are my ears; let us hear the words of eternal life. Here are my lips; we will make sacred covenants. Here are my hands; together we will receive the gifts of life everlasting. Here are my knees; kneel with me at the altars of salvation, there to become one with those we both love."[5]

When we make an effort to do our family history work, miracles occur. Let me share one miracle that happened to me. I had found information about my mother's great-great-grandfather, John Picknett, and his four children in the 1881 census. However, I found no mention of a wife. I searched through the marriage register transcripts for St. Peters Church in Redcar, Yorkshire, and found an entry in 1858 for the marriage of this same John Picknett to a Hannah Shaw. Now I had a name, a marriage date, and the ages at which they both were married. Using that age, I figured that Hannah would have been seventeen years old at the time of the 1851 census.

As I searched the 1851 census microfilm for my great-great-great-grandmother, my heart sank. I couldn't read a single word on the old film. I kept winding the film, hoping that it would clear and that I would be able to recognize something behind the black mess of ink. After about ten minutes, I decided to ask for help. Two library workers came over to my carrel to offer their assistance. I could tell from the looks on their faces that they were not optimistic. They couldn't read anything on the film either, and by way of condolence, one of the workers said to me, "That is the worst film I have ever seen."

Alone in my carrel, I bowed my head and started to cry. I closed my eyes and said a quiet prayer. "Heavenly Father, I don't understand. I am trying my best to do what is right and to help these people. I know that I am doing the right thing; I know that they want me to find their names. I cannot do this by myself. If it is thy will that these names are to be found, please help me." I looked up, almost expecting to see her name right there in front of my face, but I didn't. I turned the handle and continued my search, but still found nothing, just blackness. Still I turned, not really knowing why, when slowly some of the illegible scrawlings began to resolve into words. As if my eyes had become magnifying lenses, I could read some of the names on the page in front of me. At the bottom of the page I read, "Head: James Shaw 1803, Wife: Sarah Shaw 1793, Children: Ann, William, Hannah, James and Jane." There was Hannah Shaw, my great-great-great-grandmother, and not only that but there were all her siblings, and her parents. Since this time, I have been able to complete the temple work for this family, including the sealing of Hannah's parents and all of their children, as well as the sealing of Hannah to her husband, John Picknett, and their children.

Clearly, as Elder Richard G. Scott observed: "This is a spiritual work, a monumental effort of cooperation on both sides of the veil where help is given in both directions. It begins with love. Anywhere you are in the world, with prayer, faith, determination, diligence, and some sacrifice, you can make a powerful contribution. Begin now. I promise you that the Lord will help you find a way. And it will make you feel wonderful."[6] He also said that "when we permit the Lord to work through us to bless others, that sacred experience releases power in our own lives, and miracles occur."[7] I have felt this power flow into me in ways that I could never have imagined.

Let me tell you about another experience. My grandfather, who passed away when I was three, has only one living sibling. Her name is Enid, and she lives on the Isle of Man, a small island between northern England and Ireland. I had never met her, and knew nothing about her. No one had contacted her for more than fifteen years. I decided to try and establish a relationship. I also wanted to find out more about my grandfather. My grandmother wouldn't talk about him as it was too emotional for her, and so all I had were a couple of faded memories. I didn't even have a photograph.

I wrote to Enid, and we communicated through letters for several months. Then I decided to visit the Isle of Man. I bought a plane ticket, and on my Christmas break, set off to meet my great-aunt. It was one of the best experiences of my life. Enid and her husband Don were extremely accommodating and helpful. I had told her that I was interested in family history and asked if she could make whatever information she had accessible for me when I was there. I had no idea how wonderful this experience would be. I came home with photographs, copies of birth and wedding certificates, newspaper clippings, and obituaries. The names and dates from these sources allowed me to research and find information for more than seven hundred people in this line. Seven hundred people! That is a lot of happy people on the other side of the veil. And I now have a picture of my grandfather.

When I am doing temple work for my relatives, I say a prayer in my heart that they will accept the gospel and the ordinances being performed for them. Of course, acceptance is their choice, and I sometimes wonder whether in their own lifetimes any of my ancestors had values and beliefs similar to my own.

My great-great-grandmother Harriet Williamson wrote a poem that helps me understand what she believed in. This poem, titled "A Mother's Love," was written for her eldest child.

> *A link between us strong and sweet*
> *And let your heart to mother beat*
> *My love is with you everywhere*
> *You cannot get beyond my prayer*
> *I shall with glad impatience wait*
> *For you before the Golden Gate*
> *After earth's parting and earth's pain*
> *Never to part, never again*[8]

This poem leaves no doubt in my mind that Harriet has now accepted the restored gospel of Jesus Christ. I can only imagine how joyous she must have felt to realize the dreams expressed in her poem could be possible. Just last week in the St. George Temple, my husband and I knelt across the altar as proxies for Harriet and her husband, Myles, to be sealed together as husband and wife for all eternity. As I knelt there, my heart full, these words came again to my mind, "Here are my eyes; together we will look upon the beauty of the Lord's house. . . . Here are my hands; together we will receive the gifts of life everlasting. Here are my knees; kneel with me at the altars of salvation, there to become one with those we both love."[9] Let me ask the question that I began with: "What on *earth* are you doing for *heaven's* sake?" I invite you to discover for yourselves the rewards and joy of family history and temple work, and I repeat the question I began with: What on *earth* are you doing for *heaven's* sake?

Notes

1. Boyd K. Packer, *The Holy Temple* (Salt Lake City: Bookcraft, 1980), 255.
2. Dallin H. Oaks, "Family History: 'In Wisdom and Order,'" *Ensign*, June 1989, 6; emphasis added.
3. Joseph Fielding Smith, *Doctrines of Salvation*, 3 vols., ed. by Bruce R. McConkie (Salt Lake City: Bookcraft, 1954–56), 2:144.
4. Gordon B. Hinckley, "Rejoice in this Great Era of Temple Building," *Ensign*, November 1985, 60.
5. S. Michael Wilcox, *House of Glory* (Salt Lake City: Deseret Book, 1995), 96.
6. Richard G. Scott, "Redemption: the Harvest of Love," *Ensign*, November 1990, 7.
7. Richard G. Scott, "The Power to Make a Difference," *Ensign*, November 1983, 71.
8. Harriet Williamson, "A Mother's Love," 1 February 1885, copy in possession of the author.
9. Wilcox, *House of Glory*, 96.

THE DESIRED RESULT

Lyn H. Denna

"The furnace of affliction" is where we often find ourselves pouring out our hearts to our Heavenly Father. In affliction we learn how prayer works in our lives. The scriptures share countless examples. Miracles answered the prayers of Hannah and Sarah, who were barren; Moses, who lead the children of Israel out of Egypt; Daniel in the lion's den; Esther and her people; Alma's wayward son; and Joseph Smith in the Sacred Grove. These accounts of God's interaction with his children give hope and strengthen our faith.

But what of Lehi, who prayed for his two rebellious sons, and Joseph Smith, who prayed for deliverance from imprisonment and inhumane treatment in the Liberty Jail? Surely Abinadi must have asked for relief, and what of the prayers of Mormon and Moroni, who watched their people revel in iniquity and perish in sin? Even Jesus Christ prayed, "Oh my Father, if it be possible, let this cup pass from me" (Matthew 26:39).

I, like you, have had many prayers that I felt were answered to my satisfaction and others that were not. "It is so hard when sincere prayer about something we desire very much is not answered the way we want," taught Elder Richard G. Scott. "It is especially difficult when the Lord answers *no* to that which is worthy and would give us great joy and happiness. Whether it be overcoming illness or loneliness, recovery of a wayward child, coping with a handicap, or seeking

Lyn H. Denna, a returned missionary and graduate of Brigham Young University, has held numerous leadership positions in the Church and community. A professional homemaker, she brings beauty into her home through her outstanding skills with music, handwork, quilting, and gardening. She and her husband, Eric L. Denna, are the parents of seven children.

continuing life for a dear one who is slipping away, it seems so reasonable and so consistent with our happiness to have a favorable answer. It is hard to understand why our exercise of deep and sincere faith from an obedient life does not bring the desired result."[1]

Some of the answers to these questions come from a better understanding of the true nature of prayer. Prayer is not our avenue to let God know what we want and see if we can convince him of the necessity of our requests. The Bible Dictionary says, "As soon as we learn the true relationship in which we stand toward God (namely, God is our Father, and we are his children), then at once prayer becomes natural and instinctive on our part (Matt. 7:7–11). Many of the so-called difficulties about prayer arise from forgetting this relationship."[2]

In 1981 my husband, Eric, and I were blessed with a son whom we named Benjamin. A matter of hours after his birth, it was apparent to the doctors that all was not well with the baby, and he was transported to Primary Children's Medical Center. At the end of that very long day, the doctor sat down with us and explained that Benjamin had a heart condition called *truncus arteriosus*. At that time, the oldest living child with this defect was only eight years old.

As we drove home, we tried to understand the many ways in which our life had suddenly changed. Benjamin was our second child, and we were students living close to poverty level. We stood in a financial, spiritual, and emotional whirlwind and needed something to hold on to. We arrived to a quiet, empty kitchen, just the two of us. Eric helped me to a chair and suggested that we pray. Pray? What would we say? I was consumed with what I will call the "Poor Me Syndrome." How would we manage the impending medical bills? How could I love this sweet little soul just to have him taken from me? I had given birth only hours before. Where would I find the strength to care for our daughter and an infant in the hospital?

My husband was voice for our prayer. I did not know until years later that he didn't know himself what to say, but he knelt and addressed our Heavenly Father. Then it became natural, instinctive, as the Bible Dictionary puts it. Here we were, two children approaching a loving Father who we knew wanted to embrace us, strengthen us, help us be successful. As this relationship came into focus, words came to Eric as naturally as a light, refreshing rain. He thanked our Heavenly Father for this son and all that he came with, and for all that we would become because of his condition. As I heard these words, my heart changed too. I felt the power of God's spirit cleanse my heart of the darkness that had engulfed it. From that moment on, I began looking forward to the adventure that awaited us.

Understanding our divine relationship with our Father also helps us know what we must do to have a two-way communication. Essentially, we can't disregard what we come to know he expects of us and still expect him to grant our every wish. Elder Neal A. Maxwell has said, "Knowing and behaving are irrevocably linked."[3] Obedience to the Lord's commandments not only prepares us to know what to ask for, it conditions our hearts to hear the Lord's answers.

In my youth, I never asked the Lord if I should serve a full-time mission. I avoided asking on purpose. I was afraid that if I asked he would answer "yes," and I didn't want to serve. I had all sorts of reasons: I was too fat, too unprepared, too eager to be found by some handsome young returned missionary and go off into the sunset with him, bearing a bevy of little children who would wear spotless white pinafores and never have green, runny noses.

Although I never asked the "mission" question, I always tried to follow the commandments. Many of my prayers included a plea that the Lord would guide me in my path and help me know what I should do. I tried to be anxiously engaged in doing the right thing and staying on the right path. Through a series of events, I found myself one day sitting on my bed working on an afghan. I was listening to music written for the musical, *Threads of Glory*, commissioned by the Church to celebrate the bicentennial. My mind was floating, open to thoughts that casually passed through.

I don't think I heard a voice, although I could have—the experience was so vivid and real. But I know the Lord spoke to my heart and to my mind. In an instant, I knew I was supposed to serve a mission.

More important, I *wanted* to. Never had I received direction with such power or clarity, nor have I since. The Lord, in his tender mercies, was willing to speak to me a little louder to help soften my heart to this particular option in my life.

Obeying, with exactness, is one way we can ask God to write his will upon our hearts. Obedience on my part had prepared a conduit for our Heavenly Father to reveal his will, and at once our wills were intertwined. As the Bible Dictionary says, "Prayer is the act by which the will of the Father and the will of the child are brought into correspondence with each other. The object of prayer is not to change the will of God, but to secure for ourselves and for others blessings that God is already willing to grant."[4]

When I read this passage for the first time, I thought, *That seems simple enough! You pray, the Father reveals his will, you do it, and you live happily ever after.* But for me, it has never been that easy. Another line in the Bible Dictionary enlightened me. It is not meant to be easy! "Blessings require some work or effort on our part before we can obtain them. Prayer is a form of work, and is an appointed means for obtaining the highest of all blessings."[5]

Before Rex E. Lee became president of Brigham Young University, he was diagnosed with cancer and had undergone grueling medical procedures. At that time, his wife, Janet, experienced firsthand the work involved in prayer. She knew the fundamental elements of prayer and felt that her prayers had matured through the years, but in her fear of losing Rex, her prayers, she said, became childish again. "In the first few days after the diagnosis, I must have sounded like a two-year-old, demanding and insisting that I have my way. 'Please, Heavenly Father,' I had begged over and over, 'make him well.' . . . But these prayers did nothing to bring the healing balm I needed for my wounded spirit.

"Soon, without even realizing it, I changed my prayers. I began to instruct, reason, even bargain with the Lord. 'Surely,' I would plead, 'there are things on this earth for him to do. He is still useful here. Send him anywhere, ask him to do anything, and I will be at his side

helping. Take away everything we own, but please leave him here.'
Again, I found no peace.

"That Sunday as I bowed my head, my prayer was significantly different from my previous pleadings. 'If it be thy will,' I began, 'let Rex recover from his cancer. Thou knowest the desires of my heart, but I recognize that I do not understand all things. Please strengthen me to meet the challenges ahead, and please calm my troubled heart.' Finally peace came. . . .

"The assurance that came to me that day was not that Rex's cancer would be cured forever, but that a loving and all-knowing God would be by my side. As I quietly arose to return to the hospital, I remembered the sentiment expressed somewhere in a biography of C. S. Lewis—that we do not pray to change God; we pray to change ourselves."[6]

Faith is a critical element in prayer, faith in our Heavenly Father's desire to bless us. As parents, we must also be willing to exercise another type of faith—faith in our children's ability to get answers to their prayers. My natural inclination as a mother is to answer all our children's queries, tell them what to do, expect them to trust in *my* revelation in their behalf and then obey. Instead, we should encourage our children to practice the principles of prayer themselves, and then show them that we trust their experience. Sometimes the decisions they come to will not be life changing, but our demonstration that we trust their ability to receive revelation will be.

Two personal experiences with our sons taught me this concept. Our youngest, Tate, loves mountain biking and desperately wanted to buy a very expensive mountain bike. To me, the all-knowing mother, it was clear that he should be saving his money for his mission. The bike was an unnecessary extravagance. His father encouraged him to pray about this decision. I worried that he would receive the "wrong" answer. I wasn't ready to allow him to make this choice without my intervention. Fortunately, Eric and I took the time to discuss this at length. With infinite patience he pointed out that our son had been taught correct principles, and now we had the opportunity to support him as he applied the principles of personal revelation that he had been assured were true. Eric helped me understand that even if Tate's choice were different from what we would want, he would learn more from experiencing the process firsthand than if we continued to tell him what to do. Our Heavenly Father allows *us* this exercise of agency, and we should allow our son the same. Tate and I both learned important lessons through this experience.

The second experience involved a far less frivolous decision. In spite of four open-heart surgeries, Benjamin, the son I mentioned earlier, enjoyed a good childhood. He was fourteen years old when he once again became sick. Doctors opened his chest once more in September. By November he again had to endure an emergency surgery, his sixth open-heart repair. At this point, doctors told us that his only option now was a heart transplant. A transplant was not going to make all his troubles go away; it would only change the type of challenges he would face. On the other hand, not getting a transplant meant increased suffering for Benjamin and a painful death.

We knew that the ultimate decision had to be Benjamin's. He was tired—from too much suffering, too much pain for one so young. He had borne it with dignity, but his reserves were low and his stamina depleted. We counseled with him and sought counsel. I was convinced that going for the transplant was the right—the only—option, and Benjamin knew how I felt. Finally one evening Benjamin told us that he had decided to go for the transplant. I was relieved. He was only fourteen years old—too young to make such a critical decision. His father, however, knew that a fourteen-year-old could receive answers to prayers. After all, Joseph Smith was this tender age when God, the Father, and his son, Jesus Christ, appeared to him in answer to earnest, sincere prayer. Eric asked Benjamin if he had prayed about his choice. He hadn't. Eric encouraged Benjamin to ask his Heavenly Father what he thought Benjamin should do.

That night Benjamin hardly slept. He prayed for a while, lay in bed, then prayed some more, repeating this cycle until dawn. By morning, with his IV pumps hanging on his shoulder, this tired but peaceful young man came gingerly down the stairs. He entered the office and said, "Dad, I think Heavenly Father wants me to come home . . . and I'm OK with that."

In general conference, Elder Richard G. Scott counseled us: "Try to understand what you can. Act where you are able; then let the matter rest with the Lord for a period."[7] Shakily, trying to follow this advice, we decided to do our part: we put Benjamin on the transplant list, but we kept him at home. We had been told that unless he was actually in the hospital, he would be low on the transplant list. His health was so fragile that we knew he wouldn't last long at home. Benjamin was comfortable with this arrangement.

As expected, he quickly deteriorated until the doctors pleaded with us to bring him into the hospital for a few days to see if they could adjust his IV medications. They hoped to buy him a few additional weeks. We convinced Benjamin to go into the hospital one more time.

After a day of trying, the doctors realized they couldn't help Benjamin any more. Benjamin took his father's hand that night and pleaded, "Please, just let me go home." The doctors agreed to send him home first thing in the morning.

Benjamin and Eric were sitting on his bed discussing what they'd like to do at his funeral when a nurse came in, clearly trying to contain her emotions. She motioned Eric out into the hall. Because Benjamin had gone back into the hospital, he had been bumped to the top of the transplant waiting list. There had been a car accident. A young man's parents had just given consent to donate his heart.

Eric went back into the room to see what Benjamin wanted to do. Benjamin asked questions while his father tried to answer. Would he have to take lots of medicine? Yes. Would he still have to have the pacemaker? No. Would he still have lots of doctor's visits? Yes. Would he be able to eat regular food? No, he would still have to eat what his mother cooks, just like the rest of the family.

Finally Benjamin decided, "I'll do it. I'll have the transplant, but," he continued, "I don't understand. Why did I pray so hard and think I got a different answer from this?"

Suddenly, as though a door had been thrust open, Eric, with perfect clarity, remembered the experience of Abraham and Isaac. Abraham's test was not truly to sacrifice his only beloved son—a son he had prayed for, waited long for, and loved deeply. Nor was Isaac ultimately required to give his life as a sacrifice. Their test was to submit to the will of the Father. Through demonstrating their willingness to submit so completely that Abraham had the knife poised in the air, the test was complete.

So it was for our family. Heavenly Father needed to know if we were willing to put everything on the altar, "and," Eric said to Benjamin, "I believe Heavenly Father accepts your offering with as much joy as he accepted Abraham and Isaac's."

A celestial experience took place in a tiny, sterile hospital room because a father had the courage to invite his son to experience for himself what prayer is all about.

Each of us has the privilege of coming to a better understanding of our relationship with our Heavenly Father, obeying his commandments, and showing our willingness to submit to his greater understanding. As we do this, our prayers will guide and direct us, strengthen our resolves, provide peace, and allow us to stand in holy places.

Notes

1. Richard G. Scott, "Trust in the Lord," *Ensign*, November 1995, 16; emphasis in original.
2. LDS Bible Dictionary, s.v. "prayer," 752.
3. Neal A. Maxwell, "The Inexhaustible Gospel," *Ensign*, April 1993, 71.
4. LDS Bible Dictionary, s.v. "prayer," 752–53.
5. Ibid., 753.
6. Rex and Janet Lee, with Jim Bell, *Marathon of Faith* (Salt Lake City: Deseret Book, 1996), 62–65.
7. Scott, "Trust in the Lord," 17.

"BE THOU AN EXAMPLE OF THE BELIEVERS"

Jane Henriod Wise

An elderly friend once confided to me that sometimes when she glanced in the mirror she'd start back and say, "Who's that old woman?" I smiled, but at twenty-two I didn't really understand. As I was walking through a department store recently, the same thing happened to me. I glanced to the side, not knowing there was a mirror there, and wondered who that rather matronly woman was—and then, shocked, realized it was I.

How wonderful it would be if we were as philosophic as the apostle Paul when he described himself as an empty clay pot. He wasn't concerned about how beautiful or young or strong the pot was. He knew what was most important about him, and he called it a "treasure." It was the light, that "power of God" that illuminated the clay pot, that made it "excellent" (2 Corinthians 4:6). He wanted all followers of Christ, the Saints, the believers, to recognize this power in them.

We have that power in us, that "treasure." We are believers. What are we to do with that power and light? The Savior said, "I am the light of the world: he that followeth me shall not walk in darkness, but shall have the light of life" (John 8:12). Believers who follow Christ have "the light of life" and are named, like him, "the light of the world" (Matthew 5:14). That "light" is to "shine" forth with such radiance that others seeing our "good works" will praise and glorify God (Matthew 5:16). How do we use our light so that others will glorify

Jane Henriod Wise is a legal writing teacher at the J. Reuben Clark Law School and the editor of its publications. She also teaches for BYU's Church History Department and writes for the Tabernacle Choir's program, "Music and the Spoken Word." She practices law part-time with her father, Joseph L. Henriod. She and her husband, Stuart R. Wise, are the parents of four children.

God? Christ told us, "Ye know the things that ye must do . . . for the works which ye have seen me do that shall ye also do" (3 Nephi 27:21).

Isaiah said the works of Christ would proclaim who he was to the world. "The Spirit of the Lord God is upon me; because the Lord hath anointed me to preach good tidings unto the meek; he hath sent me to bind up the brokenhearted, to proclaim liberty to the captives, and the opening of the prison to them that are bound; . . . to comfort all that mourn; . . . to give unto them beauty for ashes, the oil of joy for mourning" (Isaiah 61:1–3). Paul later described the words of Christ when he wrote: "God anointed Jesus of Nazareth with the Holy Ghost and with power: who went about doing good, and healing all that were oppressed of the devil; for God was with him" (Acts 10:38).

Christ worked through the Spirit with power to do good and to put to right sick bodies and souls. We must do these same things, for the Spirit of the Lord is upon us too. Let's see how it works when believers' lives are filled with light and Spirit. At the feast of Pentecost, the Spirit descended on the believers. In the aftermath of that spiritual outpouring, the Saints were filled with a tremendous tide of generosity and love. They "had all things common; and sold their possessions and goods, and parted them to all men, as every man had need" (Acts 2:44–45). The believers were connected, giving to each other as they saw need, worshiping together, and spending much time in the temple. They even ate their food together with glad hearts (Acts 2:46). They were a community of saints committed to worshiping God and committed to each other. One of the hallmarks of being a believer and being filled with the Spirit is realizing that we are not alone: we have been given people to love and people who love us.

Peter and John were part of that community of believers. One afternoon as they were going to the temple to pray, a beggar who had been lame since birth stopped them at the gate. This man knew his job. What better place to beg in all Jerusalem than at the temple gate where the pious, fresh from the temple, would give him generous alms. How did Peter and John respond? "Peter, *fastening his eyes upon him with John*, said, Look on us" (Acts 3:4; emphasis added).

We have all seen people begging for money. How many of us like to make eye contact with those on the street who are begging, holding up pitiful signs: "Homeless," "Will Work for Food," "Please Help," "God Bless"? The easy thing is *not* to make eye contact because when we do, we see them as human beings and that calls forth some sort of connection and effort on our part. Many times that is more than we want to do.

But Peter and John were filled with the Spirit and with light. They had spent much time in the temple worshiping God. They didn't see just a beggar. They saw a man the way the Lord in his earthly ministry saw men and women. Remember, Peter and John now stood where the Savior had stood: to do the works that the Lord would have done. Why do you think so many sinners and outcasts were drawn to the Savior? It was because when Jesus *looked* at them, he saw children of God full of possibilities, people capable of rising up. The Lord never wrote off anyone, even if everyone else had. So, Peter and John "fastened their eyes" on this man—remember, believers have to look outside their community. Evidently, the beggar wasn't making eye contact with them. It must have been hard for that lame man to compare himself, day in and day out, with people who could walk, who had families, who were strong. So, not only did Peter and John look on him, they commanded him to "look on us." And that is what healing requires. It takes an individual's complete attention. It requires lifting your eyes above your distress to see hope.

Once Peter and John had reached out to this man, they were not about to leave him in a place where he was less than what he could be. He had asked them for alms, but Peter answered, "Silver and gold have I none; but such as I have give I thee: In the name of Jesus Christ of Nazareth rise up and walk" (Acts 3:6). That is what Peter and John had to offer—healing. They had the power that all believers have— that we have!—to offer hope in the name of Christ.

"And [Peter] took him by the right hand, *and lifted him up*: and immediately his feet and ankle bones received strength" (Acts 3:7). Peter didn't just tell the man to get up. He took him by the hand and raised him up. Believers have the power to lift people up. "And he leaping up stood, and walked, and entered with them into the temple, walking, and leaping, and praising God" (Acts 3:8).

In this wonderful story, Peter and John showed forth dramatic power as believers. The results of that power caused a commotion. We read that "all the people saw [the beggar] walking and praising God . . . and they were filled with wonder and amazement [and they] all . . . ran together unto them in the porch that is called Solomon's, greatly wondering" (Acts 3:9–11).

Unconcerned about any possible outcome, Peter and John weren't stingy with what they'd been given from God. There was no counting the costs it took for them to be an example. They weren't about to hide their lights under a bushel. They let power and light blaze forth, for they had given themselves over to Christ. They belonged to him.

C. S. Lewis often borrowed a parable from the great Christian writer George MacDonald which describes what it means to belong to Christ when he asks us to imagine ourselves as a living house. "God comes in to rebuild that house. At first, perhaps, you can understand what He is doing. He is getting the drains right and stopping the leaks in the roof and so on: you knew that those jobs needed doing and so you are not surprised. But presently He starts knocking the house about in a way that hurts abominably and does not seem to make sense. What on earth is He up to? The explanation is that He is building quite a different house from the one you thought of—throwing out a new wing here, putting on an extra floor there, running up towers, making courtyards. You thought you were going to be made into a decent little cottage: but He is building a palace. He intends to come and live in it Himself."[1]

Have we made room for him? Have we made room for the light and power within us? They are precious gifts that can change the world, both inside and out. That change can be dramatic! The scriptures are full of examples of believers wielding earth-shaking power: mountains move, the sun stops in the heavens, the heavens are closed, the heavens are opened, fire falls from the sky. The sick are healed. The dead are raised. But those outward, physical signs of God's power are not as important as the inward signs, wherein we are remodeled into a palace. Peter and John healed this man who had been lame from his birth. But more important, they gave him the one name under heaven that can save, and he leaped and danced and praised God. The outward healing that Christ gave and Peter and John performed is never just about relieving physical problems; everyone they healed eventually got sick again and died. Healing sick bodies by the power and in the name of Jesus Christ is done to keep us in *remembrance* of his power to heal sick souls and transform us. How do these things happen?

As Alma proclaimed, almost excusing himself for the plainness of this truth: "Now ye may suppose that this is foolishness in me; but behold I say unto you, that by small and simple things are great things brought to pass; and small means in many instances doth confound the wise" (Alma 37:6).

Interestingly, the very smallness of "small and simple things" can be a stumbling block for many. Naaman almost wasn't cured of his leprosy because he wanted to do something heroic, something very expensive or grand in exchange for a cure—either that, or have Elijah do something elaborate and grand to cure him. Naaman was a Syrian noble who sought out the prophet Elijah in Israel at the suggestion of his Hebrew serving maid. She had assured him that Elijah could heal his leprosy. Naaman, a powerful and rich man, traveled to Elijah's house with an elaborate retinue. Elijah, however, didn't even come out to see his important guest. He sent a servant to deliver his message: Naaman should bathe seven times in the Jordan River, an uninviting, muddy, and shallow river.

Naaman was angry and insulted at this suggestion that he thought was beneath him. But his wise servant prevailed, "My father, if the prophet had bid thee do some great thing, wouldest thou not have done it? how much rather then, when he saith to thee, Wash, and be clean?" (2 Kings 5:13).

As believers, we can't sit around and wait for the calling to perform grand gestures of outward show. Instead, we need to look for the simple good works that are required. What are some of the simple things that we as believers can do that will shine out full of light, full of power?

Let me tell you about bread. It is the staff of life. It is part of a title for Christ, the Bread of Life. It is the medium whereby we renew our covenants each week. Bread is sacred. Bread is ordinary, the stuff of our daily lives. I love to bake bread. I love to grind the flour; I love to knead the dough; I love the smell of yeast.

Not everyone feels the way I do. In fact, not many people make bread anymore on a regular basis. That's too bad because everyone loves homemade bread. And that's why our family tries regularly to give some away when we bake. It's such a small and simple thing, bread, but many stories have come back to us letting us know that power and Spirit can be found in a loaf of bread. It has comforted, gladdened hearts, and extended friendships. It has strengthened friendship and offered hope and love.

Smiles and civility can be the source of light and power. Nine years ago we met a wonderful family from Iran: Ali, Heideh, Keyvan, and Tara Vasefi. The Vasefis had moved to San Diego where we lived, and our sons started third grade together. Keyvan spoke very little English when he started school, but by the end of the year, he was fluent in English and in the highest reading group. We were friendly and helpful to the Vasefis, happy to see them at school and in the neighborhood, but we really did nothing out of the ordinary for them. Imagine our surprise when Heideh, the mother, called one Sunday morning and asked what time we attended church. Our friendliness had communicated more to them than we realized. Once they began attending church, they experienced the love and generosity of our community of believers as the ward welcomed them in. Remember how when we are in a community of believers we have people to love as well as people to love us? The Vasefis came to know the power of the Spirit of God, power in the name of Christ that can transform lives. They were baptized on March 16, 1997, and sealed together as a family a year later.

We learned from that experience that we cannot be filled with the Spirit and hide the power within us. It will illuminate our smiles, our footsteps, all that we do. Nelson Mandela, in his 1994 inaugural speech as the president of South Africa, spoke eloquently of not holding back when we are filled with power. He stated, "Our deepest fear is not that we are inadequate. Our deepest fear is that we are powerful beyond measure. It is our light, not our darkness that most frightens us. We ask ourselves, who am I to be brilliant, gorgeous, talented, and fabulous?"[2] Actually, who are you not to be? You are a child of God. Your playing small does not serve the world; you were born to make manifest the glory of God that is within you.

Have you noticed how little children can't hide their emotions very well? Their joy or sadness is written all over their faces. Their little bodies are smaller than those huge emotions they are trying to contain. It's the same way with a secret. Secrets are also too big for children to keep. They just can't hide them. As we get bigger and older, however, we have a much easier time finding room in our lives to hide things with restraint and careful language. Sometimes we hide things so deeply we can't find them ourselves. To be filled with the Spirit of the Lord, though, is to be filled with something much bigger than we are. Don't be afraid to let the Spirit shine through you, through these clay pots. Feel free to let the Spirit use you and your good works. Be brilliant, gorgeous, talented, and fabulous. Remember who you are? Paul said, "For as many as are led by the Spirit of God, they are the sons [and daughters] of God . . . And if children, then heirs; heirs of God, and joint-heirs with Christ" (Romans 8:14, 17). That's who the believers are: the Father's heirs, joint heirs with Jesus Christ. Let the Spirit illuminate your good works, that they will shine forth and bring glory to God.

Notes

1. C. S. Lewis, "Counting the Cost," *Mere Christianity* (New York: Macmillan Publishing Company, 1952), 174.
2. Nelson Mandela, as quoted in J. Bonner Ritchie, "Learning to Teach, Teaching to Learn," *Brigham Young Magazine* (August 1996): 34.

"I HAVE LOVED THE HABITATION OF THY HOUSE"

Wendy L. Ulrich

While it is easier than ever for most of us to get to the temple, getting to the temple does not, in itself, satisfy the deepest longings of our soul. We want more than to get to the temple. We want to get home—home to the Father who gave us life, home to the Savior who redeems us through his love. The temple is the house of the Lord, and it is the Lord we hope to meet there, even though we can't quite imagine how. The Lord himself has encouraged us in that expectation, however, for he has said, "And inasmuch as my people build a house unto me in the name of the Lord . . . my glory shall rest upon it; Yea, and my presence shall be there, for I will come into it, and all the pure in heart that shall come into it shall see God" (D&C 97:15–16).

How I long to have eyes that can see. I believe the ordinances of the temple are designed to endow us with such sight and to give us glimpses into the soul of God, into the infinite goodness of the Father, the merciful love of Jesus, the compassionate wisdom of the Holy Ghost. The temple embodies their great plan of happiness, focusing our hearts especially upon the atonement of Jesus Christ, the "at-one-ment." In God's house we may become more "at one" with ourselves, with other people, and with God, who is our home.

As I get older and seeing clearly gets more difficult, I find more personal meaning in Christ's ability to restore sight to the blind. But, of course, my spiritual blindness is a far more dangerous condition than the inconvenience of fading eyesight. In this perilous world, we are not

Wendy L. Ulrich is a psychologist in private practice in Michigan. She serves as a stake Relief Society president. She and her husband, Dave, are the parents of three children.

merely inconvenienced by sin; we are blinded, sickened, and injured both by our own sins and the sins of others, and in our blindness and pain we lose sight of the God who reaches after us and offers us redemption. The temple becomes meaningful to us as we learn to see God there, as we learn to receive his healing care and ponder his tender mercies in our hearts.

What in your personal life is broken or injured right now, leaving you feeling at odds with yourself? What breaches in your most important relationships need binding up? What blindness or rebellion or fear keeps you from seeing and feeling God's love for you? Each room and ordinance of the temple points us toward the miracle of atonement, of at-one-ment, with ourselves, our loved ones, and our heavenly home. Let us consider some of those rooms and the visions of God they open to our sight.

BAPTISTRY

The baptistry is the first ordinance room we can experience in the temple. We often speak of baptism as a cleansing process. Baptism, however, is not about cleansing so much as it is about dying. Coming to know God requires a change so radical it can be spoken of like a death. In this room we submit to the water as we would submit to a grave, a place where things return to their native element, dissolving and breaking apart until all is matter unorganized. This is not what we have in mind when we come to Christ for healing. When we have gone as far as our old assumptions will take us, we would prefer that God simply make our lives work again and put them back the way they were. When that fails, we hope that maybe he can change other people, or that he will change the rules of life itself. What does not occur to us is that he will ask *us* to change, and to change the very assumptions that we thought made us safe. Baptismal waters testify that old ways of understanding who we are, old ways of trying to be safe and in control, old ways of trying to get our needs met must often die and dissolve before we can be reborn as children of power.

The baptistry is the only temple room devoted solely to work for the dead. There we also remember that our ancestral heritage may include access to both spiritual blessings *and* the blinding, wounding legacy of unrighteous traditions of fathers and mothers. In fact, these traditions are part of what we may have to let go of so that we can claim our birthright in the family of God. So it is that the baptistry does more than offer new birth to the dead; it also calls us, the living, to engage in the two mortal acts of single greatest worth to our soul: to repent and to forgive. As we repent of any sinful ways we have absorbed through culture and tradition, I believe we help release our ancestors—and others who have helped shape the culture we live in—from spiritual prisons of regret and remorse which they must experience as they see their sins perpetuated in our lives. As we truly forgive them, we may also release ourselves from the bondage of our own self-loathing; for is it not them that we hate in ourselves, and ourselves that we hate in them?

When I go looking for God in the baptistry, I ask myself, What needs to die in my life right now so that I can more fully claim my birthright within my heavenly home? To what new freedoms is God calling me? Is it time to give up on the shame that is simply another form of pride? Do I need to lay to rest permanently my insistence on being in control? Is it time to bury fear of failure, of loneliness, or of death—fears that enslave my life in unholy ways? The baptistry reminds us that Jesus knows all about dying, and that we can afford to trust that the hand that pulls us down into the watery grave will also raise us again.

Washing and Anointing

Even after our baptism of death and new birth, we quickly realize that our ongoing mortal journey still exposes us to much that sullies and sickens us. We continue to need Christ's cleansing and healing power against the sins and sicknesses of our own generation. Temple ordinances allow us to experience such blessings in very direct ways. For example, quoting Elder Boyd K. Packer, "The ordinances of washing and anointing are referred to often in the temple as initiatory ordinances. . . .

"In connection with these ordinances, in the temple you will be officially clothed in the garment and promised marvelous blessings in connection with it."[1] While details of the washing, anointing, and clothing ordinances of the temple are not public, the words *washing*, *anointing*, and *clothing* all have rich meaning, which can be accessed through the scriptures.

For example, in the story of the good Samaritan, Christ speaks of a man who fell among thieves and was stripped of his raiment, wounded, and left for dead. In the scripture story, the Samaritan had compassion on this wounded one "and went to him, and bound up his wounds, pouring in oil and wine, and set him on his own beast, and brought him to an inn, and took care of him. And on the morrow when he departed, he took out two pence, and gave them to the host, and said unto him, Take care of him; and whatsoever thou spendest more, when I come again, I will repay thee" (Luke 10:34–35).

When we find ourselves emotionally wounded, psychologically naked, and left spiritually half-dead, the temple is the healing inn to which our Good Savior takes us, putting us on his beast in his place, the twelve oxen of his covenant with Israel, and paying himself the full price for our care. In the healing inn of the house of the Lord, our spiritual wounds are cleansed, anointed with healing oil, and bound up in the white dressing of God's covenant promises. We find refuge and rest in the temple inn while our wounds turn into sacred scars, which attest that we have met the enemy, been injured on the journey, but have triumphed in Christ over the power of the destroyer. The temple is much more than charity work for the dead. It is a hospital of hope for the living, where we may encounter him who comes with healing in his wings. President James E. Faust has said, "We believe in the gift of healing. To me, this gift extends to the healing of both the body and the spirit. . . .

" . . . Our temples are . . . hallowed sanctuaries [where] God 'healeth the broken in heart, and bindeth up their wounds' (Psalms 147:3)."[2]

In the initiatory ordinances of the temple, we can come before the Lord without pretense or worldly possessions to feel known and loved in all our vulnerability for exactly who we are. We see more clearly that our bodies are sacred gifts to be nurtured, valued, and learned from. Our bodies are not just vehicles we use to carry around our heads, or beasts of burden to be whipped into submission. I think we, as women, are especially prone to judging ourselves by what our bodies look like to others, rather than recognizing the goodness and love we can embody with them. Even when we are subject to hard physical labor, illness, or the brutal hand of enemies, our bodies are meant to be our tutors, our shelters, our personal temples, where our spirits and the Lord's spirit may dwell eternally.

I see the hands of God in those hands that offer me the healing ordinances of washing, anointing, and clothing in priesthood garments. Those hands seem to call on me to honor the gift of my temple-body, which, though it be destroyed, God will surely raise up again. How can we take this gift of embodiment more seriously, remembering that the God we seek is an embodied, glorified being, in whose image we are created?

Creation Room

One room in the Salt Lake Temple, known as the creation room, portrays on its walls the creation of the world. Sometimes I wonder what the creation story, repeated so often in scripture, has to do with me. But when I go to the temple looking for God, I remember that I am in the business of learning to be like him whose very identity is defined by his ability to create and engender life. Like God, I can bring order and light out of chaos and despair, whatever my circumstances may be. In fact, at the heart of the gospel of Jesus Christ is his assertion that even when we are compelled to give up our coats or walk a mile with our enemy, we can create loving options that are not merely reactive, but life engendering.

How desperately we need that lesson whenever in our relationships we strive to break out of patterns of blame and shame, anger and withdrawal, wherein no new life can be found. You know the patterns I mean—the ones where each participant knows how the script unfolds as soon as it begins, even while hoping against hope that this time it will be different. Trapped in a script of mutual blame, or of withdrawal into mutual isolation, or of yielding to too-familiar sins, how we long for the creative power of God to find a loving path out of misunderstanding and vengeance, sin and self-betrayal. How we long for the creative power to break out of the habits of addiction, perfectionism, worry, obsession, and self-recrimination in which we endlessly circle and never find peace.

The story of the creation reminds us that we have the God-given capacity to create our lives and not merely live them in reaction to others or enslaved by our own history. The creation story also reminds us that creating requires descent into the darkness, not merely playing in the light. In Abraham's recounting of the Creation, the Lord says to those with him, "Let us go down"—down into the depths of unorganized matter to order it and give it life (Abraham 4:1). We too may contemplate what it means to descend trustingly into the darkness and chaos that is at the beginning of any creative process. Nowhere is this chaos more evident than in the process of creating and recreating our lives, our personal stories and dreams. As we seek through Christ to understand our internal chaos and bring forth order, beauty, and variety, we gain hope that ultimately we can claim our creations as good and thus find joy therein.

What are you busy creating these days? Are you actively engaged in the creative process, and in learning how to be a creator like your heavenly parents? What might the temple teach us about God's creative power in the world and about how to model our creativity after his?

THE GARDEN ROOM

The room in the Salt Lake Temple known as the garden room portrays the abundance and beauty of the Garden of Eden. In the

Genesis account, God walks in the garden in the cool of the evening, and yet a distance exists between God and his innocent children. Their innocence has prevented them from experiencing firsthand the temporal pains and suffering that will potentially enable them to make choices and exercise the agency necessary to dwell with him eternally. The garden story poignantly reminds us that in the day we see ourselves as we truly are—naked, blind, sinful, and deceived—something inside us (our pride? our willfulness? our false independence?) will surely die. Yet in that dying we gain the possibility of knowing God with a depth that our premortal existence could not bestow.

Amazingly, even though their transgression will have vast and seemingly terrible consequences not only for them but also for all of their posterity, Adam and Eve do not disintegrate into either exaggerated self-sufficiency or despairing self-flagellation when they err. They simply promise to learn from their mistakes and try to do better, trusting that God knows what he is doing and doesn't hate them, even when he evicts them from his presence and doesn't talk to them much anymore. They don't get angry and they don't give up. They trust in God's will and power to save them, and they learn to walk more patiently through the world, as he walks patiently through the heavens.

The World Room

From the story of Adam and Eve, we also learn that however beautiful Eden may be, God never intended it as our final destination. The way back to God's presence is not back, but forward, through the dangers and perils of our fallen world. The world room in the Salt Lake Temple portrays this world as a dangerous place, where lions struggle for dominance and vultures soar overhead. In the Manti Temple we see armies at war. In this fallen world, we learn about the nature of power and the ongoing battle for our souls. We experience the difference between Satan's version of power, which is power *over*, as in power over others, and God's version of power, which is power *to*, as in power to do good, to love, to create, to heal. When we feel powerless because we are subject to the sins of others or to the consequences of our own poor choices, what a blessing it is to be reminded of what powers we do have, what provisions God is making to reach out for us, and what good we can yet do amid all that we cannot do. Christ has been in all these hard places with us and for us; he knows how to guide and succor us in the loneliness of this dark realm we live in. He has taken on the hard task of atoning for all our sins, and he desires all to receive this message of hope and salvation.

But we agreed to do something hard as well. We agreed to come down to this dreary world and get soiled, to face the indignity of making messes we cannot clean up. We must have understood that in mortality our goal is not merely to stay as clean as we possibly can: for if that were the goal, our best course would be never to take on the incredible risks of trying to parent, to help, to discern, or to grow. These tasks are simply so difficult that we will inevitably fail at them. No doctor lives up to the oath of doing no harm in the process of trying to heal. No bishop assumes the responsibility for feeding the flock without offending any of the sheep. No mother parents a child without bruising that child's soul a little before she is done. If the goal were to make as few mistakes as possible and return to God as close as possible to the condition we left him in, then we would be better off to lie down on the ground the day we are born and never get up. But our goal is not merely to *avoid* imperfection and failure. Our goal is to learn to do good, and in that process we will all do some harm as well. Only the atonement of Christ can make the risks of mortality worth taking.

When I am about the risky business of learning to create, heal, and bless in my Father's footsteps, it is easy to get discouraged. How tempting, when I fail, to say, "Why do I even try to discern God's voice, for I am forever getting it wrong, and at such a price? Why have children when I am such a poor parent, and my children suffer so for my sins? Why try to help others when I so often just end up hurting them instead?" Why? Because our learning is more important than our failures. How gratefully I read Christ's words, "Fear not to do good, . . . Behold, I do not condemn you; . . . Look unto me in every thought;

doubt not, fear not" (D&C 6:33, 35, 36). Such words help me to see that God's faithfulness to me, a sinner, is stronger than the cords of death (D&C 121:44).

What good work does your life call you to right now? What good work do you avoid trying for fear of failure? How might you be blessed by a reminder of God's power to save, amid all the ways that you feel powerless not to harm when you mean to help?

THE TERRESTRIAL ROOM

While there are no pictures on the walls of the beautiful terrestrial room to help ground us in the scriptures, we learn from the *Encyclopedia of Mormonism* that "at the conclusion of the temple service, those participating in the endowment ceremony pass from the terrestrial room to the celestial room through a veil."[3] That veil reminds us of our state of separation from the Lord, and we yearn to have that wounding separation healed. We remember that the purpose of the Atonement is not only to heal us and resurrect us, but also to make us "at one" with God. The Atonement invites us to partake of the sacred gift of prayer, both public and private, which allows us to seek God, despite the barriers that block him from our view. The scriptures speak of the Savior standing at the door of our soul and knocking, waiting on us to hear his voice and open the door so that he can come in (Revelation 3:20). I have come to believe, through personal experience, that despite my protestations of wanting to be close to God, I am most often the one who keeps that door closed. The Lord longs to be close to us—listening to our prayers, helping us with our problems, or simply sitting with us as we weep. He wants us to know him, to see him. Yet to my surprise, the more intimately God reveals himself to me, the more prayer can feel incredibly difficult. Spiritual intimacy is simply hard work. For me to be as honest and vulnerable as closeness with God seems to exact can be almost painful. And then, once I do let God close to me, it is harder still to endure the times of heavenly silence that inevitably come, even when my life is in order. Even the greatest prophets do not see God every day, and surely neither will I.

We ask God to teach us to pray, to teach us to see his face and live. Having asked, are we then willing to open our hearts to him, and to learn to trust him, despite the difficulties of intimacy? Are we also willing to tolerate the silence in between God's visits, without losing sight of his love, or of our worth and missions? The temple encourages our longing for God.

The Celestial Room

The celestial room and its adjacent sealing rooms are the most beautiful rooms in any temple. Sitting reverently in the celestial room, we practice stillness as we stop and wait upon the Spirit. In sealing rooms, family ties are sanctified and the blessings of exaltation are pronounced. In these final rooms of our temple journey, we contemplate eternal relationships with one another and with the Lord. We ponder what is required of us to build relationships worth perpetuating for eternity both with people and with God. The sealing blessings foreshadow the final blessing: our sealing to God, a promise described in Doctrine and Covenants 132:23–24, "If ye receive me in the world, then shall ye know me, and shall receive your exaltation; that where I am ye shall be also. This is eternal lives—to know the only wise and true God, and Jesus Christ, whom he hath sent." The temple teaches us to see and receive the Lord, that we might begin eternal life today.

Every ordinance of the temple points us toward the face of God. Every temple room embodies his redeeming power. We make covenants that give us access to the Atonement, and we learn the symbols that testify of the Atonement's workings in our lives. As we follow the path of atonement from our first new birth to our final redemption, the temple teaches us to imagine the impossible—that we, though mortally wounded and spiritually blind, can see the Father's face and live, both in this life and in the next. The temple sings redemption into the marrow of our bones. It is a vast echo chamber for this sweet and urgent message to each of us from the realms of glory: I love you, I love you, I love you. The temple resonates with the song of redeeming love.

We go to the temple not only to save the dead but also the dying, and we are the dying who need to be saved and healed within the loving arms of Jesus. We go to the temple to find and claim our life, and to find and claim eternal life, which means that we go to the temple to find the only true God, and Jesus Christ, whom he has sent—sent to rescue us, heal us, and bring us home. We absolutely don't deserve, and are absolutely worth, the full price of our Savior's blood. We are not, and cannot make ourselves, worthy of his great sacrifice for us, but we are inherently of such worth that God has organized the universe to save us, one person at a time. I testify that God has the will and the power to save and to exalt us. The only thing in the universe that can override that power is our unwillingness to believe and respond when he calls us by name and tells us who we are. Our sins will not stop him if we will repent. Our brokenness will not stop him if we will come to him for healing. This promise rightly belongs at the center of the temple of the soul.

I truly believe that the Lord is not intending to build one hundred temples, or even two hundred temples, but thousands upon thousands of temples, and we are the temples he is trying to build, through temple ordinances and the gospel of Jesus Christ those ordinances embody. We are God's true temples, his living, breathing house. "Ye are the temple of God," Paul taught, "and . . . the Spirit of God dwelleth in you . . . for the temple of God is holy, which temple ye are" (1 Corinthians 3:16–17). In our innermost chambers, we are temples of holiness to the Lord.

Notes

1. Boyd K. Packer, *The Holy Temple* (Salt Lake City: Bookcraft, 1980), 154–55.
2. James E. Faust, "Spiritual Healing," *Ensign*, May 1992, 7.
3. *Encyclopedia of Mormonism*, 4 vols. (New York: Macmillan, 1992), s.v. "symbolism," 3:1430.

Teaching Children
about Sexuality

Brad and Debi Wilcox

Some parents worry that by speaking frankly with their children about their bodies and their sexuality they are somehow promoting or condoning promiscuous behavior. Our experience has taught us the opposite is true. The most sexually active teens are usually the least informed. It is silence and ignorance, not open communication, which often lead to poor choices. The more solid sexual information young people receive from their parents, the more capable they are of making righteous and mature choices. The home is where facts and values can be combined and presented with balance. As parents we may not feel we are the best qualified to address this topic. Nevertheless, as we assume responsibility for teaching our children about sensitive things we share experiences that can strengthen the bonds between us.

Five key words—all starting with *p*—will guide us as we teach children about sex: *private, probing, point blank, positive,* and *perspective.*

Speak in private. Privacy may help us avoid feelings of awkwardness. Even family home evening may be too public a setting to meet the needs of everyone gathered without embarrassing some and overwhelming others. Personal conversations allow us to teach more sensitively and effectively. Debi remembers how awkward it was when her parents once taught some facts of life in family home evening. She and her twin brother were very curious and asking all sorts of questions

---

Brad and Debi Wilcox are the parents of four children. Brad, a popular author and speaker, is an associate professor of teacher education at Brigham Young University. He recently served as the bishop of a student ward. Debi is a registered nurse and serves in her ward as a Primary teacher.

while her older brother and sister were mortified and her younger siblings were clueless.

Ask probing questions. Once we are in private, we should ask *probing* questions that will help us know when not to overload children with more information than they really need or want. We love the classic tale of the overanxious mother whose six-year-old asked, "Where did I come from?" The mother took a deep breath and launched into an oration on the facts of life, when the little girl interrupted, "Mom, all I was wondering was where I came from. My friend Stephanie says she came from Omaha." The surest way to estimate just how much children know or want to know is by probing. For example, a child asks, "Where do babies come from?" A parent might reply, "What made you think of that?" Another child asks, "What does adultery mean?" The parent may respond, "What do you think it means?" A teenage boy says, "I just don't understand girls." The parent could ask, "Why? What do you mean?" Probing questions are not an attempt to change the subject or avoid giving a straight answer. Rather, they offer a chance to listen as well as speak—to gather enough information to respond effectively.

Offer point-blank information. When we have determined what a child knows and what we need to teach, we must not hesitate to offer *point-blank* information. We need to be factual, honest, and direct, even when we feel uneasy. If you don't know an answer, it's okay to say, "You know, I'm not quite sure about that. Let's find out together." Willingness to talk to our children honestly, despite uneasiness, will strengthen our children's confidence in us. While frankness is important in all the answers we provide, we should use proper vocabulary instead of gutter or slang terms in our discussions. Such terms communicate irreverence for a sacred topic.

Be positive about the subject. We must also remember to be *positive*. Sex doesn't have to be discussed grimly or solemnly. A light and positive touch can make discussion easier. Too often we unintentionally convey negative messages about our children's bodies with our tone of voice or word choice. We teach object lessons by chewing up gum or crushing flowers and then saying, "If you have sex, this is you." One Latter-day Saint sixth grader asked his teacher about AIDS. The teacher said, "I'd love to talk to you about that, but first go home and ask your dad." The boy said, "I did, but all he said was that AIDS had to do with sex so I wasn't supposed to worry about it." Then this sixth grader asked, "So, what about sex?" His father responded, "Sex is the second worst sin next to murder." The father was probably intending to communicate that adultery and fornication are grievous sins. However, consider the message this boy received instead.

Some religious groups see our physical bodies as a burden, a problem, a temporary hindrance from which we will one day be free. They see the body as ugly, sinful, or bad. Latter-day Saints know that is not true. Joseph Smith said, "We came to this earth that we might have a body and present it pure before God in the celestial kingdom. The great principle of happiness consists in having a body. The devil has no body and herein is his punishment."[1] In "The Family: A Proclamation to the World," the First Presidency and Council of the Twelve state, "All human beings—male and female—are created in the image of God. Each is a beloved spirit son or daughter of heavenly parents, and, as such, each has a divine nature and destiny."[2]

Our bodies are wonderful gifts essential to fulfilling our divine destiny. Some of the greatest tests, challenges, and lessons of our lives are associated with our bodies, which have appetites and needs that are new to our spirits. Children must learn about those needs and desires, about their bodies, how they grow, mature, and procreate.

Discuss sexuality from a gospel perspective. Along with being positive, we always need to discuss sexuality within a gospel perspective. A lot of books address the topic of sexuality for young people, but very few do so in the context of Latter-day Saint values, doctrines, and standards. Many books describe sex as nothing more than a biological urge to be satisfied, an itch to be scratched. Masturbation is considered appropriate—even healthy. Homosexuality is often presented as an acceptable lifestyle, and teenagers are told that sex before marriage is all right as long as the partners really care about each other. Some books that attempt to offer values-based advice suggest only that those who engage in sexual activities be safe and responsible. Abortion is sometimes condoned, even encouraged. Such teachings are incompatible with our Heavenly Father's plan for our happiness.

Many outside the Church claim that petting, masturbation, and viewing pornography are normal and healthy adolescent behaviors, but while sexual desires are normal and healthy, engaging in sexual activity is not the best way to deal with those desires. We remind young people that when they are struggling with strong desires, they should say to themselves, "Good. My body works. One day in marriage I will be grateful for these feelings," but then strive to keep appetites and passions within the bounds God has set.

The gospel is true. Jesus Christ lives, loves us, and leads us today. It is not inconsistent to bear testimony at the same time we have discussed sexuality. Spiritual things and sexual things are not opposites. Within the bounds the Lord has set, they complement each other. They can strengthen each other and coexist beautifully. How grateful we can be for the standards, guidance, and perspective the gospel provides. We don't just have the rules. We have the reasons to keep them.

Notes

1. Joseph Smith, *Teachings of the Prophet Joseph Smith*, sel. Joseph Fielding Smith (Salt Lake City: Deseret Book, 1976), 181.
2. First Presidency and Council of the Twelve, "The Family: A Proclamation to the World," *Ensign*, November 1995, 102.

MUSICAL PARENTING

Connie Cannon

When our first child hit kindergarten, I began to develop what I now believe was "first-time mother syndrome." I felt frantic that this child was already in school and was an expert at nothing except getting into mischief. Why had I not used those first five years to turn him into a genius of some sort? I realize the ridiculousness of that now, but at the time I was troubled over it. Then a dear friend introduced me to the Suzuki method of teaching music to children. The minute I heard about it, I knew it was what I was looking for. That was in 1977. By the end of 2001, all of our six children, five of whom are boys, will have gone through the program to one extent or another. Basically, I have spent a good part of my time, life, and money over the past twenty-four years helping my children become somewhat proficient in music. In this article, I'm not attempting to promote a particular method; rather I'd like to share my enthusiasm for anything that establishes music in the heart of a child.

I had no idea teaching my children music would be so hard when we began, nor, on the other hand, that it would yield so many benefits. After a successful performance, someone inevitably will ask me, "Do your children like to practice?" I am always stunned. Of course not. If any of you have a child out there who likes to practice, consider yourself one in a million. You're probably going to win the lottery too. Or be hit by lightning. There just aren't many kids who come to earth

---

Connie Cannon graduated from the University of Utah with a bachelor's degree in history and a teaching certificate, which she put to use before starting her family. She and her husband, Jim, have taken all six of their children through the Suzuki method of learning music. She owns and manages her own company and is currently a teacher in Relief Society.

loving to practice. It's hard work. It takes concentration. And as I'm painfully aware, if carried too far, forcing a child to practice can damage relationships. I've wondered from time to time if I'm nearing the brink. Once I asked our kids, for the sake of dinner conversation, what they would engrave on my headstone if I checked out that night. They all immediately said in unison, "She made us practice."

Last December, my fourteen-, sixteen-, and eighteen-year-old boys played background music at a big company Christmas party. Afterwards, the hostess invited them to eat dinner and seated them by a gentleman who was kind enough to make conversation with them. "Well, boys," he said, "what is your inspiration for being the great musicians you are?" They all looked at each other and burst out laughing. "*Inspiration?*" Curtis finally said, "Our mother *beats* us."

Friends suggest that Cate must surely have been easy, since she's made the harp such a big part of her life. She was actually worse than any of her brothers. At age five, Cate would pretend to be asleep when we arrived at her lessons. What do you do with a child who goes limp? Yes, I did drag each of them at least part of the way. Yes, I asked myself many times if I should just give it up. But the benefits kept me going.

Looking back to 1977, I believe the Lord was responding to my continual prayers that I become a better parent. One of my biggest problems was, and still is, that I am task-oriented to the point of being downright mono-dimensional. I tended to be glued to a list of tasks, ignoring my kids even though I was a stay-at-home mom. Though I read to them daily, and sang to them often at the piano, I knew in my heart it was not enough. The music regimen I stumbled onto at that time was the structure I needed to remind me to focus 100 percent on each child for a given amount of time each day.

My husband, Jim, and I both discovered that the times driving to and from lessons and performances were excellent bonding times. I'd be dishonest, though, if I let you think the children were always thrilled to bond with me. I was not enough of a draw by myself. So I would usually try to come up with something more attractive, like food. The time I spent eating powdered sugar doughnuts with Heber in the

parking lot of the "Sev" at 7:30 on Tuesday mornings were times of
learning what was going on with Heber. I liked that. And he liked the
doughnuts. It made going to cello lessons at 6:30 A.M. palatable.

In addition, music expanded the children's social horizons. Each
child sooner or later bonded with other kids from the music world.
They discovered another group of wonderful people, in addition to
school and neighborhood friends, that they looked forward to seeing.

Listening to great music is an actual assignment in the Suzuki program. I found that my spirits lifted as we played the great classics in our
home. Of course, the spirit of the mom in any home is key to the
atmosphere there. When this music was playing, I felt energized,
upbeat, and inspired. My heart felt right, and I was a better person. The
truth is that the Spirit was in our home when there was beautiful music
playing, and I know the kids felt it also.

I sat in a rocking chair and cried the day our oldest quit the violin
at age fourteen. I would have been less sad had I realized the many
wonderful gifts he had developed by then and would retain. One of
these was an appreciation for what is beautiful. When he was seven,
eight, and nine, I remember playing *The Moldau*, a piece by the Czech
composer Smetana. The music suggests little streams running together
into a huge and powerful river. I described this to him as we drove
along in the car. Fifteen years later, we traveled to Czechoslovakia to
pick up this son from his mission. As we drove along this very river, the
Moldau, which runs right through the center of Prague, Elder Chris
said, "I have a surprise for you guys." He pulled out a cassette tape of
Smetana's *Moldau* from his pocket, popped it in the player, and
recounted for us the description I had given him so many years before,
with more enthusiasm, I noted, than even I had for the piece.

He had memorized a lot of music by the time he was fourteen, and
I was amazed at the amount he retained. He actually took his violin on
his mission and remembered enough to play many lovely pieces for
sacrament meetings and other occasions. In his final meeting there, we
thrilled to hear him play Pachelbel's wonderful "Canon in D."

Memorization is an important exercise in developing the brain. In fact, research has shown that the study of music helps train the mind to learn. Children with musical training score higher on scholastic tests and may develop more active imaginations. In addition, the daily grind of practicing helped my children develop self-discipline. This transferred somewhat to schoolwork, scouting, athletics, or whatever the kids were interested in.

Developing a talent also develops self-esteem. President Harold B. Lee once spoke about how important self-esteem is to our ability to love the Lord, live his commandments, and love others. To do these things, he said, we must first love ourselves.[1] Developing our talents is one way we come to appreciate ourselves. Four years ago, Heber, our fifth child, was at the vulnerable age of thirteen. In seventh grade, there is little peer support for playing stringed instruments, especially for boys. Junior high school is probably the pinnacle of kid-to-kid cruelty, rudeness, and teasing. I knew try-outs were coming up for a school talent assembly, but I also knew better than to encourage Heber to play his cello there. In some ways, he was the most resistant to my musical tyranny, so I didn't want to push it. But I wanted him to participate in the assembly. I offered to get a bunch of his friends together and help them prepare a funny singing routine. Heber was lukewarm about the idea. I needed to leave town for a couple of days, and when I returned he said, "Hey, Mom, I made the talent assembly." "You did? What was your talent?" "My cello," he said with a bit of resignation. I was shocked. "Your cello? What are you going to play?" "Oh, I guess the first two movements of the *Eccles Sonata*," he said with a yawn. "Who is going to accompany you?" "You, I guess."

The morning of the talent show, he came upstairs in his tuxedo. I was growing more shocked by the minute. As we walked in the door of the auditorium, I was sick. A big rock band filled the stage with drums, guitars, and kids dressed like they were in rock bands. I saw a group of girls in leotards, and a boy on a unicycle riding up and down the aisle. I thought, *This is going to be the all-time social disaster for Heber.* Why was I allowing him to throw his pearls before swine, so to speak?

But he seemed to be fearless. When our turn came, he walked on stage in a tuxedo, with a cello and *his mother, of all things*. He sat down and played a relatively flawless version of the *Eccles Sonata,* and when he finished, the students brought down the house. They actually clapped so long and hard for him that the assistant principal had to get up and tell them to stop. They had no idea Heber could do anything like that, partly because he really didn't want them to know, and partly because he comes across as just a goof-off. Performance is the ultimate motivator for practice as well as a tremendous builder of self-confidence and self-esteem.

Music can communicate across continents, cultures, races, and language barriers. Recently I accompanied Chad, our youngest, to Poland, where he and fifty other children performed several concerts to demonstrate the success of the Suzuki method in America. It was a sweet experience to sit in an audience filled with people who knew little about our language, culture, country, or religion but who knew everything about Handel, Bach, Mozart, and Copeland. They were touched by these young artists and demanded several encores. After the performance, we knew we had a bond, and though we had a serious language barrier, we were communicating. Music unifies. It brings people, it brings families, into harmony.

On their own—without any tyranny on my part—each of our children has also developed a love for singing that has led them to high school madrigals, concert choir, and barbershop groups. The youngest two just got back from a high school barbershop trip to southern California. They loved their experience there so much that they have taken to rounding up ten or twelve guys every Sunday night to go serenading. Last week they serenaded several girls who lost elections or cheerleading tryouts. During hymns in sacrament meeting, I love to hear them blast forth with tenor and bass harmonies.

All in all, I feel some assurance that whatever they do or do not do with their music, it has had a profound effect on their lives—an effect that I didn't even anticipate when we started. That effect is the deepening of the soul. I know that a part of my own heart and soul, possibly the deepest part, is reached only by music. Perhaps when we left the

Lord's presence, he told us that even though a veil of forgetfulness would fall over our minds, he would give us reminders of our time with him to help us remember our mission. The most powerful of these reminders for me is music. It is the medium, besides prayer, that brings me the closest to him.

Whenever I listen to or sing truly great music, such as Handel's *Messiah*, I'm pretty sure that I've sung it or something like it before, in some distant past. I like to imagine that I was one of the heavenly hosts singing praises on that miraculous night of the Savior's birth . . . and perhaps I was. Perhaps we all were. After all, what else would we have been doing?

Note

1. Harold B. Lee, "Understanding Who We Are Brings Self-Respect," *Ensign*, January 1974, 2–6.

Family Work
Is God's Work

Kathleen Bahr

I am a mother of four sons: Alden, age 13, and Jonathan, 8; and two from Russia who recently joined our family: Dmitry, age 9, and Anton, age 7. My husband and I treasure our little boys. We want them to grow up strong, able to resist the evil influences surrounding them. We want our boys to be good friends, to support each other, to be the ones who will reach out and help others in need. We want our family ties to endure: we want to be a forever family, a covenant family, a Zion family.

I don't doubt that all Latter-day Saint parents want their families to be able to withstand the gale-force winds that are toppling families everywhere. This is not an easy task. In 1996 President Gordon B. Hinckley identified four simple ways to set families on a clear, strong moral course: we should teach and learn goodness together, read good books together, work together, and pray together.[1]

Note that in addition to goodness, good books, and prayer, he specifies working together. Why do you suppose it is *work* that is on President Hinckley's short list, and not *play*? Today's families generally see play as the more valuable family activity; we usually hurry to get work out of the way so we have time to play together. Play is worthwhile, but it differs from work in at least one critical respect: work requires more of us. It requires cooperation, unselfishness, and self-sacrifice. And why do these things matter? There are many reasons, I

Kathleen Slaugh Bahr, an associate professor in marriage, family, and human development at Brigham Young University, has a Ph.D. from Michigan State University. She is the wife of Howard Bahr and the mother of four sons. She has served as Relief Society president in her ward.

am sure, but one important reason is because these are the attributes that will enable us to become one, to become a Zion people.

President Spencer W. Kimball identified three fundamental things we must do to "bring again Zion:" "First we must *eliminate* the individual tendency to selfishness that snares the soul, shrinks the heart, and darkens the mind. . . . Second, we must *cooperate completely* and *work in harmony* one with the other. . . . Third, we must lay on the altar and *sacrifice* whatever is required by the Lord."[2] How do we learn these attributes? How do we teach them to our children? By working together. If we want our children to learn to be unselfish, we teach them how by sharing the work at home. As families, we can learn to cooperate completely, work in harmony, and sacrifice for each other— at home, together.

I remember, however, that during my childhood it always seemed easier to "work in harmony" at a friend's house than at my own; because at a friend's, work took on an aspect of play. At home, work is really work. Selfishness surfaces. We feel more at ease with those in our own homes and therefore have an easier time expressing our desires to do our own thing, in our own time, and in our own way. Even as adults, many of us can work quite well with the sisters at Relief Society and quite well with the people at our offices, but when we come home, it's tough going.

Our selfishness surfaces more in our homes and our families than almost anywhere else. And so, my sense is that if we want our children to learn to be unselfish we must teach them how. We must teach them how to work in harmony and how to sacrifice. We can do so by making appropriate sacrifices for one another and in our own homes.

The scriptures teach us that it is through small and simple things that great things are brought to pass: "Be not weary in well-doing, for ye are laying the foundation of a great work. And out of small things proceedeth that which is great.

"Behold, the Lord requireth the heart and a willing mind; and the willing and obedient shall eat the good of the land of Zion in these last days" (D&C 64:33–34).

Do you sometimes grow weary with your daily family work? Does family work seem too simple a thing to take so much effort? I think we've all answered yes to these questions. We get weary with all the laundry, dishes, dusting, and so on that must be done on a daily basis. But do not hesitate to follow Nephi's admonition to liken the scriptures to your own life (1 Nephi 19:23). The Lord says, "be not weary in well doing, for ye are laying the foundation of a great work." Family work is perhaps the best example of "well doing" that there is. It is through this well doing that we lay the "foundation of a great work." That great work is your children. Never underestimate what great things can be done through the small, simple means of working together in the home as a family.

Still, you may ask, How can working together at home strengthen families, when sharing the work at home usually leads to more contention than harmony or spirituality? Does this Brigham Young University student's experience sound familiar? "One day a week we deep clean the house together. My parents divide us into teams. We hate this. They force us to work together. We get along much better when we aren't working so close together. Usually it ends up in a yelling match, and then my parents freak out. My mom starts crying because we aren't getting along, and therefore we aren't righteous enough and she's failed as a mother. Then my dad gets upset because Mom is upset. The result? We are forced to spend more time together preparing for eternal life as a family. Cleaning the house is a miserable experience for everyone."[3]

I suspect most of us identify to one degree or another with this student's experience. In a recent study, teens identified conflicts over household chores as the most common source of problems between them and their parents. Compared with issues about use of the car, friends, money, curfew, grades, and the way youth dress, "home duties" emerged as the most frequent source of conflict. Family work is also a major source of conflict between husbands and wives, right along with money and sex. Why is conflict over household work so common? Because selfishness is common.

Family work is actually a gift from God, designed to bless our lives and to lead us back to him. Family work not only enables us to care for our temporal needs, but also to ensure our spiritual salvation. Without this vision, however, we are unlikely to change family work patterns in our homes. Only by going against the grain of what the world tells us, can we learn to see the value of simple, ordinary daily housework.

In one sense, we all know the work we do in our homes is important. We often quote President Harold B. Lee's statement that the most important work we will do in this life is the work we do within the walls of our own homes. But very few of us think of household work in connection with that quote. What work was he referring to? A few years ago I was involved in a research project where we asked that question of Church members in different parts of the country. Their responses? Scripture study, family home evening, family prayer. Then we asked, "What do you think gets in the way of doing this work?" They said: doing laundry, cleaning house, washing dishes, chasing after children.[4]

When I began this research project, I tracked down the original source of President Lee's statement. I must confess that I was surprised to discover that he hadn't said, "the most important work you and I will ever do will be within the walls of our own homes." What he had said was "the most important of the *Lord's work* you and I will ever do will be within the walls of our own homes."[5]

I remember feeling puzzled. I knew ordinary daily work was an important way to teach children some very valuable things, like how to be a responsible family member. I understood that such humbling work as changing a baby's diaper helped forge powerful bonds between mother and child, or father and child. But was this ordinary, daily work—doing laundry, washing dishes, cooking and cleaning—really part of "the Lord's work"?

I have learned in the years since that the answer to that question is a resounding "yes." As I have studied the scriptures and the teachings of modern prophets, my vision of the importance and power of daily household work has expanded.

Adam and Eve were cast out into "the real world," a world that differed from the garden in at least one major respect: it required a lot of hard work. In this telestial sphere, death overcomes anything that does not expend a great deal of energy staying alive. Through this daily work of nurturing life on earth and nurturing the lives of children, we develop the attributes of godliness. As writer Wendell Berry says, it is in these daily tasks of homemaking that love becomes flesh and does its worldly work.[6]

It is important to note that although Adam and Eve were each given a specific area of stewardship for the care of their new earthly home, they did not work alone; they worked together! In Moses 5:1 we learn that Adam worked to bring forth the fruit of the earth, with Eve working by his side. And we later learn that even though Eve bore the children, Adam joined her in teaching them (Moses 5:12).

Family work makes up a vital portion of the Lord's work, not because it will lead to success as the world measures success—with money—and not because it is a good source of power or gain. It is the Lord's work because it is the work of nurturing of life, and family work is an essential means to that end.

Another scriptural clue to the power of family work is found in Matthew 25, in the parable of the sheep and the goats. The Savior is teaching what is required to be either on his right hand or his left hand in the kingdom of his Father: Did you feed the hungry? Clothe the naked? Did you care for the sick? Did you take care of those who were in need? He says it matters that we do these services for "the least of these." This scripture *does* apply to our neighbors and to the needy in Africa or Guatemala, but I suspect that "the least of these" also includes members of our own family. For too many of today's parents and children alike, caring for our own has become a low priority. Our own family members have too easily become "the least" among all the other demands on our time.

If this vision of family work was taught in the beginning, how have we lost sight of the saving power of ordinary family work? I suspect the adversary has had an interest in blinding us to the power of this work.

He uses every means possible to do so. Consider what has happened over the last century or so. As families moved from the farm to the city, the work of the father became separate from the household. Fathers began supporting their families on money earned in the workplace, rather than on the homestead. The father took on a more singular role as "provider." His wife and children no longer plowed the fields beside him. Society began equating success with the monetary success achieved by a provider, who left the home for a long, hard day of work. When the father came home, he was supposed to rest and relax. (An early home economics text said that the mother was supposed to have all the children dressed in their Sunday clothes when the father came home from work. This way, they would be presentable. The house was to be totally clean, and father was supposed to be able to sit down and relax so he would be refreshed to go back to work the next day.) The adversary took this opportunity to devalue work at home, to make us believe that fathers did not have a significant role to play in the home—their role was to provide for the family *outside* of the home. His work became the measure of the family's success. We came to believe that the family could get along without the active, hands-on participation of fathers and husbands, that fathers didn't need the growth that might come from working in the home, side by side with their wives and children.

Conditions during World Ward II gave Satan opportunity to convince women of the same thing: that work done in the home was not as valuable as work done outside the home. Many women who were forced to work outside of the home during wartime found that they enjoyed the work they did. Soon, society began comparing paid work and family work on an economic scale. It became easy for women to feel as if they were underappreciated in the home, where the benefits were less tangible than the praise and monetary rewards offered by a career.

Today, when many mothers are still forced to work to help provide for their families, Satan has found other means of devaluing work in the home. He easily preys on the feelings of many mothers that they have to do all the work themselves, that they don't want to burden their husband or their children. But this daily work is priceless.

Conflicts arise as we try to work together in families because the world's ideas about how to work are mistaken. For example, we have been taught to run our homes like businesses, expecting the work to be done fast and efficiently. From hard experience, mothers learn that "fast and efficient" does not work well when applied to work at home. How might work go differently if we replaced this business pattern with the pattern of the temple?

In her essay, "My Home as a Temple," Kristine Manwaring considers that patterning our homes after temples does not mean our homes must have the same decor as a temple, or be kept as clean as a temple. For one thing, the temple has a full-time cleaning staff, and the temple has no children running around to mess things up. If we look deeper at the way things are done in the temple, we can learn a lot. For one thing, work there goes on at the pace of the slowest member of the group. Using that pattern in our homes, when we work together, we need to adjust our pace to accommodate the slowest member of the group—the youngest child, the disabled child, the person least able to do the work easily.[7]

My now-thirteen-year-old son taught me this lesson when he was just six years old. My husband and I both teach at BYU, and we arrange our teaching schedules so one of us can always be home with the children. On one occasion my husband was out of town, and I had a faculty meeting to attend. It is difficult to find a baby-sitter in the daytime, so I was going to take my children to the meeting with me. Alden was about six, and Jonathan about two at the time. I had Alden and Jonathan in the bathtub. I got Jonathan out of the tub and was getting him dressed. Alden was big enough to get out and get dressed on his own, so I told him to hurry and do so. But he just sat there. As I ran past the bathroom I said in a stern voice, "Hurry! I'm going to be late for my meeting. You get out of that tub!" And nothing happened. When I checked on him next he was out, but sitting on the floor buried under a big bath towel, just sitting there, motionless. Again I barked, "Alden, hurry! I am going to be late!" Alden responded from under the towel, "I can't hurry, Mom. I'm a butterfly and if I move my wings before they are dry, I'll hurt them."

His words gave me pause. *Isn't that the truth,* I thought. *He is a butterfly, and if I force him to move his wings before they are dry, I will hurt them.* Through the years since, I have tried, though I still often fail, not to say "hurry, hurry, hurry" so often. I need to learn to work at my children's pace. I need to allow my children to work at their own pace.

Another common source of stress and conflict is thinking that children should be free to choose what they want to do, and that we have no right to insist or assign. Is this really what agency is about? I think not. The Lord doesn't say, "Do whatever you please." The Lord gives us commandments and expects us to follow them. Just as he has high expectations of our capabilities, we need to have high expectations of our children. We can teach these expectations in loving ways, but our children need to know their participation in family work is not optional.

Here again Alden taught me an important lesson. It was his turn to mow the lawn. In previous years, he had mowed the lawn with his father, but now he was big enough to push the mower on his own. Our lawn slopes, so it requires some muscle to push the mower up and down. Alden was supposed to mow the lawn in the morning when it was cool, but he dawdled, as children do, and pretty soon the day was slipping by. Because it was getting hot, he complained that he couldn't do it. I responded unsympathetically, "I'm sorry, buddy boy, but this has got to be done, and you are the man to do it." Now there are times when the day is hot and we wait until the evening when things have cooled off to do our jobs. But on this day, I felt I must insist that he stay with it. It seemed important at that moment that he learn that he should not put off doing his work. So I said, "I'll bring you lemonade. I'll be your cheering section. But you have to mow the lawn." With much whining and complaining, he finally got the lawn mowed. Then he stood at the top of our little hill, looked over what he had done, and said, "Isn't it amazing? When you do something you thought you couldn't do, you feel like you can fly." I thought, what if I had deprived him of the lesson that he can fly? What if I hadn't hung in there with him to say, "You can do this; you are more capable than you think"?

Insisting that children help when they would rather do their own thing will not damage their self-esteem. To the contrary, it will help them discover their true worth, their great worth to you and to their Heavenly Father. It is a way of saying, "I need you. You are an essential member of our family. We cannot get along without you, and we cannot get along without your help."

The importance of this lesson has come to me more forcefully since we adopted our two little boys from Russia. Initially they did not like the idea that they needed to help do household work. They seemed to think they were on some kind of extended vacation. The first time I asked Dima to vacuum the floor, he refused. So I took his hand, placed it on the vacuum, and with my hand holding his firmly in place, we vacuumed the floor. The next Saturday I informed him it was again his turn to vacuum, and we had to repeat the process. He was a very reluctant helper. But the third Saturday, he got up and began vacuuming without being asked! And he did a good job, and he sang as he worked. Through sharing in the work, he had learned that he belonged, that he was a valued member of our family.

This does not mean that he always helps out willingly. The lesson needs to be taught over and over. But each time he helps, and each time I tell him, "Thank you for doing a good job," he learns again that he belongs, that he is needed.

Sometimes I have asked myself, what if I paid him for doing this work? Would the learning be different? I think it would. This is another area in which we sometimes desire to follow the "home as a business" mentality. Many of us have been taught that we should pay children for doing household work. We justify this because it is a common practice in the world to pay people for the work they do, and we figure our children need to learn how to live successfully in that world. But paying children to work at home changes the learning in one very significant way. Helping out around the house becomes something you do for money instead of something you do for the family.

In 2 Nephi 26:31, we are taught that "the laborer in Zion shall labor for Zion; for if they labor for money they shall perish." We want our family to be a Zion family, so I interpret that scripture to mean "the laborer in our family shall labor for the family; for if they labor for money they shall perish." Why perish? Because working for money transforms this opportunity to love and serve others into a self-serving operation. Money is a powerful incentive, and parents are tempted to use money as a motivator because it works. But it also undermines other good reasons for doing the work. Consider this. If a child makes her bed, and I ask, "Why did you make your bed?" she may answer, "Because Mom asked me to," or "Because it needed to be made," or "Because I like my room to look nice." But if you pay her a dollar to make her bed, and I ask the same question, "Why did you make your bed?" odds are she will answer, "Because Mom paid me."

When we pay children to do household chores, we risk teaching children to love money, not work. And we risk teaching them that those with money have the power to buy the work of others, while avoiding humble, serving work themselves. We deprive them of the opportunity of learning to work because it is a good thing to do, because the work needs to be done, and because this is the way we learn to love and serve each other.

Learning to work together harmoniously in our homes is not easy, but the rewards are worth it. Remember, it is by small and simple means that great things happen. Begin small. When you begin a task, invite a child to join you. If your children have assigned chores, offer to work along with them. Don't be discouraged if all does not go as well as you intended. Remember, family work is a major source of conflict in families. But conflict may not always be a bad thing. It can be part of the process of learning to overcome selfishness and to put others' needs ahead of our own self-centered interests.

Also, expect this effort to extend over the life of your family, because this is the great lesson of mortality: Will we use our time, and the gifts we have been blessed with, to bless the lives of others, or mostly for our own pleasure or gain? As we work together, we and our children learn to sacrifice our self-centered interests in order to do the right thing, the moral thing, the small and simple things that will help bless the lives of others.

This kind of sacrifice has the power to bind us together in our families, to help us become one. The Savior taught this lesson before his crucifixion in a powerful yet simple way as he prepared his disciples for his departure. "He riseth from supper, and laid aside his garments; and took a towel, and girded himself. After that he poureth water into a basin, and began to wash the disciples' feet, and to wipe them with the towel wherewith he was girded" (John 13:4–5). When Peter realized the Savior was going to wash his feet, in essence he responded, "No way are you going to wash my feet; that is servants' work." And how did the Savior respond? "Jesus answered him, If I wash thee not, thou hast no part with me" (John 13:8). The Savior's simple message seems to be: Until you are willing to do humble, serving work for each other, you will never be one with him. As he caught a glimpse of that eternal principle, Peter responded, "Lord, not my feet only, but also my hands and my head" (John 13:9). The Savior continued teaching the powerful lesson that the servant is not greater than the master, nor the master than he that is served (John 13:12–17).

Family work, the daily work of nurturing life, caring for one another in our homes, is the Lord's work. Through this humble service, we learn to set aside our pride and our self-centeredness and become one as we learn to love and serve one another. "Be not weary in well-doing, for ye are laying the foundation of a great work. And out of small things proceedeth that which is great. Behold, the Lord requireth the heart and a willing mind; and the willing and obedient shall eat the good of the land of Zion in these last days" (D&C 64:33–34).

Notes

1. Gordon B. Hinckley, "Four Simple Things to Help," *Ensign*, September 1996, 7–8.

2. Spencer W. Kimball, "Becoming Pure in Heart," *Ensign*, May 1978, 81; emphasis added.

3. Dianne S. Smith, unpublished data. Used by permission.

4. Ruth Brasher, Carol Ellsworth, and Carolyn Garrison, research project.

5. Harold B. Lee, *Stand Ye in Holy Places* (Salt Lake City: Deseret Book, 1974), 255–56; emphasis added.

6. Wendell Berry, "Men and Women in Search of Common Ground," *Home Economics: Fourteen Essays* (San Francisco: North Point Press, 1987), 118.

7. Kristine Manwaring, "My Home as a Temple," in *Strengthening Our Families*, ed. David Dollahite (Salt Lake City: Bookcraft, 2000), 94–96.

A TALENT FOR SPIRITUALITY

Carol B. Thomas

Popular author and lecturer Lucille Johnson once said, "If you're a good mother 60 percent of the time, you're a good mother." This thought comforted me and has become my mantra for many years.

So, if we only have to be good mothers 60 percent of the time, why is parenting so hard? In this life, our Heavenly Father gives us guidelines . . . that's all. In part, that is because every child is so different. There is not one right or wrong way of parenting for everyone. As parents, we must learn as we go, always turning to our Father in Heaven for help.

In some ways parenting was easier in the past. Elder Dallin H. Oaks said, "One of the great influences that unified families in prior times was the experience of struggling together in pursuit of a common goal—such as taming the wilderness or establishing a business. This principle is so important that one commentator suggested, 'If the family lacks a common crisis, hire a wolf to howl at the door.'"[1]

In our day, many wolves come unbidden to our door. But our children often don't recognize them for what they are. My goal is to give you hope and share some ideas that might help you in your parenting. At the outset, I have one request: please don't allow yourself to become overwhelmed with guilt over mistakes you may have made—a little guilt goes a long way. The most important thing is to start from where

Carol Burdett Thomas, a native of Salt Lake City, serves as the first counselor in the Young Women General Presidency. She is a former member of the Relief Society General Board. She and her husband, Dr. D. Ray Thomas, are the parents of seven and the grandparents of nineteen.

you are; don't look back and assess your track record. Take what ideas sound good to you, and if they work for you, great.

Over the years, I have read many good books and articles on parenting. What advice do I have to offer that you won't get elsewhere? It is this: *Teach your children to develop their talent for spirituality.* Most of us don't think about spirituality as a talent. Elder Bruce R. McConkie of the Quorum of the Twelve Apostles once said, "Above all talents— . . . chief among all endowments—stands the talent for spirituality."[2] Spirituality is learning how to listen to the Spirit and *then* letting it govern our lives. "Our tendency—it is an almost universal practice among most Church members—is to get so involved with the operation of the institutional Church that we never gain faith like the ancients," noted Elder McConkie, "simply because we do not involve ourselves in the basic gospel matters that were at the center of their lives."[3]

To help children develop their talent for spirituality, I'd like to suggest three things, "basic gospel matters," that you've probably heard a thousand times before:

1. Teach your children to read the scriptures regularly.
2. Teach your children to depend on the Lord and really pray.
3. Teach your children to ponder and meditate.

TEACH YOUR CHILDREN TO READ THE SCRIPTURES

Reading scriptures invites the Spirit into my life more quickly than anything else I know of. Elder Carlos E. Asay taught that scriptures are the depository of spirituality. If that is what you want, that is where you go to get spirituality.[4]

A friend of mine is an elementary school teacher. One of her students, a boy named Bobby, was very disruptive. His parents had even taken him to a child psychologist for help. Then, almost overnight, his behavior, as well as his reading skills, improved dramatically. My friend asked Bobby's mother what had caused the change. She answered, "Oh, I really am embarrassed to tell you because it is something we should have been doing all the time." Then she said, "We have begun reading scriptures together as a family. That's the difference."

Her words reminded me of a letter sent to the general Young Women office. "When I was in the 7th grade, I was really struggling in my math class," this young woman wrote. "My test grades were lower than normal and I wasn't understanding even though I was studying hard. I began reading the Book of Mormon every night. The next test in that class I received an A. I was ecstatic. At that moment I didn't realize what had helped me. I had gained a greater understanding of math as a result of reading the Book of Mormon. I still read almost every night and feel that doing this has made me capable of understanding concepts easily that others struggle with."[5]

At various times, we tried to have formal scripture reading as a family. I wish I could tell you that it was successful. We stopped and started so many times. The important thing was that we tried. And I did have success with something: When the children were in elementary school—about ages eight, nine, or ten—sometimes I would lie on their beds with them at night and tell them scripture stories. Because I didn't know every detail, I had to read the story the night before so I could retell it with testimony and feeling. The children enjoyed this and went to sleep feeling peaceful. These stories helped give them a love for the scriptures.

When was the last time you told your children the story of the Prophet Joseph Smith in the Sacred Grove? When I need to feel the Spirit quickly, I read the First Vision, the story of a fourteen-year-old boy who became the greatest prophet to ever live, second only to the Savior. And it all began because he listened to the promptings of the Spirit. When was the last time you bore testimony of this magnificent story?

Several years ago, Elder F. David Stanley spoke at our stake conference. He told us that as a new general authority, he had been invited to counsel with President Thomas S. Monson in his office. President Monson had said, "I would like to teach you the revelatory process." What an exciting prospect! I listened intently, wondering what magical formula President Monson had shared with Elder Stanley. President Monson described three steps to receiving revelation. First, analyze the scriptures regularly. Second, cross reference all the scriptures back and forth. Third, look for pure revelation to come by the gift of the Holy Ghost.

I thought of Lehi's experience in the first chapter of the Book of Mormon—when he "cast himself upon his bed [and] was carried away in a vision." The Lord came to him and gave him a book. As he read the book, he said he was "filled with the spirit of the Lord" (1 Nephi 1:7–8, 12). Teach your children that as they read their scriptures, they too can be filled with the Spirit of the Lord. They probably will not have a vision as Lehi did, but their minds will be enlightened and they will be filled with a spirit of peace.

"Faith is . . . born of scriptural study," said Elder Bruce R. McConkie. "Those who study, ponder and pray about the scriptures, seeking to understand their deep and hidden meanings, receive from time to time great outpourings of light and knowledge from the Holy Spirit . . . a sudden rush of ideas."[6] I like the phrases: *deep and hidden meanings; great outpourings of light and knowledge; sudden rush of ideas.* Are we teaching our children how to receive their own revelation?

TEACH YOUR CHILDREN TO PRAY

Our Heavenly Father wants us to pray. When he says, "Pray always," does he mean *always*? I think he does.

During his brief ministry to the Nephites following his resurrection, the Savior mentions prayer at least twenty-eight times (3 Nephi 11–18). Prayer must be extremely important to him. Are we teaching our children to pray as they walk down the halls at school, before a hard test, or when they're out with friends?

My daughter Becky has eight children, including two sets of twins. Most every night before bed—and it's usually late—she and her husband gather the family in a central hallway, hold hands, and have family prayer. Then they hug and run off to bed. When I asked what had prompted praying this way, my son-in-law said that he noticed his sons, ages fourteen and sixteen, were pulling away from him and didn't want to be hugged anymore. He had thought to himself, *My parents didn't have this trouble. What did they do that we're not doing?* He remembered how his family prayed. Then he said, "Ever since we've been praying this way, I don't have any trouble hugging my boys."

Pray with your children . . . pray *for* your children. Let them hear you plead to our Father to bless them with their schoolwork, finding friends, or whatever they may need. One friend of mine prayed with her child whenever he got in trouble. The child would be reluctant, too embarrassed to want to participate in a prayer right then. But, she says, her prayer for him always softened his heart. A child is teachable when his heart is softened—then he can feel the Spirit of the Lord. Another family has "prayers on the stairs." Kids arrive with hair wrapped in towels or dripping wet, others are dressed and ready to race off to school. If the parents miss one or two, they try to pray with them before they leave too.

Teach Your Children to Ponder and Meditate

President Hinckley has invited us to meditate often. That's not easy when our lives are overfull. We have "Time To Do Everything Except Think," suggests an April 2001 *Newsweek* article. Whether we realize it or not, we all need solitude. It helps to center us, calm us. It helps us define ourselves and what we really believe. I love Sister Marjorie Hinckley's philosophy. She did not believe in planning every moment of every day for her children. She wanted them to lie on their backs, listen to the birds, and watch the grass grow.[7] The Lord invites us to ponder and meditate when he says, "Let the solemnities of eternity rest upon your minds" (D&C 43:34).

Mothers have the right and the obligation to turn off the TV, especially during the dinner hour. Help your children have quiet time, away from the world and its distractions, a time when they can feel the Spirit. True spirituality is communion with God. If our children are so busy taking every kind of lesson imaginable, they won't have time to count the petals on a flower or the stars in the sky. We must teach them the joy that comes from being still.

In a recent visit with my daughter, I was again impressed with the power we have as mothers—for good or ill. My ten-year-old grandson tried so hard to please his mother. My daughter still has a need to please me. And, even though my own mother is ninety years old, I need her approval. It is all part of the cycle of life. The mother/child relationship is powerful. Because of its sacred nature, we must treat it with great respect. We must never, never give up on a child. Our children look to us, even when they're grown. They always need our approval.

Helping our children feel good about themselves strengthens their own inherent goodness and spirituality. Sometimes at night before our children went to bed, I counted their talents. I would say, "Let's count your ten talents tonight." My daughter says she always loved that, even though she wasn't sure she believed what I said. Children are like sponges; we can never compliment them enough. Some days we may have to search hard to give a compliment, but the search will be worth it. Former Relief Society general president, Elaine L. Jack, shared that during her four boys' teenage years, on those days when she couldn't think of anything good about them, she would say, "Gee, you breathe well."

Nothing we do in life is more important than mothering our children. And as we strive to deepen our family talent for spirituality, our most effective teaching will come by our examples. Not everything we do will be successful, but remember my mantra: "If you're a good mother 60 percent of the time, you are a good mother."

Notes

1. Dallin H. Oaks, "Parental Leadership in the Family," *Ensign*, June 1985, 9.

2. Bruce R. McConkie, *The Millennial Messiah: The Second Coming of the Son of Man* (Salt Lake City: Deseret Book Co., 1982), 234.

3. Bruce R. McConkie, *Doctrines of the Restoration: Sermons and Writings of Bruce R. McConkie*, ed. Mark L. McConkie (Salt Lake City: Bookcraft, 1989), 236.

4. Carlos E. Asay, "Look to God and Live," *Ensign*, November 1978, 52–54.
5. Letter on file in general Young Women office.
6. McConkie, *Doctrines of the Restoration*, 238, 244.
7. In *Glimpses into the Life and Heart of Marjorie Pay Hinckley*, ed. Virginia H. Pearce (Salt Lake City: Deseret Book, 1999), 54–55.

"Do Well Those Things Which God Ordained"

Virginia U. Jensen

One Sunday morning a few weeks ago my phone rang early. On the other end of the line was the precious voice of my three-year-old granddaughter, Kate. Kate had just recently graduated from the nursery to the Sunbeam class in Primary. At first she didn't want to go into opening exercises with all the "big kids." But because her mom served in Primary and her older brother and sister were there too, she felt secure and joyfully went into her new class.

In that early morning phone call, she presented a problem she faced and a solution she had come up with. She said, "Grandma, my brother and sister are sick, and Mom has to stay home from church to take care of them. I think I'm brave enough to go to Primary by myself if you will come and sit in the back." The deal was made. I sat on the back row of Primary during opening exercises. Kate sat on the front row with her class and her teacher. Every once in a while she would turn around to make sure I was still there. When her class was dismissed at the end of opening exercises, she confidently marched past me and blew a kiss.

Of all the church work I had performed during the previous week, none brought me more joy or had the eternal significance of that small act of service to a member of my family. In a simple way, I helped Kate be where she needed to be on Sunday morning, learning what she

Virginia U. Jensen is the first counselor in the Relief Society General Presidency. A homemaker, she and her husband, J. Rees Jensen, are the parents of four children and grandparents of seven. She has served in numerous volunteer and Church service missionary assignments and enjoys gardening, grandchildren, and family activities.

needs to know and do to successfully walk the path that leads back to Heavenly Father.

Like Kate, each of us needs the steadying hands of loving family members on the trek back to our eternal home. It is in our earthly homes we have the greatest opportunities to reach out to one another, to provide that substantive, steadfast help that is necessary for an eternally successful completion to this life's journey.

President Joseph F. Smith reminded us that "to do well those things which God ordained to be the common lot of all man-kind, is the truest greatness. To be a successful father or a successful mother is greater than to be a successful general or a successful statesman."[1] My life experience has taught me that all women striving for righteousness have a deep understanding of President Smith's statement.

Indeed, faithful women bring to all their relationships a profound respect for family and the roles they play in their own families. A single friend who has no children tells of a temple recommend interview she had with a member of her stake presidency. When the priesthood leader giving the interview reached the question about family relationships, he stopped and said, "You don't have a family. I don't need to ask you this." My friend, who is a devoted daughter, sister, and aunt, replied, "I don't have a husband and children, but I do have a family. I take my family responsibilities very seriously. I work hard at them. I would like to report. Please ask me the question." And he did.

Our family responsibilities mean a great deal to us, whatever our circumstances. This is as the Lord would have it. After all, Eve was called "the mother of all living" long before she bore any children. I'll never forget a lovely young woman—probably in her late thirties or early forties—who stood in a large meeting of stake Relief Society leaders recently and said, "I have never married and have never borne children, yet I am a 'mother in Zion.' We must learn to use the word *mother* to unite us and not divide us."

My hope is that all of us, sisters of Zion in many lands, will unite in a sacred recommitment to the holy calling of mothering and to "doing well those things which God ordained." Each of us—single or married, having borne children or able to nurture and bless God's children whom we haven't given birth to—has much to offer.

Other prophets of this dispensation join President Joseph F. Smith in teaching us how to view our roles. President David O. McKay said, "Motherhood is . . . the highest, holiest service to be assumed by mankind. It places her who honors its holy calling and service next to the angels."[2] We faithful sisters of The Church of Jesus Christ of Latter-day Saints, every one of us, do honor mothering and motherhood. The world, however, doesn't declare that message. In fact, it proclaims the opposite message in word and deed. The world praises women for many things, but rarely for that service which "God ordained."

Children, who are our literal legacy from the Lord, require our diligent, prayerful, loving mothering. And whether a woman has children in her home or not, each woman can exercise her gift of mothering in her extended family, in her Church callings, and in a variety of other settings. I would like to talk about three vital aspects of mothering: testimony, teaching, and time.

TESTIMONY

President Heber J. Grant declared, "The mother in the family . . . is the one who instills in the hearts of the children, a testimony and a love for the gospel . . . ; and wherever you find a woman who is devoted to this work, almost without exception you will find that her children are devoted to it."[3]

The faith of mothers often becomes the faith of children, even if it takes years for mothers to witness the fruits of their influence. Monica, the mother of St. Augustine, spent years praying for the salvation of her son. As a child and young man, Augustine lived a life of disobedience and laziness, "feeding upon the lusts of the world." Though it seemed he would languish in sin forever, he was never beyond the reach of his mother's example. Slowly he began to study the Bible, seek friends who could teach him more about Christianity, and resist the temptations of the flesh. Near the end of Monica's life, she and Augustine lived together in a house overlooking the sea, where they spent their evenings discussing the things of God. When she died, he resolved to live the way his mother had always prayed he would, and so he devoted himself to the Lord's service. After seventeen years of Monica's fervent prayers for her son and her enduring faith in Christ, Augustine spent forty-three years as a servant of God.[4]

Like Monica, women who live their testimonies of our Heavenly Father, our Savior, and the restored gospel of Jesus Christ bless generations.

Do your children and family members know you have a testimony? Does your knowledge of the restored gospel and the plan of salvation steady your children as they search for footing in a world of shifting values?

Recently, one of my adult children shared with me her frustration about how hard Sundays were for her. She said something I have heard from many women, "Sunday is my most difficult day of the week." As we talked, I thought back to the time when I was a mother raising young children and serving in a Relief Society presidency. My husband was always gone on Sunday morning serving in his Church assignment. It was extremely challenging to help my children get ready for church, get all the materials in the car I needed for Relief Society, and choose an outfit for myself to wear that went well with baby spit-up. Because it was the Sabbath and I wanted my children to feel the importance of this special day, I always tried to have a nicer dinner than on weekdays. Keeping peace and calm in the house so that a reverent spirit of worship would permeate the day was especially challenging. Truthfully, I felt like I failed most of the time. But I kept trying. And now, here was my daughter experiencing the same trials I remember so well.

As we talked, without even thinking, my testimony just started spilling out. I said, "It won't last forever, and besides, the gospel is true and it is worth all the difficulty." We then talked about the great things the Church does for us and our families. It was a sweet moment, and I was grateful for my testimony of the truthfulness of the gospel of Jesus Christ and his plan for us during our time on this earth. Your testimonies, both spoken and seen in your homes through your example, are treasured resources in strengthening family members.

Raising a child is not for the faint of heart. And have you noticed there are precious few cheerleaders on the sidelines in the game of motherhood? I have a friend whose son was a mighty spirit packed into a little body. His eagerness to learn and do were a tremendous challenge for his mother. He never tired of watching a half-gallon of orange juice spread under the refrigerator. He was fascinated by the splat of eggs dropped one at a time from the kitchen counter onto the floor. In an attempt to thwart these efforts, his beleaguered mother secured the refrigerator door with a rope. A smart and creative boy, he quickly figured out how to undo it. This mother spent the first five years of her son's life on her knees—not just cleaning up orange juice and eggs but also in fervent prayer for peace, stamina, and insight. She begged her husband to trade jobs—she would go to work, and he could stay home. But the mantle was hers, as President Smith put it, "to do well those things which God ordained to be the common lot of mothers." I am happy to report that everyone survived. Our zealous young man will go on his mission this month.

As you are on your knees and as you listen for the voice of the Spirit, your testimony will grow stronger. What a gift to be able to speak your heart to the Lord and have the promptings of his Spirit to guide your daily interactions with your family members. In Latter-day Saint family life, testimony is an all-important element. We love, nurture, and pray with and for each family member. Generation after generation of righteous children, youth, and adults come from homes where mothers' and family members' lives reflect their testimonies.

TEACHING

In one of his fables, Aesop tells this story: "A mother crab and her son went scurrying over the sand. The mother chastised her child: 'Stop walking sideways! It's much more becoming to stroll straightforward.' And the young crab replied: 'I will, Mother dear, just as soon as I see how. Show me the straight way, and I'll walk in it behind you.'"[5]

The world offers far too many substitute teachers to show our children alternate paths if we do not endeavor to teach them how to walk "the straight way." Any woman who doubts the significance or centrality of her place in the Church should realize that prophets learn their first gospel lessons in their homes from their mothers. The home is where our children learn about the Savior and the important gospel truths that will lead them back to their heavenly home. It is the mother who most consistently encourages her sons to advance in the priesthood and to prepare to serve missions; it is the mother who teaches her daughters to dress modestly and live worthily to enter the temple. Every mother is a teacher. No formal degree is required, but your determination to instruct prayerfully and lovingly and according to God's plan is prerequisite to your success—and theirs.

Patrick Henry said in the closing scene of his life: "I have now disposed of all my property to my family. There is one thing more I wish I could have given them, and that is the Christian religion. . . . If they had that, and I had not given them one shilling, they would be rich, and if they had not that, and I had given them all the world, they would be poor."[6] Every one of us, by honoring our mothering role, can give some part of our "Christian religion" to the children and youth in our lives.

We live in a time of values upheaval, when many standards have been discarded. Behavior is widely accepted now that just a few years ago was considered shocking. We must teach our children the things of God, the mission of Christ, and their plan for eternal happiness. Just as we strive to sustain our children temporally, we must teach them the lessons of eternity or we deprive them of what they really need to survive spiritually.

It doesn't take much outside influence to lead a child off the straight and narrow path. Hence, our consistent, loving teaching must be like a guidepost that our youth can rely on to make the way straight, even amidst a deluge of confusing worldly beckonings. A parent himself, President Joseph F. Smith undoubtedly understood all that constitutes the "common lot" of mothers and fathers. No wonder he strongly urged us "to do well those things which God ordained," for if we don't, the price is excruciatingly high. Now is the time. Home is the place.

Time

Although eternity lies before us, mortal life is the period in which children of God learn the lessons that enable eternal progression. Focusing our all—time, energy, spirit, and heart—on our God-ordained role brings the greatest rewards for ourselves and our family members. We can easily become confused, however, and spend our time and energy in the name of many good things that seem important while neglecting that which is of highest value—our families. With so many things competing for our time, it is easy to become distracted; and the prize is so great that Satan wants us to get sidetracked. Women have many choices and many obligations, but strengthening our family members remains the single most important thing we can do with our time. President Gordon B. Hinckley counseled: "As long as [your children] are in your home, let them be your primary interest. . . .

" . . . Let your first interest be in your home . . . let nothing stand in the way of [your] role as a mother."[7]

The Savior taught us about priorities when he said, "Lay not up for yourselves treasures on earth, . . . but lay up for yourselves treasures in heaven, . . . for where your treasure is, there will your heart be also" (3 Nephi 13:19–21). An old fairy tale tells the story of a mother who learns the hard way what her treasure really is. While out in the forest picking strawberries with her young daughter, the mother discovers a large cave filled with golden treasure and guarded by three maidens. Told she can have as much as she can hold, the mother releases her child's hand to gather the gold coins in her apron. In shock she discovers that by choosing the gold she has forfeited her child's company for one full year. When the mother returns to the cave the following year, she sees the maidens, the gold, and her child. Again the maidens tell her she can have as much gold as she can carry, but the mother runs eagerly to her child and enfolds the child in her arms. "Take the little one home," the maidens tell the mother, "for now your love is greater than your [other desires]."[8]

Make your family your treasure. Make home a place of building testimony, a place of teaching life's important lessons, and a place of refuge and renewal for family members. Wholeheartedly give them your time, energy, and avid attention. Children need mom to be there. Families need quiet time, unhurried time, pondering time, time for discovery, time for testimony, time for teaching.

Only you can determine the most important use of your time. But remember, the routine, small acts that take place in the home are the building blocks of eternal relationships. In the informal discussions at the dinner table or while working at daily tasks come the moments to teach and observe. In the day in and day out of family life, children can come to know and love Heavenly Father and our Savior, Jesus Christ, in ways no Church activity can ever duplicate or teach.

President Joseph F. Smith taught us a potent truth when he counseled us "to do well those things which God ordained to be the common lot of all man-kind." The daily business of motherhood often seems common indeed, but you, the women of Zion, are uncommonly good. Thank you for doing well those things which God ordained.

May the Lord bless you in this most important work of nurturing his children. May you be there when they are very young and need the strength of your testimony. May you be there with eternal truths when they need your teaching. May you just be there—consecrating your time and your devotion as you honor the holy calling of mothering.

Notes

1. Joseph F. Smith, *Gospel Doctrine: Sermons and Writings of Joseph F. Smith* (Salt Lake City: Deseret Book, 1986), 285.
2. David O. McKay, Conference Report, October 1942, 12–13.
3. Heber J. Grant, *Gospel Standards*, comp. G. Homer Durham (Salt Lake City: *Improvement Era*, 1941), 150.
4. Laura M. Adams, "Monica, Mother of Augustine," in *The Moral Compass: Stories for a Life's Journey*, edited by William J. Bennett (New York: Simon & Schuster, 1995), 540–42.
5. Aesop, in *Moral Compass*, ed. Bennett, 522.

6. Patrick Henry, as quoted in *The New Dictionary of Thoughts* (Garden City, N. Y.: Standard Book Co., 1961), 561; also in David O. McKay, "Applied Christianity," *Improvement Era*, December 1937, editor's page.

7. Gordon B. Hinckley, "Your Greatest Challenge, Mother," *Ensign*, November 2000, 98, 100.

8. In *Moral Compass*, ed. Bennett, 520–21.

"The Heart of Her Husband Doth Safely Trust in Her"

Natalie Curtis McCullough

When I was about fourteen years old, my parents took me to see *Camelot*, an exciting new movie musical. *Camelot* is the story of a king who longed for order and civilization in an age of medieval terrors. King Arthur envisioned a round table where the most virtuous men sat in equal alliance for the cause of right. One favored and exceptional knight named Lancelot was more pure, more visionary, and more powerful than any other knight at the table . . . until he fell in love with the king's wife, Guinevere. Lancelot and Guinevere's infidelity to the king poisoned and ultimately destroyed Arthur's enlightened dream for England.

This magnificently scripted movie was about the repentance, forgiveness, and compassion required in real love. And it was about the tragic and enormously far-reaching consequences of adultery. I remember my feelings as an adolescent when Lancelot and Guinevere first realized their love for each other and when Arthur recognized that their pain at betraying him was as great as his own. I cried as I watched. Whatever the failings of my age and gender, I knew disaster was being courted. I anguished for Arthur when he looked into his best friend's eyes and saw in them love for his wife. I was stirred to the depths when King Arthur went into his round room and determined to return the bitter cup of betrayal with forgiveness. It was more than I could bear.

Natalie Curtis McCullough received a bachelor's degree in English from the University of Utah. She is a guest presenter for Human Pursuits, the Western Humanities, and volunteer for the Salt Lake Foster Care Citizen Review Board. She currently serves as stake Young Women president. She and her patient husband, Jim, are the parents of four children.

My heart swelled for the tortured lovers, and I fell into uncontrollable sobbing. All this was before intermission.

My mother finally asked my father to take me out into the lobby and explain to me that this was just a movie. It wasn't real. (They never had time to argue about why it was Dad's job to take me out if Mother knew what to say to me, but it is a useful pattern I have faithfully replicated.) The fact that I could hear them discussing me over the movie and my own sobs was not making us popular with the other theater goers.

Finally, as the love songs got more dramatic and tortured, I became so upset that my father took my arm and led me out to the theater lobby. I do not believe he had any way of being prepared for the drama that was to continue off screen, so to speak. I, on the other hand, was prepared for his words of comfort, having heard my mother teach them to him just moments before. He no sooner spoke them than I lashed out with all the vehemence, illogic, and righteous indignation of a teenaged girl in the throes of romantic distress.

"This is not make-believe!" I told him. "This is real to me. People can't help how they fall in love. You think I'm too young to understand. But I know when something's real." I no doubt gasped for breath before continuing, "It is so unfair to King Arthur. He loves them both." The look on my father's face—innocent, kind, tolerant—was something no mere actor has ever matched. I believe he was stunned by the sincerity and depth of my passion. He was alarmed by my grief about the love triangle being played out on the screen. He took me in his arms and said something to the effect, "OK. You are right. The people are pretend, but their predicament is real. The story is true, and it is tragic."

I have never felt so validated. We went back into the theater, and I continued to sob. Every song brought renewed spasms of grief. My mother continued to nudge my father to take me out of the theater, as our unpopularity was turning to something generally reserved for political candidates who have tied in an election. But he said to leave me alone, that my heart was appropriately breaking.

Even at the peak of hormonal instability (and well before I realized that all romantic distress has some foundation in hormonal instability), I understood and would not be distanced from the poignant truth about the power of love between men and women, about marriage and betrayal and enlightened vision and how royalty should behave.

I have never forgotten the anguish I felt during that movie. I have never gotten over my love and adoration for King Arthur and his dream for Camelot. His vision was much more than a dream about noble Knights of the Round Table and courts of law replacing violent rule. His vision was about the legacy of a righteous man who ruled himself. I still believe his story is absolutely true to the truth. And I believe it spoke so forcefully to my heart because, fundamentally, we are covenant kings and queens in training. We, too, must have a higher vision for our lives than the pleasure-seeking peasantry, as it were, in the great drama of the plan of salvation.

So who plays Lancelot to our marriages? He is whatever threatens our fidelity and devotion to our spouses. He may be the allure of our career successes, our concern for status and material possessions, our vanity over intellectual ability. Lancelot comes as our worst fears and uncontrolled anger. He is even our children or friends if they stand between us and our loyalty and attention to a spouse. The most devastating form of Lancelot in a marriage relationship is indifference. And the frightening thing is that Lancelot, the usurper, comes in the guise of all that is pure and strong and desirable. His comical lines, "C'est Moi, C'est Moi I'm forced to admit, I'm simply the best by far," underscore a profound doctrinal truth.

The Savior is frequently referred to as the bridegroom, with the church as his bride, and those things of the world that we worship in his place are represented by the metaphor of the unfaithful lover. "Who can find a virtuous woman?" the scriptures say, "For her price is far above rubies. The heart of her husband doth safely trust in her" (Proverbs 31:10–11). Isn't that the loveliest prose? The chapter ends with these words, "Favour is deceitful, and beauty is vain: but a woman that feareth the Lord, she shall be praised. Give her of the fruit of her hands; and let her own works praise her in the gates" (vv. 30–31).

Give her the fruit of her hands . . .

If we really believed in the law of the harvest, wouldn't we behave honorably? The problem is that even though we know intellectually that we will reap what we sow, we get impatient with the seasons. Emotionally, we want continual springtime and no winter.

I wonder if we recognize those seasonal patterns in our lives often enough. I know I don't. Camelot generally represents the period of perfection in King Arthur's court, the time when "Might for Right" was the ideal, when autumn leaves were magically whisked away before sunrise, and Guinevere and Arthur were true in their devotion. All was order and beauty. It lasted only for a brief moment. My "I want everything to be Camelot right now" mentality shows so little tolerance for the life process. For proper seasons.

I think it is hardest to overcome the "Camelot" syndrome in marriage because the intimacy of an everyday relationship encompasses so many levels of emotion and personality with such high stakes. I want every part of my marriage to be right at all times (so that the prospect of eternity seems like a blessing). But the very power of the marriage covenant is that it binds us to each other in our imperfections, through our winters so to speak.

I love this thought from Clarissa Estés' book, *Women Who Run with the Wolves:* we should practice "tending to [our] marriage like the orchard it is."[1] Marriage as an orchard is a scriptural pattern to contemplate. What is an orchard if not an archetype for the whole? An orchard is where there is tending and grafting, nurturing and hard labor. One must be continually on the lookout for pests and disease, which start out small but can be devastating if left unchecked. An orchard requires continuing education to learn the newest and best methods, fertilizers, and hybrids. It demands order and thoughtful planning. Any successful orchard is pruned to keep the focus on the fruit, not letting the tree itself go woody. Think about that as an image for refocusing our passions, interests, and desires heavenward.

What I love most about the concept of marriage as an orchard is its seasonal nature. There is the time to plant and prune, to nurture, and, yes, to harvest. But there is an equal and opposite fallow period. What a necessary and appropriate season is dormancy, space to turn inward. Time to rest and time to heal. No relationship is only harvest. This image is a worthwhile pattern to process. We cycle! Every year brings a winter—some mild and some harsh, but a period of dormancy, in predictable patterns. We cannot force any relationship to be only harvest. Why do I forget this? Why am I so easily surprised by the pattern of seasons?

German poet Rainer Maria Rilke (1875–1926) said it this way:

> *I live my life in widening rings*
> *which spread over earth and sky.*
> *I may not ever complete the last one,*
> *but that is what I will try.*
>
> *I circle around God, the primordial tower,*
> *and I circle ten thousand years long;*
> *and I still don't know if I'm a falcon, a storm,*
> *or an unfinished song.* [2]

What a lovely pattern, that we circle the same issues in widening rings, maybe even for ten thousand years, but we are never finished. We never run out of cycles. How I would like to be finished with the lessons of faith, charity, or repentance. But I seem to need to learn them in progressive patterns, widening circles of understanding. This repetitious learning is another one of the blessings Heavenly Father has specifically reserved for us as royalty in training. He offers us life as a glorious process.

What is covenant-making but widening rings? Most of us at any one time will be discouraged with a child, unhappy with a sweetheart, angry with a neighbor or coworker, feeling on the fringes, or threatened by health or financial issues. These issues are the life process. We do not solve these problems once and for all so much as we get a broader view of them and put them into perspective. We cycle through them. We cry like Esau out of our abundance, "Isn't there a blessing reserved for me?" and do not realize that our problem may be the blessing. Our heartache or our loneliness or our disillusionment is part of the orchard of our life—if we understand it and, like King Arthur, will be governed by it.

The commitment to rule ourselves is the basis of a fulfilling marriage. Consider the example of Father Lehi. When Sariah and Lehi's sons do not return from their journey to obtain the plates in Jerusalem, Sariah complains against Lehi for putting her sons' lives at risk and for being a visionary man (of course, this was probably the very thing that attracted her to him in the first place). She says: "Behold, thou hast led us forth from the land of our inheritance, and my sons are no more, and we perish in the wilderness" (1 Nephi 5:2).

Now Sariah is not a silly woman. She does not complain of losing her silver, linens, and tapestries, her comfortable home with servants, her women friends or her tennis foursome, except in a very general way. She only notes that because of Lehi's visions, they have traded the land of their inheritance, which includes their children's opportunities and future, for a tent in the wilderness where the family will likely perish. And she believes her sons may already be dead. These seem like reasonable complaints, even for a woman of substance.

Father Lehi acknowledges Sariah's point of view. He does not look off with longing to the River of All Righteousness and clean his ears with a stick when she starts to nag. He does not pick up the Liahona remote and try to mute her when she accuses him of being the source of all her unhappiness. I love Lehi. I see why he was a chosen vessel of the Lord. First, he makes his wife feel understood. Notice I did not say he understands her. What man and woman truly understand each other? But he makes her *feel* understood. Like my own sweet father in the theater lobby, Lehi validates her perception of him. He accepts responsibility for the truth when he acknowledges, "I know that I am a visionary man," and then he explains why that particular defect in a marriage partner is a blessing for him and for their family. He continues, "For if I had not seen the things of God in a vision I should not have known the goodness of God, but had tarried at Jerusalem, and had perished with my brethren" (1 Nephi 5:4).

Then he does an extraordinary thing for a man who is also the husband of a complaining woman. He comforts her by addressing her specific fear for the lives of her sons. He bears fervent testimony which speaks to her trusting heart. He says, "I know that the Lord will deliver my sons out of the hands of Laban, and bring them down again unto us" (1 Nephi 5:5). We read that Sariah was comforted "after this manner of [Lehi's] language" (1 Nephi 5:6). Well, of course she was.

Later, when the sons return as Lehi has prophesied, Lehi and Sariah rejoice together. Lehi offers no recriminations for Sariah's loss of faith. No sulking or silent treatment—"Visionary, am I?"—over the name-calling. They simply express gratitude and renewed faith after their trial. Their joy is full. How opposite from many of us who, after the trial, in place of rejoicing and gratitude choose the long descent into recriminations and blame.

I find this to be a profound pattern for the men and women who serve in the Church today. Either the husband or the wife could be the family visionary, or on the metaphorical podium. My husband, Jim, has been in a bishopric three times in our twenty-five years of marriage. That is a lot of spiritual experiences on the stand for him while I pace in the foyer with crying babies or look for missing teenagers at 7-11. He used to come home filled with the spirit of a meeting while I wondered if the same meeting would ever end.

I might have voiced an occasional, faint complaint.

Remember that after Sariah's boys returned, she expressed reciprocal testimony saying, "Now I know of a surety that the Lord hath commanded my husband to flee into the wilderness; . . . and given [my sons] power whereby they could accomplish the thing which the Lord hath commanded them" (1 Nephi 5:8). Or in other words, "Now I have the vision, too." No one points out to her, the mother, that Nephi caught the spirit of that principle several chapters ago. Hello? No, her sons return as prophesied by her visionary husband and "they did rejoice exceedingly, and did offer sacrifice . . . and they gave thanks unto the God of Israel" (1 Nephi 5:9).

What a pattern for my marriage. If only my husband and I would have compared our widely divergent experiences in worship and had a good laugh at ourselves so that I would understand and remember our vision for our family as Sariah did. Then I could have exclaimed, "Now I know that we each have meaningful contributions to this work and different seasons for being on the stand feeling the sweet Spirit or in the rest room changing foul diapers."

Being willing to understand another's point of view is the power of compassionate marriages—perhaps better named, "compassionate communication marriages," the kind that Lehi and Sariah modeled. But do not be discouraged if your marriage is not patterned after this model, yet. If we were to compare Lehi and Sariah with Jacob and Rachel, we would learn that not all scriptural marriages were perfect. Remember when Jacob was deceived and married Leah, the older sister, after working seven years for Rachel, and those years "seemed unto him but a few days, for the love he had to her" (Genesis 29:20)? That is all very romantic for the courtship period, but what about after the marriage when Rachel had a complaint? She came to her husband after Leah had given him four sons. Rachel envied her sister and yearned for a child of her own. She said to her husband, Jacob, "Give me children, or else I die" (Genesis 30:1).

I find that a compelling conversation starter. There is no beating around the bush or getting off on a tangent. I would think a man would be grateful to respond to so direct and concise a statement of need. But not Jacob. He was a better fiancé than husband, at that time. It says in Genesis that after her complaint, "Jacob's anger was kindled against Rachel:" and he said, "Am I in God's stead, who hath withheld from thee the fruit of the womb?" (Genesis 30:2).

The point is that, even though it is no more Jacob's fault that Rachel is barren than it is Lehi's fault that his sons are waylaid in Jerusalem, one man knew how to treat his wife so that she could safely trust in him and one man didn't. Most of us live with men who were more compassionate communicators before marriage.

And undoubtedly we were too. To be the one who brings compassion and healing into a relationship takes effort. It is so much easier to try to control other people's choices, to force other people's repentance or perspective or life process than to properly experience our own. What chance does the still, small voice have when I am raising my voice in the persistent whine? Maybe that is why the voice is still small, circling ten thousand years waiting for women's, wives,' and mothers' voices to gentle.

One of the repetitive themes in my marriage is the feeling that I am not properly valued or cherished by my husband. In retrospect, I usually find that the feeling is self-induced, self-maintained, and finally overcome by me, alone. (Something about the "hormonal instability" I referred to earlier.) Nevertheless, while I feel unloved, it is very painful. Not until I finally leave off recriminations about his shortcomings and get around to ruling my own responses and beliefs am I able to discern the whisperings of the Spirit, which inevitably teach me how to perform the healing miracles of marriage, in widening rings.

One woman had just finished a busy week of children's sporting events, recitals, and school responsibilities, and had also entertained and supported her husband through his successful regional conference. Despite the abundant harvest of the Spirit which blessed their efforts during the day, by Sunday evening she was exhausted. She was feeling pretty invisible for all the love and labor expended, especially when her children wandered away without acknowledging the evening meal and her husband left at the same time to watch TV for some needed decompression. Making a snap decision to spend a few days alone at their ski resort condominium to regroup, she cleaned up the Sunday dishes and slipped out of the house without telling her husband where she was going.

He called her early the next morning and asked her what was going on. She was incredulous that he had no idea why she left. She said— nicely, I am sure—that she hoped he would manage the household, somehow. When she didn't come home for another day, he drove up into the mountains to talk to her. She explained that she believed he didn't love her. She named some of his obvious acts of indifference.

Though her husband displayed some Jacob tendencies, he had much of the greatness of Lehi. He wanted to show her that he cared. He listened to her grievances and repeated back to her what she was feeling to see if he really understood. As it turned out, he had just a few faint complaints for her, as well. As she sat in front of the fire, her hostility diffused by his patient ear, she had to hold the painful mirror of reality up to her own behavior. An amazing thing happened. After they expressed their frustrations and apologized for inconsiderate behaviors, her heart changed. She felt safe to share a problem she hadn't been able to articulate for a period of time. This was the main cause of her emotional ups and downs and really had nothing to do with her husband. As he listened to her, she felt genuinely loved. She could see more clearly some of the unreasonable emotional demands that accompanied her outward devotion and hard work. They shared a glimpse of the same vision.

Most of us don't have to run away to get perspective. A brisk walk or hiding the television remote accomplishes the same thing. But it is sweet to me this wonderful Regional Representative probably spoke on the importance of healthy marriages the morning before his wife left. And she, for her part, pushed him to emotional distance by her own unreasonable neediness. If she didn't know what was upsetting her, how could he? When he acknowledged her unhappiness, he showed compassion for her distress. When she finally looked through his eyes, she healed something in herself.

These are not priesthood miracles of giving sight to the blind or causing the lame to walk. But they are miracles of compassion, which equally heal our blindness and infirmity. And women, as well as men, have the power to perform them.

I recently came across a passage of scripture in the gospel of Luke, which seems to describe a miracle based on compassion rather than faith. The Savior came out from teaching in the synagogue on the

Sabbath and saw a woman "which had a spirit of infirmity eighteen years, and was bowed together, and could in no wise lift up herself." Jesus said to her, "Woman, thou art loosed from thine infirmity" (Luke 13:11–12). It doesn't appear that she asked for his blessing or even knew who he was. We are told "he laid his hands on her: and immediately she was made straight, and glorified God" (v. 13). Then the ruler of the synagogue was indignant because Jesus healed on the Sabbath, and probably worse, the miracle was wasted on an old, Hebrew woman—a person utterly without stature or significance.

Jesus called the ruler a hypocrite, but he called the distressed woman "daughter of Abraham" (Luke 13:16), allowing for all of the prestige and honor associated with that revered name to be added to her miraculous healing. First, he had compassion on her, then he healed her physical infirmity, and last, he bestowed upon her the reminder of her spiritual birthright, or royal lineage. I believe that this incident gives us a pattern for healing our own marriages.

This layered healing comes partly to our marriages through the blessing of repentance, the great swelling desire to try again, to stay on for the duration. And we are blessed by the reality of consequences, which soften and make teachable our erring hearts.

I can find no happy ending to infidelity: either physical or emotional, either to our covenants or to our sweethearts. Lancelot ended up in mortal combat with the man he most loved, and Guinevere lost both her loves and entered a convent, symbolic of utter sterility, for there was no place far enough to hide them from the harvest of hurt they brought upon themselves, the man they both loved, and upon the hundreds of innocents in the court and beyond. The destruction of the kingdom of Camelot was not so tragic to me as was the waste of a marriage, the poisoned orchard.

The fact is that we need our imperfect spouses for our perfecting. While it is true that we are here to learn to rule ourselves, doing so in the context of a marriage may be the ultimate crucible. In the marriage covenant we must act with absolute fidelity, learn compassion, recognize patterns and seasons, and practice coming into the presence of the

Lord as royalty. The development of these attributes is miraculous, for by them the deeply compassionate gift of being "safely trust[ed]" by the hearts of our husbands becomes possible (Proverbs 31:11).

Notes

1. Clarissa Pinkola Estés, *Women Who Run with the Wolves: Myths and Stories of the Wild Woman Archetype* (New York: Ballantine Books, 1995), 322.
2. Rainer Maria Rilke, in *Ahead of All Parting: The Selected Poetry and Prose of Rainer Maria Rilke*, trans. Stephen Mitchell (New York: The Modern Library, 1995), 5.

"Honour Thy Father and Thy Mother"

JoAnn Ottley

Tevye, the long-suffering father in *Fiddler on the Roof*, sings at his daughter's wedding words that express the poignant feelings we all have as we watch our babies disappear into grownups: "Is this the little girl I carried? Is this the little boy at play? I don't remember growing older. When did they?"[1] It isn't much of a stretch to see the heart-tugging similarity between watching our children grow up and watching our parents grow old. For me this is a particularly tender comparison right now. I can't help wondering, is this the vibrant, laughing mother I remember? Is this my strong, heroic "Dad-who-can-do-anything"? When did that wretched illness steal her mind and shrink her beautiful body to a mere skeleton, making us pray for her release? When did Dad become an old man with a fringe of cotton-white hair, begging his legs to sustain him long enough to get the few steps to his wheelchair? (Though his soul, however, is as large as ever, and he still keeps us all laughing!)

We are commanded to honor our parents that our "days may be long" (Exodus 20:12). Yet caring for infirm parents brings many challenges as well as rewards. Understanding this subject is like trying to take a sip out of a fire hose. Let me briefly discuss three questions dealing with elderly parents that seem crucial to me.

JoAnn South Ottley, soprano vocalist, recording artist, and former vocal coach for the Tabernacle Choir, was caring for both her aged father and her disabled sister at the time of this presentation. Her father passed away in July. In 2000, she and her husband, Jerold Ottley, received presidential citations from Brigham Young University and were honored by the BYU Management Society as "Distinguished Utahns of the Year." She and Jerry are the parents of two and the grandparents of one.

How Can We Balance the Added Needs of Parents with Our Own Pressing Lives?

Picture this: A dog balanced on one hind paw on a large ball. His front paws are extended upward, holding a long, thin, candy-striped rod. On the rod at each end are parrots. Each parrot is riding a very small unicycle and holding in its beak a long, thin stick with a small flag on it. In the center of the candy-striped rod held aloft by the dog balancing on the ball is a large cat. The cat is doing a handstand on one front paw, the rest of its body skyward. Balanced on the highest hind paw of the cat is, believe it or not, a goldfish bowl—full of water—with, yes, a goldfish.

This feels like my life, perhaps yours too. At this moment I am precariously balanced, and any unexpected change—not just a cannonball from left field but even a mere feather at the wrong moment—may reduce me to shambles. And when I get myself back together and up on the ball again, my life looks very different.

Seventeen years ago, as my precious mother started down the long, sad road of Alzheimer's, I faced a daily rebalancing act, often without warning. Never, ever, did I truly feel that I learned how to balance. My dear dad didn't balance his load; he simply gave everything he had. During those eight years of her illness, I, however, was the dog on the ball, continually off-balance, always re-examining the load and my capacity to even get up on the ball, let alone add more pieces. Only in hindsight do I realize that I didn't do too badly. My balancing act took many forms over those years, and I got a lot of bruises from falling off and re-adjusting, but somehow, with help from around me and above me, I did what needed to be done.

Nine years have passed since Mom died. Dad is now nearly ninety, and his needs are continually increasing. Last year, my sixty-one-year-old sister, single and in poor health, had a stroke, a suspected heart attack, and a ruptured disk in her lower back, leaving her permanently disabled and in need of a great deal of care. A few weeks after the worst of her trauma, my Dad hemorrhaged, requiring hospitalization, surgery, and a period of rehabilitation. A short time later, he was hit by a car while crossing a busy intersection in his electric wheelchair. He was not injured seriously, but it was traumatic all the same, for all of us. This was one of those cannonball-out-of-left-field times for me, and there were days when I felt sure I was about to move into the "cared-for" category myself. Again, hindsight is benevolent. We made it. I've "redone my load" and it's working . . . this week.

This historical (and sometimes hysterical) overview may lead you to believe that I have much wisdom to offer. Not so. I still get up every day, rebalance, and think of that wonderful dog. I never know when or if the next crisis will come.

So, to address the question of how we balance the needs of parents with the demands of our own busy lives, my advice is: Be sure of your foundation, adjust your load, trimming as necessary, and stay flexible—the load is always shifting and you must be ready to bend. An infirm parent may face a temporary illness or a lifetime disability. The parent may or may not recover. We rarely know for sure. Being there for elderly parents is an exercise in living with uncertainty. To maintain your balance you may, periodically, need to step off the ball to reassess and get on more sure footing.

Upon What Resources, Family and Community, Shall We Draw?

Before we make any decisions about helping elderly parents, we have to determine their needs. That assessment needs to be ongoing. If someone needs a trip to the grocery store and I bring her flowers, I have done a good deed but missed the greater need. Sometimes a need is simple—maybe a phone call every day instead of once a week, maybe an extra visit. Sometimes the need is greater—meals, housing, or help with doctors' appointments. Sometimes the need is for all-out, full-time care, day and night, for a short time or a long time.

When we know help is needed, we must simply dig in and find out what's available. The first resource, of course, is family. A family that can offer cooperative care among members has great power not only to ease burdens and provide needed care, but also to bind itself together. Is it easy or comfortable? Not likely. Is it rewarding and worthwhile? Is it the Lord's way? Yes.

In the condominium community where we live, at least two families we know of (the "children" being in their mid-sixties) have sold their homes and moved into their parents' condo homes to care for them. One couple, very successful professionals as well as active church and community volunteers, moved from the East coast to care for the husband's mother. They are living in the basement of his mother's home. And, by the way, he has just been called as bishop of her ward.

During the late stages of my mother-in-law's life, the family members took care of little things, like cleaning, threading needles, and running errands. In the final stages of her life, we took turns taking meals, sitting with her, sometimes through the night, and my husband, her baby, would sit on her bed and sing hymns to her. The greatest of the care, however, was on the shoulders of her daughter, who lived next door and gave long-term, heroic care.

May I insert here a small aside. Honoring our parents continues posthumously. Because many unfortunate things happen when it comes time to settle a family estate, large or small, let me share an example that impressed me deeply. After my husband's mom passed away at age ninety-three, the oldest brother called a family council to consider the will and decide on the small estate, which was primarily the family home. The children decided, in full love and agreement and gratitude, that the sister should have the home in recognition of her selfless care for their parents. I think Grandma and Grandpa—and the Lord—smiled.

Every family is unique and continually changing. We should all simply do the best we can with the issues we have: money, relationships, distance, and health. All go into the mix. That's where other resources come in.

Let me mention specifically community resources and assisted living. Our communities now offer some amazing programs and choices. As I searched through possibilities for my disabled sister and father, I found an array of choices. Housing is available in a wide range of choices and costs. My dad has a studio apartment in an independent-living senior residence, which was his choice. Our family has helped take care of him there for over a year, but his needs are increasing. We do not know what his future needs may be.

Magazines, books, geriatric physicians, counselors and attorneys, and AARP (the American Association of Retired Persons) are all good resources for help in determining what is available. However, I'd like to say a few words about a resource you may be inclined to either over-look, on the one hand, or overwork, on the other. It's you. Perhaps the hardest question of all in caring for loved ones in need is "How much is enough?" I wish I had an answer. I don't, because in our attempts to be Christlike, giving, and unselfish, we can also damage ourselves as a resource for other very important people in our lives. We can damage sacred relationships, we can damage our physical and emotional health, and we can create financial hardship for those around us.

We often find, on the other hand, that we gain both wisdom and strength as we go. This returns me to the question of balance. Does a dog come to mind? It's also good to remember that difficult situations are lightened by laughter. I am so grateful for a family that laughs together.

In summary, I would suggest we try to look at the whole picture, counsel with those around us who can see that picture, know when we've crossed the line between too much help and too little, stay flexible, and continually seek spiritual guidance from the Lord.

How Do We Give Sensitive, Loving Care?

A wise Church leader suggested that it is much easier to do the *how* and *what* of a thing if we first know *why* we do it at all. I believe him. Examining why we care for our elderly parents will help us be better caretakers. An easy answer for me would be simply that my parents are worthy of any honor I can possibly give them. I love them dearly and fully. But what if they weren't worthy of my honor? What if parents haven't been lovable? Then the *why* of the question takes on new significance.

You will remember that Moses wanted in the worst way to bring the children of Israel to a higher law. After generations of bondage, however, they were seemingly unable to progress toward a higher way, and the Lord was merciful enough to give them a pared-down law, a law he knew they could abide if they chose. That pared-down law was the Ten Commandments—the bare bones of spiritual laws, if you will. To me that means that the commandment to honor our fathers and mothers is not to be taken lightly. It's left as a core item, not peripheral, and is simply unconditional. We are to honor our fathers and mothers, regardless. And what's more, the apostle Paul points out that that commandment is "the first commandment with promise": "That thy days may be long upon the land which the Lord thy God giveth thee" (Ephesians 6:2; Exodus 20:12). Moses later added: "and that it may go well with thee, in the land which the Lord thy God giveth thee" (Deuteronomy 5:16). In other words, the condition for maintaining an inheritance in a promised land is personal righteousness—obedience to the commandments, which includes honoring parents.

This is why we care for our elderly parents with sensitivity and love. It is a commandment intended for *our* eternal benefit, as well as theirs. In caring for them—whether they have earned our love and respect or not—we exercise faith, virtue, knowledge, temperance, patience, kindness, and through it all, charity, the pure love of Christ. You may recognize the list. Those are the qualities listed in 2 Peter, the qualities of godliness (2 Peter 1:5–7). In caring for our frail earthly parents, we become like our Heavenly Parents. As we honor even less than ideal parents, the struggle to love and care for them helps move us to our best. One physician, a leader in hospice work in California, stated that our task is not simply to learn to love, but to *become* love.[2] In commanding us to honor our fathers and mothers, God has designed the perfect workshop for the class in love.

How then do we care for them with sensitivity and kindness? Using any means we can find. What makes them feel loved? What makes their tired eyes sparkle as we show them the love and care only their children can give? What comforts them, eases their loneliness, helps fill their days? Love takes an infinite number of forms, and we can find new ones every day.

I see looks in my own children's eyes now, as they see my husband, Jerry, and me heading down that path. What is ahead for these parents who were so on top of everything, so vigorous and so awake? Now they're not moving around so easily, not quite so swift with either the answers or the questions. Are these the parents I remember? I've often thought of a good parent-child relationship as being like birds playing together in the sky, wheeling, diving, and turning in a playful aerial ballet. As families, we dance together. We hope to fly together for eternity. Even in the challenges that come in late life, the joy, the laughter, the love can be part of our life journey with those who gave us life.

Notes

1. Sheldon Harnick, "Sunrise, Sunset," from *Fiddler on the Roof* (Sunbeam Music Inc., 1964).
2. Gerald G. Jampolsky, *Teach Only Love*, (New York, N.Y.: Bantam Books, 1983), 63.

APPRENTICES AT WORK

꧁꧂

Carol S. Middleton

A few years ago I read President Hinckley's biography, *Go Forward with Faith*. In chapter 10, "Life with Father," I found many wonderful parallels between President Hinckley's family and the family in which I was reared. One of President Hinckley's daughters commented, "It didn't matter whether or not Dad had ever done something before. . . . If he decided something needed to be done, he saw it through. I don't think it ever occurred to him that he couldn't do something, and I can't think of one thing he tackled that he didn't pull off."[1]

Like President Hinckley, my dad could make, fix, or build anything. When I was born, my parents were building their second home—by themselves! I was put in a playpen close by my parents while my older brothers, who were five and three and a half, learned to entertain me, move things around, and hand tools to our parents. First they finished a basement apartment, and we moved into it as my parents continued work on the main and second floors.

My dad was working full time, was the president of a professional organization, and served on the high council. This schedule limited his building time to Saturdays and available evenings. A Mr. Carsey laid the bricks, but my parents did everything else, with some help from my grandfather. As time and money permitted, work progressed on the house.

By the time my sister was born, the main floor was completed. In fact, Dad painted the living room while Mom was in the hospital.

Carol S. Middleton developed a strong work ethic from her family while building their home together. She and her husband, Anthony W. Middleton Jr., are the parents of five children. She serves as a Relief Society teacher in her ward.

Work on the second floor continued, and when my youngest brother was born in October 1952 (six years after construction began), the house was completed, and we each had our own bedroom.

I remember Mom saying that it was our responsibility to keep our own rooms clean, which included making beds daily, picking up clothes, and so on. If we didn't want to take care of our rooms, she said, we would have to hire someone to do it for us. I'm sure she never thought that we would take her up on that, but my brothers were real con artists, and my sister and I were very gullible. We were hired for a quarter a week each to make their beds daily, pick up their dirty clothes, and vacuum and dust weekly. They told us how lucky we were to make so much money, and we believed them for quite a while.

Our house was built on what was originally a quiet cul-de-sac. But the end of the street opened up onto a busy street, and apartments were built nearby. When zoning in the neighborhood was changed from residential to commercial, my parents knew that they needed to look for another place to build a home.

By this time it was 1962, and my two older brothers were on missions. When the oldest returned, another family building project was scheduled to begin. This brother had had experience working for a very good homebuilder and had also worked with a sheetrocker, so he was able to provide technical direction for the family effort.

My father's journal details the stage-by-stage process of building another home. He noted, "This was a family project, not only for the boys but for the girls as well." When the electricity was connected, we uncrated the refrigerator and put it in the hall because the kitchen was still under construction. We plugged it in and stocked it with food so we could eat more conveniently while we worked. When the plumbing was hooked up, we moved in. The front porch was complete, but the sidewalks and steps weren't. We came in and out of the house through the garage. One day we heard an unexpected knock on the front door. My mother answered to a door-to-door salesman, who said, "Lady, that sure is a big step." Steps and sidewalks were soon completed.

One Saturday, my mother's sister Elizabeth and her fiancé, Ern, dropped by to see us. We were trying hard to get things looking as nice as possible for an open house in their honor a month later. They found us in the midst of pouring a slab of concrete for the patio. To quote my dad, "Both Carol and Jan, much to Ern's amazement, were busy feeding the concrete mixer." We all pitched in to do whatever needed to be done.

In addition to building three homes, our family also built together a twenty-two-foot boat, a camper, a freezer, a motor home, and an electric car. The following story about my sister Jan illustrates our self-reliance. After Jan graduated from high school, she had the privilege of driving "Big Fellow" to work at the F.A.A. building close to the airport. (We gave most of our cars nicknames.) On this particular day, she walked out to the parking lot with her boss. When she put her key in the ignition, it wouldn't start. Jan's boss came to her rescue and applied his "superior knowledge" in starting a car. He couldn't get it started either, but in fiddling around under the dashboard, he pulled a chain that set the windshield wipers going. (This was the handiwork of my brother Kent to repair the broken wipers.) After the boss's unsuccessful efforts, Jan opened the hood, picked up a hammer that we kept in the car, removed the air filter from the top of the carburetor, and with the hammer gave the carburetor the appropriate whack. She put the air filter back on the carburetor, closed the hood, and, to the amazement of her boss, started the car.

My brothers, sister, and I learned to do things as we worked side by side with our parents. Essentially, we were apprentices; we worked alongside our parents to learn a lesson or skill. Even Jesus, who was spoken of both as a carpenter and a carpenter's son, must have learned those skills while working alongside Joseph, because this was the custom of the time.[2]

In an apprenticeship relationship, we learn not only skills from our parents but we learn their values. President Howard W. Hunter said, "Our Heavenly Father loves us so completely that he has given us a commandment to work. . . . He knows that we will learn more, grow more, achieve more, serve more, and benefit more from a life of industry than from a life of ease."[3]

As with many principles, the value of work may not be fully apparent while we are in the process of learning, but it becomes more apparent in retrospect. Almost sixty years have gone by since my parents' first child was born, certainly a long enough time to see how effective their methods have been over the years. All five of their children have become productive citizens, all are active in the Church, and I am the only one of the five without a Dr. in front of my name.

Perhaps the most striking achievement of our apprentice work with our parents is the closeness we felt as we worked together as children. That closeness has carried over into our adult relationships with each other. We have had bumps in the road of life just like any family, but we continue to enjoy each other's company. All of us know there is total support from the others in any time of need. Even though our parents have both passed away, they instilled in all of us the value of working together and playing together. I am grateful to them.

Notes

1. Virginia Hinckley Pearce, as quoted in Sheri L. Dew, *Go Forward with Faith: The Biography of Gordon B. Hinckley* (Salt Lake City: Deseret Book, 1996), 161.

2. See, for example, James E. Talmage, *Jesus the Christ: A Study of the Messiah and His Mission According to Holy Scriptures Both Ancient and Modern* (Salt Lake City: Deseret Book, 1983), 110.

3. Howard W. Hunter, *The Teachings of Howard W. Hunter*, ed. Clyde J. Williams (Salt Lake City: Bookcraft, 1997), 158.

"AS SISTERS IN ZION, WE'LL ALL WORK TOGETHER"

⚜

Mary Ellen Smoot

Whether we are serving in Primary, Young Women, or Relief Society, we are all Relief Society sisters, and wherever we serve, we can help create an atmosphere in our wards where everyone feels included, everyone feels loved, and everyone feels nourished. As sisters in Zion, we all work together.[1]

In the Young Women organization we say, "We are daughters of our Heavenly Father, who loves us, and we love him."

In Primary we say, "I am a child of God. I know my Heavenly Father loves me, and I love him."

In Relief Society we say, "We are beloved spirit daughters of God, and our lives have meaning, purpose, and direction."

We invite you to study the purposes of the women's organizations of the Church and gain an understanding of the power they have to reach every individual. No matter how large the Church becomes, it is also no larger than our own ward boundaries. We can better feed our Father's sheep, and more effectively, if we are united. We can bring new members into the fold as we work together. Unitedly we are striving to assist families to seek Christ and his teachings.

May I share some ideas with you about how to help families accomplish the great task of reaching every child, young woman, and adult? Let me assure you that the Lord has established a pattern for this—and

Mary Ellen Wood Smoot has served as Relief Society General President since April 1997. She loves family history and has written histories of parents, grandparents, and their local community. She served with her husband, Stanley M. Smoot, when he was called as a mission president in Ohio, and they later served together as directors of Church Hosting. They are the parents of seven children and the grandparents of forty-seven.

for all things. How can we accomplish this great task? In the Doctrine and Covenants 52:14 we read, "And again, I will give unto you a pattern in *all things*, that ye may not be deceived" (emphasis added).

Our prophet, President Gordon B. Hinckley, has taught that the pattern for bringing all to Christ is in a Christ-centered home and that we can save our nation by saving our homes. "Society's problems arise, almost without exception, out of the homes of the people. If there is to be a reformation, if there is to be a change, if there is to be a return to old and sacred values, it must begin in the home."[2] To live according to "old and sacred values," we must strengthen our homes. We must reform our homes to reflect these values. Every good thing begins at home.

The auxiliary organizations are set up to assist Church members—not the other way around. It is the responsibility of parents to teach gospel truths in their homes. Imagine what would happen if everything we planned as auxiliary leaders in wards and stakes were evaluated as to how the activity would affect the family and whether it would bring families to Christ?

A few months ago, I was staying with my grandchildren one night while their parents were out of town. A book on their shelf, titled *Our Home* and written in 1899, caught my eye. I was intrigued by some of the chapter headings: "Influences of Home," "Home Training," "Joys of Home," "Books for the Home," "Music for the Home," "Self Culture," "Individual Rules of Conduct," "Contentment at Home," "Dignity at Home," and many more. In those days, it seemed, family members were more devoted to creating happy, productive homes. Family members had to work together daily to accomplish all that was needed for the health and benefit of the family.

One passage from the book struck me as particularly wise counsel: "The distinctive characteristics of the home life are manifested most strongly when the labors of the day are ended and the family gather round the fireside for the evening. One hour of evening home life is worth a month of the ordinary daily experience. It matters little where our days are spent if we spend our evenings at home."[3]

You may say, "You can sure tell that book was written in the nineteenth century. Who gets a chance to have evenings with family gathering around the fireplace in the twenty-first century? It's almost impossible even to have family prayer and eat dinner together." It does require effort, but I want to testify to you that whatever it takes to spend time as a family is worth it. Develop your knowledge and talents together. Return to sacred values. Strengthen the home!

I know one sister with a large family who gathers her five smallest children right after school and nurses the baby as her other children sit on their chairs at the kitchen counter doing their homework. Her way of doing things may not be your way, but that's the beauty of following a righteous pattern. Each of us brings our own cloth, woven with our strengths and talents, but we don't sew just any pattern. We follow the pattern the Lord has set for creating eternal families. Where do we find the Lord's pattern? In the scriptures and in the prophetic utterances of his prophets and servants. The pattern for raising a righteous family can be found in the scriptures, "for in them are *all* things written" (D&C 18:4; emphasis added). Not just *some* or *many*, but *all* things. This is a promise we can each count on. As we search the scriptures, we will find the answers and direction we need concerning our own families.

When you sew or crochet or knit, you need a pattern to guide you, or the finished product will not turn out as you had planned. In the same way, when we follow the Lord's pattern, our lives turn out as planned and we receive promised blessings. I would like to highlight three essential pieces of the Lord's pattern.

One piece of the Lord's pattern is personal and family prayer. We simply cannot do without it. It's like the bodice of a dress, the piece that holds so many of the other pieces in place. Only with prayer can we achieve our potential and become all that our Heavenly Father would have us become. No matter how hectic the day begins or ends, don't forget to pray: "Cry unto [the Lord] in your houses, yea, over all your household, both morning, mid-day, and evening" (Alma 34:21).

Sarah Bitner insisted upon regular family prayer every morning and

evening. She would ask the Lord to send guardian angels to watch over
the children during the day and bring them home safely. Young Ada
Bitner, influenced by her mother's prayers and her father's love of learning, traveled with her sisters Sarah and Ella to Chicago to learn the
Gregg Shorthand Method. Upon her return to Salt Lake, she began a
teaching career at the LDS Business College. Girls in a commercial
school were, according to one newspaper article, as scarce as typewrit-
ers, but Ada was teaching typing, shorthand, and English at the age of
nineteen.

After eight years of teaching, Ada left her professional life and
married Bryant Hinckley, a widower and father of eight children.[4]
Prayer as well as love was certain to have been a part of her decision.
Ada had been taught where to go for guidance and help. Through faith
and prayers she developed the strength and courage to face what was
certainly not an easy life. She was blessed with five additional children
of her own, the first being our beloved prophet, President Gordon B.
Hinckley.

Make daily personal and family prayer a practice in your life. It will
have a tremendous impact on every person in your family. In structur-
ing your home life, pray to discover your own particular talents and to
find ways to use them.

A second piece of the Lord's pattern for happiness is daily scripture
study. In the scriptures you will find strength and wisdom. In the scriptures you will come to know the Savior and feel his peace.

Let me introduce you to some other sisters in Zion: the sisters who
were in charge of selecting a theme for the 2001 women's conference.
This committee of twenty-one competent and devoted women were
asked to suggest a scripture. Each of them studied and prayed, and then
they worked together to reach a consensus. Only when all twenty-one
felt good about the scripture that was chosen was it submitted for
approval. This process is relevant to us because it is a pattern for our
own problem solving. If we will turn to the scriptures for knowledge
and guidance, we will be blessed. If we "teach them diligently unto
[our] children [and all within our responsibility,]" as the Lord has

admonished, they will be blessed (Deuteronomy 6:7). In the scriptures are the answers we seek.

A final important piece of the Lord's pattern is service. "O ye that embark in the service of God, see that ye serve him with all your heart, might, mind and strength" (D&C 4:2). Each of you is already in his service as you love his children, young and old, and look after their needs.

Allow me to introduce you to one more sister. Jessica McGovern grew up in Minnesota. As a young child, she remembers watching the news and grieving over the tremendous devastation she saw caused by the frequent tornadoes in that state. Sometimes she would lie in bed awake, wondering who was going to help those people and what she could do. She dreamed of a building. In the building were forklifts, trucks, and a vast array of other resources.

As an adult, when Sister McGovern found the gospel, she also found many opportunities to serve, but she never found the kind of organization she had dreamed of as a child. Not long ago she moved to Utah and was called to assist with a service project for the women's conference. In April 1999, she walked into the Humanitarian Service Center and the sight almost took her breath away. There before her very eyes was the building of her childhood dreams. She felt so blessed to be participating at last in projects that would assist and bless others' lives in the way she had been shown in her childhood dream.

Sister McGovern, the sisters of the women's conference committee, Sister Ada Hinckley, and so many more sisters are valiant servants who have chosen to follow the Lord's pattern and find great joy in it. Each of you has a story to tell as well. Each of you is a sister in Zion who could be highlighted in this way. Your faith, hope, and charity make you remarkable and are what qualify you for the work.

My heartfelt prayer is that we will all work together to do the Lord's will and accomplish his purposes in these latter days. The power is in us; the tasks lie before us. May we earnestly pray, diligently study, and lovingly serve so that our families, homes, and indeed the whole world will be blessed and strengthened by God's pattern.

Notes

1. "As Sisters in Zion," *Hymns of The Church of Jesus Christ of Latter-day Saints* (Salt Lake City: The Church of Jesus Christ of Latter-day Saints, 1985), no. 309.

2. Gordon B. Hinckley, *Standing for Something* (New York: Random House, 2000), 165.

3. Charles E. Sargent, *Our Home: or, Influences Emanating from the Hearth-stone* (Springfield, Mass.: King-Richardson, 1899), 173.

4. Bryant's first wife's parents raised the two youngest children.

LEARNING FROM PRIESTHOOD LEADERS

Coleen K. Menlove

A few weeks ago my three-year-old grandson, Jacob, came running into the kitchen and called out to his mother, "What are you doing?" She replied, "I am feeding little Emily. What are you doing?" Jacob answered, "I'm keeping the commandments." Children have such great potential for knowing what's important.

Recently I visited a Primary where the Primary president asked, "Who is our prophet today?" The children responded without waiting to be called upon: "President Gordon B. Hinckley." The leader then asked, "What does President Hinckley do?" The children were not as quick to respond to this question, so she answered by saying, "He conducts the business of the Church." I thought, *Yes, and so much more.* Feelings of respect and honor for our prophet and the office he holds filled me. I wanted to share my testimony of the blessings of a living prophet of God on earth today. I wanted the children to know that the hymn they sing in Primary, "We Listen to a Prophet's Voice," declares the truth.

> *We listen to a prophet's voice and hear the Savior too.*
> *With love he bids us do the work the Lord would have us do.*
> *The Savior calls his chosen seer to preach the word of God.*
> *That men might learn to find the path marked by the iron rod.*[1]

Coleen K. Menlove has served as Primary General President since October 1999. She received a bachelor's degree from the University of Utah and a master's degree from Brigham Young University. She has served on Church writing committees and the Young Women General Board. She and her husband, Dean W. Menlove, are the parents of seven children and grandparents of eight.

The holy priesthood of God has the keys that offer saving ordinances of the gospel of Jesus Christ. Righteous priesthood leaders have the authority and power to govern and bless the Lord's people. "As sisters in Zion" we can be part of the mighty work of God as we assist and work with priesthood leaders. A three-step pattern of faith will help us learn from our priesthood leaders. The pattern is: sustain, listen, and respond.

Our priesthood leaders have received the power of God for the purpose of blessing our lives. Sustaining them is not a mere formality but the way we acknowledge God's love and his desire to bless us. When Sister Smoot and I visited San Salvador in February of this year, the people had experienced three major earthquakes. We visited a family who was living in the backyard area of their property. The walls of their home had fallen down around their feet just four days before. The father had used the tin from the original roof to make a covered area for cooking and sleeping. He told us how he had managed to get his family, including his ten-year-old daughter who is paralyzed, to safety. The Church had delivered bricks and cement to rebuild their home. Nevertheless, on this Saturday, this father, as the bishop of the ward, was completing the forms for sustaining the officers of the Church in ward conference the following day. In the midst of a disaster, he was preparing to offer his ward members the opportunity to raise their hands to sustain the general and local officers of the Church. The act of sustaining those who are called can in itself bless us.

Each year eleven million members throughout the world participate in the act of sustaining. Each has an opportunity to commit to the words of the Savior, "whether by mine own voice or by the voice of my servants, it is the same" (D&C 1:38).

It requires faith to surrender our will and follow the direction of those in authority. Submitting or surrendering is not something mortals do well. But we are not talking about surrendering to human beings nor to another person's will. We are talking about surrendering to God's will and his authority upon this earth.

President James E. Faust counsels: "Some women may feel it subverts their agency to be directed by the power of the priesthood. This feeling comes from misunderstanding. There should be no compulsion, duress, or unrighteous dominion involved in priesthood authority."[2]

Men are called, ordained, and set apart to administer the saving ordinances of the gospel of Jesus Christ. This is more than the service of organizing the work of the kingdom, this is doing the work of the Savior, bringing individuals and families unto Christ. Elder Dallin H. Oaks explains, "The Lord's servants must do the Lord's work in the Lord's way or their efforts will come to naught."[3]

The Lord's way is for men and women to be directed by priesthood authority and for both to receive inspiration from the same source— the Lord. This means we are to follow the true order of heaven for leadership in the Church. It is our privilege and right to know the mind and will of God, but that information may come through someone else. Yes, we are entitled to direct personal revelation for ourselves, but this does not preempt priesthood inspiration in administering the Lord's work. When we sustain our local priesthood leaders with the same conviction and joy that we sustain the prophet—with heart and soul—we are blessed.

The second step in the pattern of faith is to listen with understanding. Elder M. Russell Ballard counsels: "I cannot stress enough the importance of listening to and following the prophet and the apostles. . . . Think of it! Think about the value of having a source of information you can always count on, that will always have your eternal interests at heart, and that will always provide inspired truth. That's a phenomenal gift and guide."[4] The Savior counsels, "He that hath ears to hear, let him hear" (Matthew 11:15). Faith can direct ears and hearts to hear beyond the words. We must listen with a desire to understand the perspective of priesthood leaders. When we listen more and talk less, we learn more. In 1 Timothy we are counseled to "learn in silence" (2:11). Why? Because listening allows the Spirit to enlarge and expand learning beyond our own understanding. We can take the next step from sustaining to knowing the truth of the teachings of our priesthood leaders. That places us truly on the same team. President Gordon B.

Hinckley admonishes: "In this world, almost without exception, we must work together as teams. It is so obvious to all of us that those on the football field or on the basketball court must work together with loyalty one to another if they are to win. It is so in life. We work as teams, and there must be loyalty among us."[5]

I have personally found it helpful to record not only the directions I receive from priesthood leaders, but also the impressions I feel from the Spirit. A well-worn file folder contains priesthood teachings and my impressions. I review this folder to remind myself of principles that will help me with various challenges I face in my Church calling and in my family.

The third step in the pattern of faith is to respond promptly. This year in a January meeting for the general auxiliaries, our priesthood adviser encouraged us to follow President Hinckley's example and reach out to lift others. I felt a desire in my heart to follow that counsel and be more encouraging and more appreciative. After the meeting I hurried over to the Joseph Smith Memorial Building to pick up some supplies. I saw a mother and grandmother there with three children. I generally greet children when I see them, but I was in a hurry this time.

Then the words of my priesthood adviser rushed back to my mind. I stopped and spoke to the children. The father and grandfather joined the group. I learned they were in Salt Lake for a family member's temple wedding. As I lingered, I told this family how I appreciated their goodness. Standing in their midst, I felt the Spirit bless me, and our tears flowed. Teachings of a priesthood leader and promptings from the Spirit can be simple, yet can bless our lives in important ways.

President Hinckley has said: "I feel to invite women everywhere to rise to the great potential within you. I do not ask that you reach beyond your capacity. I hope you will not nag yourselves with thoughts of failure. I hope you will not try to set goals far beyond your capacity to achieve. I hope you will simply do what you can do in the best way you know. If you do so, you will witness miracles come to pass."[6]

Last fall my Relief Society visiting teacher gave me a small Grateful Heart book with blank pages and invited me to record my blessings daily. In the blessings I have recorded over the past six months, many pertain to the counsel and blessings I have received from priesthood leaders.

I love joining Primary children singing this truth: "We listen to a prophet's voice and hear the Savior too. With love he bids us do the work the Lord would have us do."[7] Our ears can be attuned to the words of prophets and other priesthood leaders as if they are from the Lord himself. We are blessed as sisters in Zion to join with priesthood leaders bringing families unto Christ. Let us respond to a prophet's plea. President Gordon B. Hinckley has said: "Stand on your feet and with a song in your heart move forward, living the gospel, loving the Lord, and building the kingdom. Together we shall stay the course and keep the faith, the Almighty being our strength."[8]

Notes

1. "We Listen to a Prophet's Voice," *Hymns of The Church of Jesus Christ of Latter-day Saints* (Salt Lake City: The Church of Jesus Christ of Latter-day Saints, 1985), no. 22.
2. James E. Faust, "A Message to Our Granddaughters," 12 February 1985, *Devotional and Fireside Speeches, 1984–85* (Provo, Utah: Brigham Young University Press, 1985), 77–82.
3. Dallin H. Oaks, *The Lord's Way* (Salt Lake City: Deseret Book, 1991), 5.
4. M. Russell Ballard, "Here Am I, Send Me," devotional address, Brigham Young University, 13 March 2001 (http://speeches.byu.edu/devo/2000-01/BallardW01.html).
5. Gordon B. Hinckley, "Stand up for Truth," *Speeches (Brigham Young University) 1996–97* (Provo, Utah: Brigham Young University Press, 1997), 17 September 1996, 21–26; see also *Teachings of Gordon B. Hinckley* (Salt Lake City: Deseret Book, 1997), 320.
6. Gordon B. Hinckley, *Teachings of Gordon B. Hinckley* (Salt Lake City: Deseret Book, 1997), 696.
7. *Hymns*, no. 22.
8. Gordon B. Hinckley, "Stay the Course—Keep the Faith," *Ensign*, November 1995, 72.

COUNCILS: THE PATTERN
OF HEAVEN AND EARTH

Margaret D. Nadauld

One of the most effective ways that "sisters in Zion [can] all work together"[1] to strengthen families is in councils. Councils are the pattern of heaven and earth. Scriptures teach about the Council in Heaven, and we know of the Council of the Twelve Apostles. Many of us participate in councils that affect us and our families more personally. I would like to focus on informal councils as well as those that are more structured.

Informal councils, or "Kitchen Councils" as I like to call them, involve parents and children. To illustrate, let me share an experience I had while I was traveling on an assignment in another country. After a long, busy day of training assignments, we returned to the home of the family we were staying with and were greeted by two teenage daughters. I was so impressed that as the mother went to the kitchen to prepare dinner, her daughters joined her. Side by side in the kitchen they peeled and chopped vegetables for the soup. As they worked, they talked about what had happened at school that day, who had called on the phone, and what had happened in the mother's day. They also coordinated activities they were involved in. They were counseling together!

No sooner was the soup on the stove than the daughters began to set the table, without any instruction from the mother. They did a beautiful job. It was obvious that this happened often. The twelve-year-old

---

Margaret D. Nadauld serves as the Young Women General President and is a member of the board of trustees of Brigham Young University. She has taught high school English and served as a member of the Relief Society General Board. She and her husband, Stephen D. Nadauld, a former member of the Second Quorum of the Seventy, are the parents of seven and grandparents of five.

240

folded the napkins into fancy shapes. Flowers were set in the center of the lovely table. Shortly the doorbell rang and in came the seventeen-year-old daughter's nonmember friend who had come for dinner and then to join us for the fireside later in the evening. As we sat around the table for a delightful dinner hour, the father, the mother, the daughters, and visitors, chatted about important things and simple things; but we developed bonds of understanding and friendship in that sweet and simple kitchen council.

It was so much easier for the girls to listen to what their mother had to teach them as they worked casually side by side, hands busy, than if the mother and father had sat the children down in a formal setting and said, "Now we want to teach you about what we've learned in our meetings today. Please pay attention to us." Of course, formal teaching has a place in our families. But there is also power in informal teaching.

A study conducted by the Church indicates that "gospel learning in LDS families is more like a conversation than a meeting."[2] A nationwide study shows that the majority of Americans eat dinner together five nights a week. Nine out of ten respondents said they consider shared meals important, and they all said they converse, catching up on the day's activities, planning the next day's schedules, and discussing current events.[3]

Something I had taken for granted seemed meaningful to my husband when he wrote, "Our family spends time in Manti, often in the kitchen of the wonderful, old, restored family home. Margaret's mother gathers the family around her, her daughters and daughters-in-law, and now the granddaughters and the wives of the married grandsons. These gifted, insightful women counsel with one another and talk about the truly important issues of life. We see the effects of those informal kitchen councils almost every day."[4] In this setting, we really did discuss important things—gospel principles and politics, fashions and family home evenings, menus and motivating children.

In today's world, the many women who do not live close to extended family can enjoy the benefits of wonderful informal councils with church "family." When we lived two thousand miles from my mother, it was at Relief Society Homemaking meetings that I learned from my dear "sisters" the details of pregnancy and delivery while anticipating the birth of our first child. The sisters in our ward became "mother" to me with valuable counsel at this very important time.

We have many other opportunities in our church family to counsel together, including informal visiting or counseling with the Relief Society, Primary, and Young Women presidencies on matters of mutual concern. One Relief Society presidency became aware of the personal needs of the Young Women presidency in their ward. The Young Women president was expecting a baby that week, her counselor had sick children and a husband who traveled, and the road show was coming up. Can you relate?

As this sensitive presidency counseled together, it became clear to them that one of the greatest acts of service and relief they could give would be to their sisters in the Young Women presidency. They got busy, as only Relief Society sisters can, and took the load of the road show from the shoulders of the Young Women presidency. In addition, they came in with meals and household help, much to the relief of the Young Women presidency. What a wonderful example of sisters in Zion working and counseling together on an informal basis to bless lives.

Now let's talk about sisters following the formal pattern of councils as they work together in ward and stake council settings. Elder M. Russell Ballard reminds us in his classic book, *Counseling with Our Councils*: "Because women possess the power of faith, of purity, and of charity, they have much to contribute in councils." He writes, "It is a short-sighted priesthood leader who does not see the value of calling upon the sisters to share the understanding and inspiration they possess."[5] Elder Ballard's words are instructive for not only priesthood leaders, but for sister leaders in the Church.

Those who attend ward or stake councils have an obligation to participate in at least two ways. First, we should represent our organization. The benefits are great as we use the insight and resources of the ward council as a problem-solving body. In ward council, a Young Women leader can share the concerns of parents of a less-active fourteen-year-old girl and ask the ward council for help. The Relief Society might suggest mobilizing the visiting teachers to show an interest in this young girl and learn her needs from her mother. The elders quorum could send a young man of Aaronic Priesthood age with the older home teacher to befriend and invite the girl to Mutual activities. The Primary president could invite this artistically talented young woman to help the children with an art project on an activity day, helping her feel needed. These suggestions would be in addition to what the Young Women were already doing through their organization.

Sister leaders in ward or stake councils, besides representing their organizations, should also represent their personal point of view, which certainly includes being a defender and protector of the family. When activities are discussed, a woman can voice her perspective on how an activity will affect the family. Can it be planned in ways that will bless families? Can the timing of the activity be organized to strengthen families? The First Presidency teaches that "as we strengthen families, we will strengthen the entire Church."[6]

In November 1999 I attended the World Congress of Families held in Geneva, Switzerland, where representatives from many nations met to discuss how to strengthen families. A representative from one country explained that where he comes from, before a law can be implemented, the government is required to conduct a "family impact study." I compared this to the United States where we routinely conduct "environmental impact studies." We are concerned about how what we do will impact the environment. Among other things, we are interested in protecting endangered species.

I very much like the idea of a family impact study to determine what we can do to protect and nurture an endangered species—the family. In Church councils women can be advocates for the "family impact study."

As we work with each other and with priesthood leaders may we be blessed with a spirit of cooperation. In formal and informal council settings may we understand that we are all on the same team striving to build testimonies, build faith, and bring Heavenly Father's children to Christ.

Notes

1. "As Sisters in Zion," *Hymns of The Church of Jesus Christ of Latter-day Saints* (Salt Lake City: The Church of Jesus Christ of Latter-day Saints, 1985), no. 309.
2. Study performed by the Church Research and Information Department on Religious Activities in the Home (copy filed in the general Young Women offices).
3. National Pork Producers Council, "The Kitchen Report," survey for National Eat Dinner Together Week promotion, 1996.
4. Stephen D. Nadauld, in *The Arms of His Love: Talks from the 1999 Women's Conference Sponsored by Brigham Young University and the Relief Society* (Salt Lake City: Bookcraft, 2000), 136.
5. M. Russell Ballard, *Counseling with Our Councils* (Salt Lake City: Deseret Book, 1997), 53.
6. "Letter from the First Presidency" (dated 11 February 1999), *Liahona*, December 1999, 1; see also "News of the Church: Keeping Children Close to the Church," *Ensign*, June 1999, 80.

How Do I Teach This?

Virginia H. Pearce and
Tricia Henriksen Stoker

For a teacher, there are two parts to a lesson: What am I going to teach? and How will I teach it? We'd like to consider those elements in relation to the Relief Society and Melchizedek priesthood curriculum, *Teachings of Presidents of the Church*.

THE CURRICULUM—WHAT TO TEACH

Tricia: For the past six months I have had the humbling challenge and blessing of serving on a *Teachings of Presidents of the Church* writing committee. I now more fully appreciate and understand the value of the new curriculum. Some family and ward members have asked me, "Why is it important to study the teachings of past presidents of the Church?" "Why are the new manuals a collection of quotes instead of stories from the presidents' lives? I much prefer the stories." Elder Jeffrey R. Holland has commented: "Our prophet [Gordon B. Hinckley] is calling for more faith through hearing the word of God."[1] *Hearing the word of God.* Remember that the Lord said, referring to the Prophet Joseph: "For his word ye shall receive, as if from my own mouth" (D&C 21:5). The Lord also said, referring to those who are

Virginia H. Pearce received a master's degree in social work from the University of Utah. She and her husband, Dr. James R. Pearce, are the parents of six and the grandparents of five. A former first counselor in the Young Women General Presidency, she serves as the Relief Society president in her stake.

Tricia Henriksen Stoker received a bachelor's degree in home economics from the University of Utah. She is currently on a Church writing committee. She is a PTA president and has been involved in community and university alumni boards. She and her husband, Stephen G. Stoker, are the parents of seven children and the grandparents of nine.

teaching the gospel: "Whatsoever they shall speak when moved upon by the Holy Ghost shall be scripture, shall be the will of the Lord, shall be the mind of the Lord, shall be the word of the Lord, shall be the voice of the Lord, and the power of God unto salvation" (D&C 68:4). Why do we use quotes from the prophets? Because their words are the same as hearing the word of God. This study of teachings, using the prophets' own words as text, becomes an exercise in learning the words of the Lord through his servants.

Each manual has two purposes. The first purpose is not what you might suppose: these books are first to be personal study guides and family resources. They have been translated into many languages and are being distributed throughout the Church worldwide. The manuals are intended to provide each Church member with a personal reference library on gospel doctrine for their own homes. The second purpose is to be a manual for study in the Relief Society and priesthood quorums.

Few Church members have the easy access to church books that members on the Wasatch Front do. My parents were called on a mission some years ago to the warm, green islands of Fiji. When they arrived in Labasa, their small branch had no ward library, no pictures, no resources, and the members led very humble lives. Out of the branch of nearly a hundred, only three families had phones, only two owned vehicles. Even if they had extra money, there would be no place to purchase church materials. The Church manuals the instructors had been given were all they had. Some members could not even afford their own set of scriptures. Imagine what is happening worldwide in branches like the Labasa Branch. Now each adult member will have his or her own set of books to take home, a personal gospel doctrine library. Eventually they will have gospel discourses from all the prophets of the Church. Can you envision the opportunity for learning worldwide these manuals afford?

Elder Holland, in giving instruction to the writing committees, emphasized that in preparing these manuals we should include more material in each chapter than can be taught in the thirty minute lessons. Haven't you heard teachers say, "Gosh, I can't get through all of this stuff"? Well, we're not supposed to. We're supposed to pick and choose what pertains to the people that we are teaching. It's challenging for those who teach to have more material than they can cover, but what an opportunity for those in our worldwide church who want to learn on their own.

The Technique—How to Teach

Virginia: As a Relief Society instructor, I read the chapter in *Teachings of Presidents,* and re-read it, perhaps many times, and then ask myself, "*How* am I going to deliver this curriculum message?" *Teaching: No Greater Call,* the Church manual for gospel teachers, offers a wealth of ideas, strategies, and methods to help teachers figure out the best way to get Joseph F. Smith, or the Doctrine and Covenants, or whatever we are teaching into the lives, the minds, the hearts, and the behavior of class members. At least one overriding principle sets this new manual apart from every other previous Church teaching manual—it is that learning the gospel is the individual member's responsibility. Of course, that principle has always been true, but perhaps it has never been so clearly articulated before. Learning the gospel is our individual responsibility. That message underlies every single suggestion or example in *Teaching: No Greater Call.* Where does that principle leave the teacher? As a teacher, what is my role if I am before a class of learners? If they are supposed to do the learning, what am I supposed to be doing?

Here is the answer from *Teaching: No Greater Call:* "What is the role of teachers? It is to help individuals take responsibility for learning the gospel—to awaken in them the desire to study, understand, and live the gospel and to show them how to do so."[2] It should make a difference in the way we teach if we say, "My responsibility is to show other people how to learn. My responsibility isn't to show them what *I* know. It is to show them how to go about their *own* learning, to give them some practice, and to help them feel a desire to learn so that they will go home knowing how better to learn because they were in this class." *Teaching: No Greater Call* details hundreds of ways to awaken learners' desires and to help build their learning skills. Let me share a few with you.

The first, and by far the largest, section in the book is about teaching by the Spirit. A teacher can bring about teaching by the Spirit in many different ways, but prayer is the beginning, along with simply recognizing who really teaches in a class. Women's conference is a great experience for most of us because we come *expecting* to be touched by the Spirit. Similarly, we turn on general conference *expecting* to be taught by the Spirit. Sometimes, you and I go to church, but we don't expect to be taught by the Spirit. We might expect a teacher to do something "pizzazzee" with the material, but that's all. The truth is that we can be taught by the Spirit in our Sunday School classes as surely as we can by an Apostle speaking at women's conference. The Spirit is the same. The speaker or teacher is a vehicle, but the Spirit is the same whether in a Relief Society room or a Sunday School room, or the Conference Center. That Spirit can teach us during Sharing Time just as well as he can in general conference. All we have to do is be present and open. We can get up Sunday morning and say, "I can't wait to find out what the Lord wants me to learn today in Church. It's been a tough week (or a great week), but I know he's got something for me there." It might be in the song, it might be in choir practice, it might be in a friend's words in the hall. I have tried this. It works. It is the miracle of really participating in church meetings.

Elder Gene R. Cook taught, "Ultimately, all true gospel teaching is done by the Holy Ghost. He is the teacher, not us. We must be careful not to get in the way."[3] As teachers, we are instruments; we are not the teachers. The Lord is the one who knows the needs of those being taught. That's actually very comforting. Called to teach the gospel, we could be terrified and feel inadequate—how can we possibly know what every class member needs to know each Sunday? But knowing that the Lord is the one who knows their needs, the one who can impress someone's heart and cause them to change, reassures us.

As teachers, our next challenge is to try to help the class members discover what we discovered when we read the material. I am confident that 90 percent of Church members don't read their lesson manuals ahead. We'd all like them to, but it probably won't happen soon. So how can we give the class members a vital experience with the words themselves, not just tell them about our experience with the material? The "Use Effective Methods" section instructs, "Choose methods that actively engage the learners."[4]

As teachers, we want the class members to do something besides listen. Even though listening is appropriate some of the time, the best methods would "actively engage" them. How about calling upon class members to read the words aloud? We've all done that—passed out papers and had individuals read a quote. Can I go on record as saying that reading aloud is one of the least effective teaching methods there ever was? It doesn't work very well. The person who is reading is so nervous she can't think about what she is reading, and the others just tune right out. The manual suggests instead that we ask questions that require learners to find answers in the scriptures and the teachings of Latter-day Saint prophets. Our approach can be: "What are some questions that will help the sisters get into the written material to find the answers?"

The "Methods" section says that when teaching adults we should use at least three teaching methods in every lesson.[5] I love those little hints, don't you? Three methods for adults; between five and seven for children. You could put a thought question on the chalkboard for them to be thinking about as they come in the class. Choose questions that invite discussion, not one-word answers. Use a worksheet. Ask individuals to share an experience. Prepare a visual to help class members understand a sequence in behaviors. Try a class choral reading. It is not illegal to do something different. Choral readings are fun; they wake people up. You can do that in Gospel Doctrine, not just in Primary Sharing Time.

When considering a method, ask: "Will this method help learners better understand the principle I'm teaching?" Not, "Oh, this story will be fun to read," or "This is a great quote," but "What principle in the material does this story or quote illuminate?" Remember the centrality of the text.

The "Understanding and Teaching Adults" section points out that adults *want* to talk about how gospel principles apply to their lives.[6] If I come to the end of a lesson without inviting someone to make an application, the principle I am teaching is far less likely to make a difference in anyone's life. Another approach would be to ask class members to write down one insight, one understanding, one prompting, one affirmation, just a word or two, that might make a difference to them. When individuals do that at the end of a class, they are more likely to understand what it was that the Spirit wanted them to hear. Good conclusions, the manual says, help learners apply gospel principles in their lives. They "are uplifting, motivating, and positive" and always allow time for testimony.[7] I believe the gospel is true with all my heart. I love teaching and I love learning. I know that each of you do too.

LEARNING FOR OURSELVES

Tricia: I attended a temple marriage ceremony some years ago performed by Elder Neal A. Maxwell. His advice to the bride and groom impressed me then and has since grown to become a compelling foundation in my life. The essence of his advice was, "Don't let this be a marriage where the husband is the theologian and the wife is the Christian." In my heart I knew I was hearing a truth that was not simply about marriages. I think sometimes we fail to balance our lives with both learning and Christian service. Both are essential to our spiritual growth.

An *Ensign* article introducing the new Melchizedek Priesthood and Relief Society manuals instructed: "We are not simply to sit in class while teachers pour gospel doctrines into us until we are full of them; we are to actively gather in these eternal truths and pray for the Spirit to be with us."[8] I admit that I'd been one who had been going to church, sitting down, and waiting for the teacher or speaker to inspire me, to throw something out at me that would make a difference in my life. I was missing my own responsibility to be open to the learning and

even to participate in the teaching. Henry Eyring, a renowned professor of physics at the University of Utah, taught me how to do that. In
his book, *Reflections of a Scientist*, he wrote: "Sometimes, because of
high council assignments and my own ward schedule, I attend more
than one [sacrament meeting] on a Sunday. I always get something useful out of them. Sometimes the talks being given from the pulpit are
rather weak. Then I may have to listen awhile before I can figure out
what the topic is, but once I have that, I start preparing in my mind a
talk on the same subject. 'What would I say if that were my theme?' I
ask myself."[9]

Joseph Smith described in his history how overwhelmed he felt at
the end of the First Vision. At home, his mother noticed him leaning
against the fireplace and asked what was the matter. He replied, "All
is well—I am well enough off. . . . I have learned for myself" (Joseph
Smith–History 1:20). That statement, "I have learned for myself," has
come back to my mind over and over again. "I have learned for myself."
Sometimes we are those who would be taught, and other times we are
those who teach, but for all of us, every time, we can—and must—
learn for ourselves.

Notes

1. Jeffrey R. Holland, "'A Teacher Come from God,'" *Ensign*, May 1998, 25.
2. *Teaching: No Greater Call* (Salt Lake City: The Church of Jesus Christ of
   Latter-day Saints, 1999), 61.
3. Gene R. Cook, *Teaching by the Spirit* (Salt Lake City: Deseret Book,
   2000), 12.
4. *Teaching*, 89.
5. Ibid.
6. Ibid., 123–24.
7. Ibid., 94.
8. "With 'The Tongues of Seven Thunders,'" *Ensign*, January 1998, 53.
9. Henry Eyring, *Reflections of a Scientist* (Salt Lake City: Deseret Book,
   1983), 18.

"That God May Know Mine Integrity"

Marleen S. Williams

One of Satan's first lies in the Garden of Eden was to tell Adam and Eve that they could hide from God and thereby avoid the consequences of choices they knew to be contrary to their Father's will. As a psychologist, I have seen what happens when a person fails to live truth as he or she has come to understand it. When we flee from the truth, trying to block it from our awareness, we cannot change and grow. And what begins as a simple sin or error becomes a lifestyle that compromises our basic integrity. Public experience and behavior becomes vastly different from private experience and behavior. Individuals who become trapped in addictions typically fit into this pattern, struggling with the secrets of a double life. This type of failure to face the truth and the desire to hold on to secret sins keeps people trapped in those sins.

The motives for holding onto secrets vary. Some rationalize that an act is "technically" defined as moral if no one knows of it or if they can rally public support for their behavior. Some hide because they fear rejection or loss of love from parents or other loved ones. Some hide because they don't want to deal with the sorrow and guilt of knowing their behavior has hurt themselves and others.

Whatever the reasons, hiding and then having to carry "the secret" keeps people trapped. Satan has always understood the power of secrets. From the beginning he put it into men's hearts to "tell it not"

Marleen S. Williams is an associate clinical professor at Brigham Young University. She has published and presented research on women's mental health and spirituality. She is currently serving as Young Women president in her ward. She and her husband, Dr. Robert F. Williams, who is also a clinical psychologist, have a combined family of nine children and eleven grandchildren.

(Moses 5:29). The chains he binds people with are the fears of their secrets being known. Secrets create shame, and shame and fear block us from the powerful healing love of Christ's atonement. Understanding and believing in the Atonement are what make repentance and growth toward integrity possible.

Life presents us daily with choices that can challenge, exercise, and thus build muscles of integrity. Rearing children is one of life's great opportunities both to learn integrity and to teach it. When children make mistakes, loving, wise parents can provide life's first lessons in the relationship of justice and mercy in the Atonement.

When our children make mistakes and sin, our hearts break because we love them. We are often flooded with feelings: sorrow, guilt, anger, fear, humiliation, and worry. We may find it difficult to understand and manage these emotional responses and may be tempted to excuse wrong behavior, justify the child, or lower standards to protect the child from painful consequences. However, doing so teaches the child to hide from the truth and from God.

On the other hand, if our own feelings of hurt, anger, and humiliation are powerful, we may be tempted to reject or abandon the child at a time when he or she most needs our love. A parent's rejection also teaches the child to hide the truth to avoid shame, fear, and loss of worth. Yet, if parents can find that divine combination that holds fast to correct, eternal, unchanging principles while still showing unconditional love, our children have a greater chance of understanding the relationship between the laws of both justice and mercy. Thus the times when our children make mistakes are our best opportunities to teach the nature of the Atonement. Without careful thinking about how we choose to react, however, we may miss these opportunities.

Our own example is the most powerful way we teach our children. If we are not consistent and clear, we may be sending our children double messages. Consider the following scenarios:

- A father regularly brings home "borrowed" office supplies from his work, then reprimands his son for stealing pencils from school.

- A mother scolds her child for hitting his brother and threatens to spank him if he does it again.
- A harried woman lectures on stress management.

To be examples of integrity, we do not have to be perfect, but rather should be constantly willing to courageously examine ourselves and admit our weaknesses to ourselves and to the Lord. We are then in a position to ask for Christ's help in doing the right thing for the right reason. He has the power to teach us how to turn weaknesses into strengths. If we submit to his will rather than depend solely upon our own willpower, we can access real spiritual power to change. It is not by *pretending to be perfect*, but by submitting to the ongoing process of perfection that we "continue in patience until [we] are perfected" (D&C 67:13). Our children will learn the necessity of submission to this process of perfection through our own example.

The scriptures describe Job as "perfect and upright" (Job 1:1). Job's strength of character, however, did not relieve him of the tests and challenges of mortality. His children all died in a tragic accident; he lost his source of livelihood and suffered painful, unrelenting health problems; and his supposed friends falsely accused him of deserving his afflictions because of sin.

As a therapist, when I read Job's account, I can identify symptoms of a serious clinical depression. Yet in spite of all these painful and difficult experiences, he did not curse God or alter his commitment to remain faithful. He stated, "Til I die I will not remove mine integrity from me" (Job 27:5). The pain of his own mortal challenges enabled him to reach deep into his soul and discover for himself the depth of his integrity.

Job's story, memorialized in scripture, parallels a multitude of faithful lives quietly and privately bearing witness to the power of personal integrity. I would like to share the story of one: her nickname is "Ted." When their youngest child was six years old, Ted's husband died leaving her with eight children to raise alone. Her children struggled to understand why their father had to die. Even working full-time, she made barely enough money for necessities and none for luxuries. On her feet all day at work and then at home caring for her children, she developed ulcerated veins in her legs that caused her constant pain but, like Job, she did not become bitter and curse God. She knew and taught her children that a kind and loving Father sustained and comforted her in trials. Instead of turning away from God, she drew closer to him.

As her children grew, the family faced even greater challenges. Five of her eight children began to show signs of a rare genetic disease that produced blindness. Other serious health problems plagued her and her loved ones. Like Job, she experienced bouts of depression, but she believed in the words of Job, "Though . . . worms destroy this body, yet in my flesh shall I see God" (Job 19:26). She continued to have faith and hope in the Atonement and the Resurrection.

Several years after her husband died, her ward began building a new chapel. Her bishop called her in and asked if she could contribute to the building fund. She told him, "I can barely make ends meet." As she left his office, she impulsively turned and said, "If God would give me a thousand dollars, I promise that I would gladly give it to you." She left his office, sad that her widow's mite was practically nothing. Within a few days, she received a request to run a drainage canal through some pasture land she owned. The earnest money agreed upon was exactly one thousand dollars. A thousand dollars would buy much for herself and her family, but she remembered her promise to her bishop. Her integrity was more important to her than anything she could buy. She gave the bishop the thousand dollars as promised.

When life doesn't give us what we had hoped for, we may be tempted to believe that God has abandoned us, but without agency we could never develop the internal strength and moral integrity to choose righteously. There is no integrity without agency. And there is no exaltation without the development of integrity. Now nearly eighty, Ted's heart is thankful instead of bitter because life's trials have brought her to know and rely upon God.

In the last day, each of us, like Job, will be "weighed in an even balance, that God may know [our] integrity" (Job 31:6). Only the Savior lived with complete integrity. The rest of us achieve it line upon line. That is the great plan of the Atonement. We continue to progress by courageously and lovingly examining ourselves, admitting our weaknesses, asking for God's help, submitting to his will for us, and trusting in his infinite love. It is through this process that we find real peace and hope. It is through this process we develop integrity.

SPIRITUAL HOUSECLEANING

Gretel Swensen

As I thought about the scripture, "Even as Christ forgave you, so also do ye" (Colossians 3:13), I remembered an incident in my life when I hung up the phone after a hurtful conversation and cried to my husband across the room, "I hate them! I never want to see them again." As soon as the words were out, I remember thinking immediately, "I haven't said those words since I was in fifth grade, or at least in high school when my older brother was teasing me." But at that moment, like many of you, I was hurt, I was angry, and my heart was broken.

How can we set aside the burdens of anger and resentment that destroy the heart and canker the soul? How can we houseclean spiritually?

I like the words "spiritual housecleaning." They make me think of spring cleaning, the time of year when I get energized and make all kinds of lists. I list things that need to be cleaned, things that need to be painted, things that need to be repaired. I like lists, and I have a lot of them. But perhaps we need to create another list, one that includes the names of those we don't like or may even hate. Names on this list are there for various reasons. More often they are on the list because of what they've done to us. They have lied about us. They have lied to us. They have stolen from us or cheated us. They have said mean things about us. Said mean things to us. Or they have hurt us in some

---

Gretel Foxley Swensen, a former member of the Primary General Board, served with her husband, Swen R. Swensen, while he presided over the Austria Vienna Mission. She has been a schoolteacher and has twice served as PTA president. She and her husband are the parents of five children and the grandparents of two. She serves in her ward as a Primary president.

other way. The list goes on. Maybe we just don't like them and can't remember why.

Maybe we personally have not been attacked. Maybe someone has done something to one of our children, said something about our husband, even hurt our dog. Maybe we have even been hurt at church.

One Sunday morning while my husband, Swen, was bishop, I was walking down the hall after Young Women and saw a member of the Primary presidency huffing towards me. "Come and get your child right now!" she commanded. "I don't want to deal with him anymore." I was stunned. I remember walking into Swen's empty bishop's office and sitting down. A moment later, my husband walked in and asked what was wrong. I told him that I could see why people leave the Church and never come back. Someone in a position of authority had attacked one of my children. On one occasion, I had a difficult time when a ward member criticized my husband. I had, I suppose, naïve and idealistic expectations that active Church members would never speak ill of their bishops—and especially not of my husband. How do we let go of such hurts? It is not easy, but we must do it before they destroy our hearts and canker our souls.

We need to think of ourselves as Jaredite barges. Each day life tosses and turns us. In spite of this, we need to keep our balance, keep our eyes on the goal. The Jaredites looked toward the promised land; we seek after eternal life. Elder Marion D. Hanks said, "What is our response when we are offended, misunderstood, unfairly or unkindly treated, sinned against, [when we are] falsely accused, passed over, hurt by those we love, our offerings rejected? Do we resent, become bitter, hold a grudge?" He then added, "The nature of our response . . . may well determine the nature and quality of our lives, here and eternally."[1]

Doctrine and Covenants 64:10 says, "I, the Lord, will forgive whom I will forgive, but of you it is required to forgive all men."

We can apply healing balm for cankers of the soul. The expressions, "cankers the soul," "having a burr under the saddle," or a "scab that keeps bleeding," all refer to something that is bothering us. No matter how uncomfortable we may feel, we can't, or rather won't, let it go. We pick at it, and it keeps bleeding. Sometimes the hurt has been festering for a long time, maybe even years. For our spiritual health, we need to deal with the hurt.

Often we don't want to deal with it. Sometimes we don't want to pray. But we need to take a look, an honest look, deep into that uncomfortable place where we all hate to go. We need to look honestly at our feelings and the reasons we cannot forgive. How can we let the hurt go, so we can heal? The following suggestions may help.

1. Fast and pray. Ask for the desire to forgive, then let the Holy Ghost guide you in the process.
2. Consult your patriarchal blessing. It tells of the love your Heavenly Father has for you. Read it and let it guide you in your actions towards those with whom you have hard feelings. Let this blessing be solace to your soul.
3. Go to the temple with your concern. Put your name and others on the prayer roll. Let Heavenly Father and the Savior help. If you are not worthy, become worthy.
4. Study others' examples. I recommend especially reading about Joseph Smith and W. W. Phelps in Jeffrey R. Holland's essay, "A Robe, a Ring, and a Fatted Calf," in the August 1985 *Ensign*.[2]
5. Seek counsel. Maybe it's time to talk to your bishop. Perhaps ask for a blessing.
6. Ready yourself to feel the Holy Spirit. Listen to the words of the Lord. Concentrate on the sacrament prayers. Read the scriptures. Ponder the words of the Prophet.

Develop memory loss. While driving in the car a few months ago, I heard on the radio: "He who buries the hatchet . . . never forgets where he put it." It made me laugh. Forgiveness—true forgiveness—means forgetting. The spirit of revenge, retaliation, and bearing a grudge is entirely foreign to the gospel of Jesus Christ. In Doctrine and Covenants 58:42, the Lord says, "He who has repented of his sins, the same is forgiven, and I, the Lord, remember them no more." If the Lord forgives and forgets, so must we.

Maybe the person who needs to forgive and be forgiven is not yourself. Maybe it's a child, a husband, a teenager, or a married child who keeps picking the scab and won't let it heal. This is where you set the example of forgiving. Create a legacy in your own home through daily acts of a mother's unconditional love. This principle is a key to repentance; not extending forgiveness often prevents us from accepting forgiveness. The influence of parents and grandparents who teach and show forgiveness never ends.

Maybe the offense takes place within the context of the Church. Sometimes even the best Church leaders may be misunderstood or, despite having the finest intentions, may even injure without meaning to. If this has happened to you, go to that leader and talk it out. Don't let pride hold you back. Such feelings unresolved do destroy the heart. They can begin to ruin the ward and your family. Don't make or repeat negative comments about Church members and leaders in front of your children. It only destroys their respect and confidence in all those who lead.

Often the person who has wronged us isn't aware of the problem. President Spencer W. Kimball said, "Generally, the hated one does not even know how bitter is the animosity against her. She may sleep at night and enjoy a reasonable peace, but the one who hates estranges herself . . . , shrivels her heart, dwarfs her soul."[3]

Stop picking at the scab. Let it heal.

Notes

1. Marion D. Hanks, "Forgiveness: The Ultimate of Love," *Ensign*, January 1974, 20.
2. Pages 68–72; also in Jeffrey R. Holland, *However Long and Hard the Road* (Salt Lake City: Deseret Book, 1985), 72–75.
3. Spencer W. Kimball, *The Miracle of Forgiveness* (Salt Lake City: Bookcraft, 1969), 272; masculine pronouns changed to feminine pronouns.

THE SCRIPTURES: LEARNING TO HEAR THE VOICE OF THE LORD

Wendy L. Watson

When our souls are still, we can hear things we otherwise would not. We can hear the voice of the Lord. And when we can hear the voice of the Lord, everything in our life changes. We are able to deal with the weightier matters; we can set priorities because our perspective is eternally clear.

One of the best places to learn to hear the voice of the Lord is the scriptures, which are the word of God. I love the scriptures. My feelings for them, my affection, has grown in ways and to extents I never imagined. I find that I want to spend more and more time with them. I am irresistibly drawn to them.

It started out simply enough. I began noticing that the scriptures responded to my every emotion. If I was worried, they calmed me. If I was happy, they celebrated with me. If I was pensive, they gave me even more space in which to ponder. If I was bewildered about a decision, they showed me the very next step I should take. In a world that is so depersonalized, the scriptures won my heart because they seemed—almost from the very beginning—to know my heart. Even though other names were written on the pages, I knew that the scriptures were written just for me. It's hard to resist that kind of personal attention.

The power of the scriptures to provide love and light and truth and

Wendy L. Watson holds a Ph.D. in family therapy and gerontology from the University of Calgary in Calgary, Alberta, Canada, and also holds degrees in nursing and psychology. She is a professor of marriage and family therapy in the School of Family Life at Brigham Young University and was chair of the BYU–Relief Society Women's Conference in 1999 and 2000.

answers is unsurpassed. Is it any wonder that I am more and more drawn to the love and the support and the direction from the scriptures? If I am doing a therapy session, scriptures come to my mind. If I am talking to a friend, they nudge their way into the conversation. When I travel, whether commuting to work or on vacation, they are my mainstay, my comfort, my security. Once in Hawaii, I left my friends at the hotel so that I could be alone—with my scriptures. I had them and my journal hidden in a bag. And there on a beach, my heart found joy, not in the surf, the sand, or the sunset, but in Paul's teaching me to "lay aside every weight, and the sin which doth so easily beset us." He taught me to "run with patience the race that was set before me" (Hebrews 12:1). That was exactly what I needed to know and to do at that point in my life. It was the first day I had ever really savored Paul's words, although I had read and even studied the New Testament many times before. That day, Paul's wisdom awakened my soul.

I know that I'm not alone in my irrepressible love for the scriptures. Many of you are in the very same situation. Who can blame a woman at the end of a long day who wishes not—as the advertisement says—for Calgon to take her away, but for Corinthians to take her away!

Just what is it that the scriptures do for us that keeps us coming back for more? What draws our hearts and minds out to them? What difference can they make in our lives?

The scriptures can help you understand the Atonement in ways you never thought you could. You experience the temple differently after immersing yourself in the scriptures, and vice versa. You find out that *every* promise President Marion G. Romney made about the Book of Mormon is true when he said: "I feel certain that if, in our homes, parents will read from the Book of Mormon prayerfully and regularly, both by themselves and with their children, the spirit of that great book will come to permeate our homes and all who dwell therein. The spirit of reverence will increase, mutual respect and consideration for each other will grow. The spirit of contention will depart. Parents will counsel their children in greater love and wisdom. Children will be more responsive and submissive to that counsel. Righteousness will increase. Faith, hope, and charity—the pure love of Christ—will abound in our homes and lives, bringing in their wake peace, joy, and happiness."[1] Could you use any of those promises?

As you infuse your life with the words of the Lord, you discover that the scriptures bring the Holy Ghost into your life in a more profound way than you have ever experienced. Conversely, you discover that the increasingly palpable presence of the Spirit in your life opens your eyes to see the scriptures in breathtakingly new ways.

You will long to learn even more from the scriptures when you discover that your patriarchal blessing reads differently after you've read certain scriptures in the Doctrine and Covenants; when the scriptures increase your ability to resist old temptations; when they change the way you pray as you read the prayers of others that have parted the veil; when you discover that you manage your time better in order to have even more of it to spend with the scriptures; when they help you—or more accurately, relentlessly nudge you—to grow into your true self and to give up living beneath yourself!

You long to increasingly intertwine your life with the scriptures when they reveal the adversary's strategies to get you off course (2 Nephi 28:20); when they increase your desire and ability to come out of the world and to come closer to the Savior than you have ever been before; when they provide you with a unique kind of safety and security because they are the iron rod to hold to as you walk through an ever-changing and ever-darkening world.

How can you resist the scriptures when they make you brighter, in every way? When they change the way you experience sacrament meeting, increasing your desire to really worship, rather than just "attend Church," changing the way you sing the hymns, which now become prayers of your heart? When they are incredibly personal and perceptive and persistent in bringing you new ideas and answers about how to live your life and how to handle its sometimes heart-wrenching problems? How can you resist spending more time with the scriptures when they seem to be new every time you read them—and yet like old friends, welcome you home again and again?

How can any of us not prefer the scriptures when they bring us the lives of common men and women, of heroes and heroines, the journals of prophets, and most important, the words of the Lord himself? When they give you the power to change, the power to live, and the power to love like you never have before?

One woman was totally enthralled with the scriptures because of the clear directions they provided her. At a most difficult time in her life, namely, the dissolution of her marriage when her husband abandoned her for a younger woman, she found the daily manna of instructions she so desperately needed right within the scriptures. Every day she took her question *for the day* to the Lord, opened her scriptures, absolutely expecting an answer, and received abundantly. She listened and followed the directions the Lord brought to her daily through the scriptures. Day after day the scriptures told her how the Lord wanted her to deal with her husband, so that her children would not be caught in the fray of the divorce.

This woman needed employment. From her daily seeking in the scriptures, she learned how to present herself at a job interview for a very desirable position within her field of engineering. She got the job. Then she proceeded matter-of-factly to take any work-related problem she could not solve right to the scriptures. (They had helped her get the job, now they could get her through it.) There she consistently found her answers.

As a marriage and family therapist, I find the scriptures are absolutely *the* best how-to books on relationships. A while ago the Spirit helped me discover in the account of the Savior's visit to the Nephites principles for families, such as: "a small voice penetrates positively," "repetition registers truth," "commendations are crucial," "believing and receiving love is beneficial," and "pure touch testifies of love."[2] Recently I have been intensely focused on solutions for marital intimacy problems. Once again the scriptures are filled with answers— when we are seeking and seeing with the Spirit. For example: several verses in Hebrews 13, when studied and prayerfully pondered, constitute a magnificent guide for marital intimacy problems. Listen to just two of the verses: "Be not forgetful to entertain strangers: for thereby some have entertained angels unawares" (Hebrews 13:2). When husbands and wives feel like strangers to each other—talking little and doing less together—that should be their first clue to start "entertaining" each other! In whatever difficult, easy, or neutral situation your marriage is in, ask yourself from time to time, "If my husband were a stranger, how would I handle this situation right now?" Then behave and speak to your spouse as you would if "entertaining" a stranger. You may begin to notice "angelic" aspects of your spouse that you have previously overlooked—the loveable, likeable, redeemable, and even adorable aspects.

Consider another verse: "Let your conversation be without covetousness; and be content with such things as ye have" (Hebrews 13:5). How different would your marriage be if you stopped telling your husband how much you wished things were different? What do you think would happen if you started to notice those things that you would like to *remain the same*—in your spouse and in your marriage. Would your husband experience more love from you if you took this approach? Remember, love is still the greatest invitation for change.

I believe that women who are immersed in the scriptures see, hear, think, and act differently than those who are not. Let me draw a distinction between reading the scriptures and immersing our lives in them. As members of The Church of Jesus Christ of Latter-day Saints, we have been immersed in the waters of baptism. I believe we also need to be immersed continually in the truths of the restored gospel following baptism. If not, we will understand and experience only enough of the gospel to feel guilty and not enough of the eternal truths to feel joy. Joy comes through immersion. A little sprinkling of the scriptures in our lives will never bring us the fulness of joy that accompanies learning, loving, and living the fulness of the restored gospel of Jesus Christ. So what happens when a woman is immersed in the scriptures?

First, a woman whose life is saturated with the words of the Lord is able to hear "whole soul" messages. Because her abilities have been enlarged and purified through the increased influence of the Holy Ghost, she can often hear unspoken sentences lodged in others' hearts. For example, when her child says "Leave me alone," she is able to hear, "*Please don't* leave me alone." When her husband says, "I'm just not celestial material," the Spirit can bless her to hear, "Please show me *how wrong I am to think* I'm just not celestial material." When her sister says, "I'm lonely," she can know that her sister is lonely not for another's company but for the best within herself. When her mother says, "I'm so tired," she is able to hear, "I'm so tired of *not being listened to, of not being taken seriously.*" Hearing the unspoken words, she can know how to respond.

Second, a woman whose life is grounded in scriptural truths can do the otherwise impossible within relationships. When her spouse pulls away, she can reach out again and again, rather than lash out in frustration or punish by withdrawing. When her friend is unforgiving of her, she can forgive the unforgiveness. When her father looks angry, she can see his pain and speak to his hurt rather than fruitlessly wrestling with his display of anger.

And speaking of anger, a third trait that sets a scripture-loving woman apart is that her feelings are positively influenced. The scriptures bring us vivid examples of conflict building and conflict resolution. The interchange between two of my heroes, Captain Moroni and Pahoran, is such an example. Read Alma 59 and 60 and watch how quickly Captain Moroni shifts from requesting Pahoran's help to offering blatant accusations and recriminations. By Alma 60, Moroni is attributing malevolent intent to Pahoran and characterizing him as selfish and neglectful. His accusations abound: "Can you think to sit upon your thrones in a state of thoughtless stupor . . . ?" "Ye have withheld your provisions." Moroni accuses Pahoran of everything from "exceedingly great neglect" to "seeking for power and authority" to being a traitor (vv. 7, 9, 17). Captain Moroni seems to have done three things that build conflict: (1) rush to judgment, (2) accuse others of negative intent, and (3) fail to remember that things are often not the way they appear.

Pahoran's response to Captain Moroni helps us understand how we can avoid retaliating when conflict is increasing. His response teaches us how to seize a potentially destructive moment and actually build the relationship rather than the conflict. Pahoran's turning-point words are found in Alma 61: "In your epistle you have censured me, but it mattereth not; I am not angry, but do rejoice in the greatness of your heart" (v. 9). How did Pahoran manage such a response? Did he read between the lines of the accusatory letter and see the great concern of Moroni? Did he attribute benevolent intent to Moroni's behavior and words and assume that Moroni was up to something good, even in the midst of his censuring? Pahoran seems to look through all of Moroni's overtly negative behavior and sees "the greatness of [Moroni's] heart" (v. 9)— and rejoices!

When a husband falsely accuses his wife of betraying him to his family; when a wife accuses her husband of not helping her enough; when a husband accuses his wife of not caring about him; when a wife tells a husband that until he changes, she doesn't want anything to do with him and in fact wishes him ill—is it still possible for the accused to see the accuser's good heart, even the accuser's great heart? When spouses follow Pahoran's example, it is. Pahoran's kind of response heals relationships and invites the Spirit to be present. Thus, a third trait that distinguishes a scripture-loving woman is that she tries to respond a little more like Pahoran over time. (Please note that, of course, seeing an accuser's great heart is very different from assuming that a chronic abuser is going to change—without something else changing.)

The fourth ability a woman immersed in the scriptures has is to discern the good in people that others overlook. I have been privileged to know several such women. They remind me of the wife of King Lamoni. Do you remember her story? King Lamoni had fallen to the earth as if he were dead. His wife asked Ammon to go and see the king who "has been laid upon his bed for the space of two days and two nights; and some say that he is not dead, but others say that he is dead and that he stinketh [now here's the line I like]; but as for myself, to me he doth not stink" (Alma 19:5).

In my clinical practice, one woman's family and friends strongly urged her to leave her husband during a difficult time in his life. To them, he "stank": he was spiritually dead, and, to their minds, dead weight for his wife. Immersed in the scriptures, she, however, perceived her husband through an eternal lens and responded, basically, "To me he doth not stink." She stayed in the marriage. The purity of her presence helped her husband experience more and more of the presence of the Spirit, and he slowly came to himself and out of his sin-induced coma.

Fifth, women whose lives are immersed in the scriptures can offer what I call a "high-level" apology—some might even say an impossible apology—the kind of apology that allows you to say to one who "hath ought against you": "I want to apologize for the negative feelings I've had about you." Such apologies purify relationships and refine the woman apologizing. Consider the healing power in the following apologies:

A mother tells her daughter, "I'm so sorry that I made your father feel so judged by me and deficient as a man. I'm sorry that my efforts to bring out the best in him only discouraged him and gave you a demeaning message about men."

A wife says to her husband, "I'm sorry I made you feel that approaching me for marital intimacy was wrong. I'm sorry I didn't realize that marital intimacy is sacred and sanctifying. Now I see that the very thing I longed for—that is, more spiritual experiences with you—is possible through uniting physically and spiritually in marital intimacy, which can draw us both closer to the Lord."

Whether you are presently immersed in the scriptures, or are merely paddling around, now and again discovering an occasional life-saver, or whether you feel you are drowning in so many other demands that you can't imagine fitting in to your life one more thing, it really is possible to find a way to increase even by 10 percent—just a tithing's portion—your love of the scriptures. We can do this. Whatever our present relationship with the scriptures, we all need to kick it up a notch. The Lord didn't give us the scriptures as a sleep inducer before going to bed or as something nice to read on a Sunday afternoon, *if* there happens to be some time.

Joy comes as we fill the measure of our creation. And the measure of our creation, our mission here on earth, becomes clearer and clearer as we are tutored by the voice of the Lord as brought to us by the scriptures. A scripture-saturated environment is a Spirit-saturated environment—a literal hot house for your spirit. The more you immerse your life in the scriptures, the more your spirit will thrive.

Sisters, it's not about color coding your scriptures—although that may help. It's about adding another level of vibrancy to your relationship with the Savior.

It's not about memorizing favorite scriptures, although that may help. It's about letting the scriptures help you remember who you are and who you have always been.

It's not about reading someone else's ideas about what certain scriptures mean, although that may help. It is about praying to have the Spirit with you continually as you read so that you can be taught what the Lord wants *you* to understand about a certain scripture to help you with your life.

It isn't about diagramming battle strategies in the Alma chapters, although there are days that may help. It's about taking the real life problems from your own battlefront and prayerfully reading by the light of the Spirit until you find the answer.

It isn't about speeding through the scriptures at a breakneck pace to meet a reading deadline, although that may help. It's about noticing those times that you don't want to move, or breathe, for fear of dislodging the feeling that has come upon you, as you have read the words of the Lord.

It's not about knowing more about the Savior's life, although that may help. It is about coming to know the Savior in a way you never have before and to attach yourself to him more than you ever have before.

It's not about learning names and dates and places, although that may help. It is about learning to take upon you the name of Christ in a whole new way.

Sisters, it's not about reading the scriptures. It's about learning to hear the voice of the Lord. And really, it's not about loving the scriptures. It's *all* about our love for the Lord.

Notes

1. Marion G. Romney, Conference Report, April 1960, 112–13; see also Romney, *Learning for the Eternities* (Salt Lake City: Deseret Book, 1977), 86.
2. Wendy L. Watson, *Purity and Passion: Spiritual Truths about Intimacy That Will Strengthen Your Marriage* (Salt Lake City: Deseret Book, 2001), 21–42.

"TRUST IN THE LORD WITH ALL THY HEART"

Barbara Ballard

My husband and I served in Toronto, Ontario, Canada, where he was mission president. As Christmastime approached the first year we were there, I thought, *Oh, these missionaries are going to be so homesick at Christmastime. What can we do to help them?* Was I naïve! They were not homesick. They simply said, "Sister Ballard, what greater place in the world could we be than in the mission field serving the Savior by proclaiming his message on his birthday?" They felt that being there was a remarkable and wonderful blessing at Christmastime. From then on, I didn't feel sorry for them. In fact, they taught the wife of their mission president a valuable truth that holiday season. I saw that their faith and their service anchored and dedicated them to the Lord. They were determined to fulfill their callings as missionaries of the Lord Jesus Christ. Our missionaries taught me that desire, coupled with commitment to a righteous goal, strengthens faith and testimony. As we read in Proverbs: "The desire of the righteous shall be granted" (Proverbs 10:24).

A few years ago I was sitting with a group of women who were wives of mission presidents. Our meeting was casual—a break from the formal teaching of the seminar we were attending. As we were telling each other a little about ourselves, one beautiful black sister related one of the most touching examples of faith and testimony I had ever heard. Their family visited the São Paulo Temple during the open house

---

Barbara Bowen Ballard, wife of Elder M. Russell Ballard, a member of the Quorum of the Twelve Apostles, has been a teacher or officer in every auxiliary in the Church. She served with her husband while he presided over the Canada Toronto Mission. They are the parents of seven children and grandparents of forty-one.

preceding its dedication. She and her husband, with their children at their side, were thrilled with what they saw and heard. They were active members of the Church, but at the time (pre-1978) her husband could not hold the priesthood because of his race. The tour came at last to the celestial room. They stood there in awe, tears flowing. They said to each other, "Take a good look at this room, for we will never be able to see it again in this life."

I can still remember how stunned I was at that moment. Think of it! They loved the Lord and his gospel so much that they were willing to give themselves to him, even though they could not participate fully in the blessings of the temple. None of us who were there that day will ever forget her testimony of faith, hope, and gratitude.

This story, of course, has a happy ending. Not too long after the São Paulo Temple was dedicated, the revelation extending the priesthood to all worthy men was given. This faithful, valiant family was sealed together for time and all eternity. This good brother, fulfilling his priesthood assignments with heart and soul, not only served as the first black mission president but later as the first black General Authority as well. This beautiful family personifies the scripture found in 2 Nephi 31:20: "Wherefore, if ye shall press forward, feasting upon the word of Christ, and endure to the end, behold, thus saith the Father: Ye shall have eternal life."

My husband, Elder M. Russell Ballard, has many examples of faithful women in his ancestry. One is Mary Fielding Smith, the wife of Hyrum Smith, the older brother of the Prophet Joseph. She is my husband's great-great-grandmother, a remarkable example of courage, inner strength, and faith.

When Joseph and Hyrum were martyred in Carthage Jail, Hyrum's wife, Mary, was left on her own with a large family to care for. Notwithstanding her many challenges, she decided to travel west with the Saints. Her history records the extremely trying circumstances as she journeyed in a wagon train headed for the Salt Lake Valley from Winter Quarters—circumstances that would have discouraged most women. Even the captain of the wagon train, who resented her being there, tried to weaken her resolve to go on.

At a point midway between the Platte and Sweetwater rivers, one of Mary's best oxen lay down in the yoke as if poisoned. All supposed he would die. All the teams behind her stopped, those in the wagons gathering around to see what had happened. In a short time, the captain came to see what was wrong. There the ox lay, stiffened in the throes of death. The captain blustered about and said, "He is dead, there is no use working with him, we'll have to fix up some way to take the Widow along. I told her she would be a burden on the company."[1] He was mistaken.

"Mary said nothing but went to her wagon and returned with a bottle of consecrated oil. She asked her brother Joseph and his friend James Lawson to administer to her fallen ox, believing that the Lord would raise him. . . . The men removed their hats. All bowed their heads as Joseph Fielding . . . knelt, laid his hands on the head of the ox, and prayed over it. . . . Its haunches started to rise. The forelegs strengthened. The ox stood and, without urging, started off as though nothing had happened. This amazing thing greatly astonished the onlookers."[2] The team went on with a renewal of strength for the remainder of the long journey.

Mary's great faith touched her young son Joseph's heart and helped him through a lifetime of dedicated service, including seventeen years as President of the Church. I believe that all mothers can leave similar legacies of faith for their children if they themselves have that faith.

A second woman of great faith is Margaret McNeil Ballard, my husband's great-grandmother. She was born in Scotland in 1845, one year after her father joined the Church. Although the family was eager to join the Saints in Utah, Church callings, including Margaret's father serving as branch president, kept them in Scotland for a time. They sailed for New York in 1856. After experiencing several more delays, eleven-year-old Margaret and her family finally began their journey west.

From Margaret's personal history, we know that measles broke out, and all of her siblings were very sick. The rest of the company began to move on without them. Because Margaret was not sick, her mother was anxious for her to remain with the company. In Margaret's own words, "My mother strapped my little brother James on my back with a shawl. He was only four years old and still quite sick with the measles, but I took him since mother had all she could do to care for the other children. I hurried and caught up with the company, traveling with them all day. That night a kind lady helped me take my brother off my back. I sat up and held him on my lap with the shawl wrapped around him, alone, all night. He was a little better in the morning. The people in the camp were very good to us and gave us a little fried bacon and some bread for breakfast.

"We traveled this way for about a week, my brother and I not seeing our mother during this time. Each morning one of the men would write a note and put it in the slit of a willow stuck into the ground to tell how we were getting along. In this way mother knew we were all right."

Margaret ends this part of her account with these words, "We arrived in Ogden on the fourth day of October, 1859, after a journey of hardships and hunger, with thankfulness to our Heavenly Father for his protecting care."

She had walked every step of the way across the plains and for a large part of the way had carried her brother James on her back. Her feet were often wrapped only in bloodstained rags.

Once in the dark of night Margaret was sent to retrieve their cow, which had wandered away. She was barefoot and not able to see clearly where she was walking. All of a sudden she began to feel that she was walking on something soft. She stopped and looked down to see what it could be. She writes: "To my horror I found that I was standing in a bed of snakes, large ones and small ones. At the sight of them I became so weak that I could scarcely move. All I could think of was to pray."[3]

Both of these women became the mothers of apostles of the Lord. Their indomitable courage came from their unwavering faith. As with them, so it is with us. My husband has taught that "our Heavenly

Father is aware of us, individually and collectively. He understands the spiritual, physical, and emotional difficulties we face in the world today. In fact, they are all part of His plan for our eternal growth and development."

"But where do we find hope in the midst of . . . turmoil and catastrophe? Quite simply, our one hope for spiritual safety . . . is to turn our minds and our hearts to Jesus Christ."[4]

My husband and I have reared seven children, two sons and five daughters. I can clearly picture in my mind each of these little ones as they first stood, balancing next to the couch or a chair. Soon they were able to stand in the middle of the floor. I still feel delight when I think of their first wobbly steps and remember the comical surprise on their little faces. In no time at all, they were off and running, and we haven't been able to keep up with them since.

As children of our Heavenly Father, we are learning to walk an eternal path. Sometimes we are unsteady; sometimes we fall. We are not perfect. But, just as we encourage our wobbly toddlers to keep trying and trying, again and again, knowing they will receive their share of bumps and bruises, we must always remember that our Father in Heaven encourages our every effort and is there to comfort us when we make mistakes. We must not lose hope or give up trying, for he has said: "Fear not, little flock; do good; let earth and hell combine against you, for if ye are built upon my rock, they cannot prevail. . . . Look unto me in every thought; doubt not, fear not . . .—even so am I in the midst of you" (D&C 6:34, 36, 32).

Righteousness has never precluded adversity. In times of trial and difficulty, what is required for each of us to be as courageous, noble, and steadfast as the women I have written of? Faith in God and in his Son, Jesus Christ. It is absolutely essential if we are to maintain balance and perspective. We must follow this admonition from the book of Proverbs: "Trust in the Lord with all thine heart; and lean not unto thine own understanding. In all thy ways acknowledge him, and he shall direct thy paths" (Proverbs 3:5–6).

The strength we seek comes through letting the Lord share our burdens. Our testimonies will be deep and everlasting, fortified with the knowledge that with the Lord's help, we can succeed.

Notes

1. Don Cecil Corbett, *Mary Fielding Smith, Daughter of Britain: Portrait of Courage* (Salt Lake City: Deseret Book, 1966), 236–37.
2. Ibid., 237.
3. Personal history of Margaret McNeil Ballard in possession of the author.
4. M. Russell Ballard, "The Joy of Hope Fulfilled," *Ensign*, November 1992, 33, 32.

KNOWING WHO YOU ARE—
AND WHO YOU'VE ALWAYS BEEN

Sheri Dew

Sisters, you are just spectacular! You're not perfect, but you are spectacular! From Siberia to Seattle, you have won my heart and my deepest respect. I believe there is more righteous courage and determination inherent within the sisters of this church today than there has ever been among any group of women who have ever lived. And I want to tell you why.

Recently, my sixteen-year-old niece Megan and two of her friends came for a sleepover. As we talked that evening, one of them asked me what it had been like growing up on a farm in the *olden days*. (This is not as bad, however, as what happened a few days ago when a handsome young returned missionary said to me, "Sister Dew, if I were just forty years older . . ." Anyway, I told Megan and her friends that in the "olden days," I had been painfully shy and had absolutely no self-confidence.

"How did you get over feeling that way?" Megan asked. A pat answer was on the tip of my tongue when I stopped, sensing that these terrific young women were receptive to more. So I told them that the reason was a spiritual one: That it wasn't until I began to understand how the Lord felt about me that my feelings about myself and my life slowly began to change. Their questions then came in a flurry: How did I *know* how the Lord felt? And how could they find out how He felt about them?

Sheri L. Dew is the second counselor in the Relief Society General Presidency. She grew up in Ulysses, Kansas, and graduated from Brigham Young University with a degree in history. A popular speaker and writer, she is executive vice-president of publishing at Deseret Book Company.

For several hours, scriptures in hand, we talked about how to hear the voice of the Spirit, about how eager the Lord is to unveil the knowledge stored safely inside our spirits concerning who we are and what our mission is, and about the life-changing difference it makes when we know.

My message to you, my dear sisters, whom I love, is the same: There is nothing more vital to our success and our happiness here than learning to hear the voice of the Spirit. It is the Spirit who reveals to us our identity, which isn't just who we are but who we have always been. And when we know that, our lives take on a sense of purpose so stunning that we can never be the same again.

As a people, we talk and sing constantly about who we are. Three-year-olds know the words to "I Am a Child of God." The Proclamation on the Family declares that we each have a divine destiny. The second Young Women value is divine nature. And the very first words in the Relief Society Declaration are, "We are beloved spirit daughters of God, and our lives have meaning, purpose, and direction." And yet, with all our talking, do we really believe? Do we really understand? Has this transcendent doctrine about who we are—meaning who we have always been and, therefore, who we may become—permeated our hearts?

Our spirits long for us to remember the truth about who we are, because the way we see ourselves—or our sense of identity—affects everything we do. It affects the way we behave, the way we respond to uncertainty, the way we see others, the way we feel about ourselves, and the way we make choices. It affects the very way we live our lives. So, I invite you to ponder in a new way not just who you are but who you have always been.

President Lorenzo Snow taught that "Jesus was a god before he came into the world and yet his knowledge was taken from him. He did not know his former greatness, neither do we know what greatness we had attained to before we came here."[1] But President Snow also taught that during the Savior's life "it was revealed unto Him who He was, and for what purpose He was in the world. The glory and power

He possessed *before* He came into the world was made known unto Him."[2] Sisters, just as the Savior came to remember and to know exactly who He was, so may we.

Unveiling this knowledge would be easier if we could remember what happened in our premortal life. But we can't. We can't remember the glory of our former home. We have forgotten the language we spoke there and our dear companions with whom we associated. We cannot recall the "first lessons [we learned] in the world of spirits" (D&C 138:56) or the identities of our heavenly tutors. We cannot remember what promises we made to ourselves and to others and to the Lord. Nor can we remember our place in the Lord's heavenly kingdom or the spiritual maturity we achieved there.

There are, however, some remarkable things that we do know. We know that *we were there*, in the heavenly councils before the foundations of this earth were laid. *We were there* when our Father presented his plan, and we saw the Savior chosen and appointed, and we sanctioned it. *We were there* among the heavenly host who sang and shouted for joy (Job 38:7). And when Satan unleashed his fury against the Father and the Son and was cast out of heaven, we were there, fighting on the side of truth. In fact, President George Q. Cannon said that "we stood loyally by God and by Jesus, and . . . *did not flinch.*"[3] We believed. We followed. And when we fought for truth in the most bitter of all confrontations, we did not flinch.

Because of our premortal valor, we were chosen to be born into the house of Israel, which lineage President Harold B. Lee called the "most illustrious lineage" of all who would come to earth,[4] and which Elder Bruce R. McConkie said was reserved for those who sought the greatest of all premortal talents, the talent of spirituality.[5]

Now we are here, separated from the safety of our heavenly home, serving a mission in this lone and dreary world—a mission to prove whether or not we want to be part of the kingdom of God more than we want anything else. The Lord is testing our faith and our integrity to see if we will persevere in a realm where Satan reigns. Happily, despite taking this test in the stormy twilight of the dispensation of the fulness of times, we have once again chosen to follow Jesus Christ. We have chosen to follow Him because we remember Him and we recognize Him.

We are among the elect whom the Lord has called during this "eleventh hour" to labor in His vineyard, a vineyard that "has become corrupted every whit" and in which only a few "doeth good" (D&C 33:3–4). We are those few. God, who saw the "end from the beginning" (Abraham 2:8), foresaw perfectly what these times would demand. Thus, said President George Q. Cannon, "God . . . reserved spirits for this dispensation who [would] have the courage and determination to face the world, and all the powers of the evil one," and who would "build up the Zion of our God, fearless of all consequences."[6]

Can you imagine that God, who knew us perfectly, reserved us to come now, when the stakes would be higher and the opposition more intense than ever? When He would need women who would help raise and lead a chosen generation in the most lethal spiritual environment? Can you imagine that He chose us because He knew we would be fearless in building Zion?

I can, because of what the Spirit has repeatedly whispered about you as I have sought the Lord in your behalf during this calling. Though we are sometimes far too casual about our spiritual lives; though we sometimes get distracted by the world and live beneath ourselves—the fact remains that we have always been women of God. We have repeatedly made righteous choices, on both sides of the veil, that demonstrate our faith and our faithfulness. We have bound ourselves to the Lord with the most binding covenants of mortality. We have been and are so much more valiant than we think. We have more divine potential than we yet comprehend.

The Lord told Abraham that he was among the "noble and great ones" chosen for his earthly mission before he was born (Abraham 3:22). And President Joseph F. Smith saw in vision that many— *many*—choice spirits reserved to come forth in this dispensation were also "among the noble and great" (D&C 138:55). Said Elder Bruce R. McConkie: "A *host* of mighty men and *equally glorious women* comprised that group of the 'noble and great ones.' . . . Can we do other than conclude that Mary and Eve and Sarah and myriads of our faithful sisters were numbered among them? Certainly these sisters . . . fought as valiantly in the War in Heaven as did the brethren, even as they in like manner stand firm . . . in mortality, in the cause of truth and righteousness."[7]

So, sisters, what about us? What about you and me? Is it possible that we were among the noble and great?

I believe it is more than possible. The Prophet Joseph taught that "every man who has a calling to minister to the inhabitants of the world was ordained to that very purpose . . . before this world was."[8] President Spencer W. Kimball added that "in the world before we came here, faithful women were given certain assignments."[9] I cannot imagine that we who have been called to bear and rear and lead and love a chosen generation of children and youth this late in the final dispensation were not among those deemed noble and great.

Noble and *great. Courageous* and *determined. Faithful* and *fearless.* That is who you are, and that is who you have always been. Understanding that truth can change your life, because this knowledge carries a confidence that cannot be duplicated any other way. I doubt many of us feel noble *or* great. But then neither did Enoch, who was stunned when the Lord called him into service: "Why is it that I have found favor in thy sight, and am but a lad, and all the people hate me; for I am slow of speech?" (Moses 6:31). The Lord responded to Enoch by promising to walk with him and give power to his words. This encounter with the Lord gave Enoch a new vision of himself, and the result was magnificent, for so powerful was his word that his people were "taken up into heaven" (Moses 7:21). But that happened *after* Enoch understood who he was and that he had a mission to perform.

Saul, who made sport of persecuting Christians, was instantly converted after seeing the Savior and learning that he was a chosen vessel (Acts 9:5; 22:15). There surely wasn't a Christian breathing who would have described Saul of Tarsus as "chosen"—at least not based on his earthly conduct. He must have been chosen before. And when Saul understood that, he changed his life and his name. The apostle Paul's conversion was at least partly about coming to understand who he had always been.

As we come to understand the same thing, we will feel a greater sense of mission and more confidence living as a woman of God in a world that doesn't necessarily celebrate women of God. We will cheer each other on rather than compete with each other, because we'll feel secure in our standing before the Lord. And we'll be eager to stand for truth, even when we must stand alone—for every consecrated woman will have times when she must stand alone.

Satan, of course, knows how spiritually potent the knowledge of our divine identity is. He hates women of the noble birthright. He hates us because he is almost out of time, while we are en route to everlasting glory. He hates us because of the influence we have on husbands and children, family and friends, the Church, and even the world. It is no secret to him that we are the Lord's secret weapon.

Thus it should not surprise us that the master of deceit is going all out to keep us from comprehending the majesty of who we are. He offers an array of seductive but sorry substitutes—everything from labels and logos to titles and status—hoping to preoccupy us with the world's artificial identifiers. Not long ago a book listing *The 100 Most Influential Women of All Time* caught my attention. I was interested to find out who the 100 most influential women of all time had been. Here's what you'll find interesting. Eve, the mother of all living—now catch the irony here, the woman without whom we wouldn't even be here—didn't make the list. Come on! This pitiful list demonstrates how absurd the world's view and valuation of women is.

In a prominent magazine, a recent cover story entitled "The Quest for Perfection" promoted a definition of perfection that was disgusting and, frankly, evil. It listed every available lift, tuck, and augmentation, while not so much as mentioning virtue or values, marriage or motherhood—or anything, for that matter, that matters to the Lord.

Clearly, Satan wants us to see ourselves as the world sees us, not as the Lord sees us, because the world's mirror, like a circus mirror in which a 5'10" woman appears two feet tall, distorts and minimizes us. Satan tells us we're not good enough. Not smart enough. Not thin enough. Not cute enough. Not clever enough. Not *anything* enough. And that is a big, fat, devilish lie. He wants us to believe that there is no status in being a mother. That is a lie, an evil lie. He wants us to believe that the influence of women is inherently inferior. And that is a lie.

Yet we often buy into Satan's superficialities. After speaking in a general women's meeting on satellite, I received a letter that said this: "Sister Dew, I can relate to you because I can see that you know what it means to have a bad-hair day." Sisters, this was no news flash; I've had *years* of bad-hair days. We obviously don't always see beyond our hair and our clothing, but the Lord does. For he "seeth not as man seeth; for man looketh on the outward appearance, but the Lord looketh on the heart" (1 Samuel 16:7).

Thus Satan's all-out attempt to prevent us from understanding how the Lord sees us, because the more clearly we understand our divine destiny, the more immune we become to Satan. When Satan tried to confuse Moses about his identity, saying, "Moses, son of man, worship me" (Moses 1:12), Moses refused, responding: "I am a son of God" (Moses 1:13). He knew who he was because the Lord had told him, "Thou art my son; . . . and I have a work for thee" (Moses 1:4, 6).

Surely one reason Moses prevailed while the great deceiver ranted and railed was that Moses knew clearly who he was. So it is with us. We will never be happy or feel peace; we will never deal well with life's ambiguities; we will never live up to who we are as women of God until we overcome our mortal identity crisis by understanding who we are, who we have always been, and who we may become.

The Spirit is the key, for as President Joseph F. Smith taught, it is through the power of the Spirit that we may "catch a spark from the awakened memories of the immortal soul, which lights up our whole being as with the glory of our former home."[10] It is the Spirit that allows us to pierce the veil and catch glimpses of who we are and who we have always been. Thus our need to be able to hear what the Lord, through the Spirit, has to say.

Asking in faith, fasting and praying, repenting regularly, forgiving and seeking forgiveness, worshiping in the temple where we may "receive a fulness of the Holy Ghost" (D&C 109:15), and being obedient all help us better hear the voice of the Lord in our minds and hearts (D&C 8:2). Conversely, there are things we cannot do—movies we cannot watch, clothes we cannot wear, gossip we cannot spread, Internet sites we cannot visit, thoughts we cannot entertain, books we cannot read, and dishonesty we cannot tolerate—if we want the Spirit to be with us.

I can think of nothing more deserving of our energy than learning to better hear the voice of the Spirit. When the Nephite Twelve pleaded with the Father for "that which they most desired," it was the gift of the Holy Ghost (3 Nephi 19:9). Why? Because the Holy Ghost "will show unto [us] all things" (2 Nephi 32:5), including who we are. I know this is true. One day while rocking a niece who was then three months old, I was overwhelmed with an impression about the valor of her spirit. My tears flowed as I rocked and wondered just whom I was rocking. Now that my niece is older, I have told her about that experience, hoping to encourage her onward.

Similarly, when I was that shy farm girl, both my mother and my grandma often told me that there was something chosen about me and my generation. I couldn't quite imagine it, but my spirit wanted me to believe. So I quietly hung on their words and hoped they were true. Is there anything more meaningful a mother or a grandmother or any of us can do for the youth we love than help them begin to see who they *really* are?

As vital as this knowledge is, however, it alone doesn't make mortality fail-safe. President Lee warned that there are many who may "have been among the noble and great" but who "may fail of that calling here in mortality."[11] In other words, "many are called, but few are chosen" (D&C 121:40). And, frankly, we do the choosing, because the sobering reality is that whether or not we live up to our premortal promises is entirely up to us.

But the effort required is well worth it, for if we could comprehend how glorious a righteous woman made perfect in the celestial kingdom will be, we would rise up and never be the same again. We would gladly take upon us the name of Jesus Christ (Alma 46:15)—which means following Him, becoming like Him, and dedicating ourselves to Him and His work. Women of God who honor their covenants look differently, dress differently, and act and speak differently from women who have not made the same covenants. Thus women of God who know who they are have unusual and sometimes unexpected influence.

There is a shop in New York City I visit when I am there. Frankly, I don't care for the shop's atmosphere, but because they carry skirts long enough for a tall woman, I endure the experience. On a recent visit, I made plans to meet a friend at this shop, and when I walked through the door, a saleswoman was already waiting for me. "Mizz Dew?" she said with a charming accent. "Yeah?" I responded. "Follow me. Your friend is waiting for you downstairs." I had never had such a warm reception, but then, for the next hour, my friend and I became acquainted with this delightful European woman. After a while she said, "There is something different about you two. What is it?" "Do you really want to know?" we asked her. When she nodded yes, I said, "Sit down." For an hour, my friend and I told her what made us different. Since then we've sent materials explaining more. And we've just sent her something else—missionaries who will call on her using our names.

What does knowing who we are and who we have always been have to do with bearing record and testifying of Jesus Christ? It has everything to do with our mandate to take the gospel to every nation, kindred, tongue, and people. Once we understand who we really are, we are not only beholden to the Lord to help others discover the same truths but we simply cannot be restrained from doing so. If a missionary moment can unfold in a stuffy New York dress shop, it can happen anywhere. And it will happen as the joy of the gospel and the reality of our mission lights our faces and energizes our lives.

I know a woman who responded to a nonmember friend wanting to sell her cosmetics by saying, "You can give me a facial if I can talk about the gospel." Both agreed, and both attended women's conference this year. There is no more persuasive missionary messenger than a woman of God who knows who she is and who is thrilled with what she knows. I hasten to add that the most important missionary work we will ever do will be within our families, as their conversion is our highest priority.

Our objective through all of this isn't to build a bigger Church. It is to bless the lives of people—mothers and fathers, sons and daughters—who deserve to know who they are, who they have always been, and who they may become.

Let's not make this harder than it needs to be. We can begin by simply praying for opportunities to serve, for we will do more missionary work through our examples than we ever will pounding a pulpit. Last year the sisters in an Arizona ward provided service, no strings attached, to a nonmember family whose infant son was undergoing open-heart surgery. Those simple acts of kindness launched a remarkable sequence of events, and not long ago that family was baptized. Now she and her husband and their three darling little boys are beginning to find out who they are.

Repeatedly, President Gordon B. Hinckley has pleaded with us to "become a vast army with enthusiasm for this work."[12] In the general Relief Society meeting held in September 2000, I invited every sister to look for missionary opportunities. And at the 2001 general Young Women meeting, Sister Margaret Nadauld asked every young woman to reach out to one girl and bring her into full activity this year. Within a week, several of my teenage nieces had already made contacts with nonmember friends. They enlisted immediately in the army.

Can we do any less? If the women and young women of this Church would join together in this glorious work, we would become a vast, enthusiastic part of the Lord's army. None of us can reach everyone, but we can all reach someone—and over time, many someones.

The gospel kingdom will not move forward as it must until we as mothers and sisters and favorite aunts become full and eager participants.

Sisters, I am asking you today to respond to our prophet's call to enlist in the Lord's army. And in doing so I make this promise: That as soon as we, the sisters of this Church, commit fully to this work, it will explode in an unprecedented way because of our unique, nurturing influence and because of the spirit that attends righteous women. It will flourish because youth who see their mothers and leaders fearlessly sharing the gospel will do likewise.

More than twenty years ago President Kimball prophesied: "The female exemplars of the Church will be a significant force in both the numerical and the spiritual growth of the Church in the last days."[13] He was talking about us. Imagine the impact if this year every woman with a testimony helped one other woman gain a testimony and begin to find out who she is and was and may become.

I'll take the challenge. Will you join me? Ask the Lord to help you, and He will. Begin by reading Doctrine and Covenants 138 and Abraham 3 about the noble and great ones, and see what the Spirit reveals to you about *you*. When you understand that *you* were chosen and reserved for now, and when you live in harmony with that mission, you'll be happier than you have ever been before.

Listen to these words from President Gordon B. Hinckley: "Woman is God's supreme creation. . . . Of all the creations of the Almighty, there is none more . . . inspiring than a . . . daughter of God who walks in virtue with an understanding of why she should do so."[14]

"Rise above the dust of the world. Know that you are daughters of God . . . and that there is for you a great work to be done which cannot be left to others."[15]

My dear sisters, will you seek to remember with the help of the Holy Ghost who you are and who you have always been? Will you remember that you stood by our Savior without flinching? Remember that you were reserved for now because you would have the courage and determination to face the world at its worst and to help love and lead a chosen generation. Remember the covenants you have made and the power they carry. Remember that you are noble and great and a potential heir of all our Father has. Remember that you are the daughter of a King.

God is our Father, and his Only Begotten Son *is* the Christ. May we rejoice in once again standing tall for the Savior and serving with valor and vigor in his vineyard. And may we be fearless in building up the Zion of our God—because we know who we are and who we have always been.

Notes

1. Office Journal of Lorenzo Snow, 8 October 1900, 181–82, Archives of The Church of Jesus Christ of Latter-day Saints, Salt Lake City, Utah.
2. Lorenzo Snow, Conference Report, April 1901, 3; emphasis added.
3. George Q. Cannon, *Gospel Truth: Discourses and Writings of President George Q. Cannon*, sel. Jerreld L. Newquist (Salt Lake City: Deseret Book, 1987), 7; emphasis added.
4. Harold B. Lee, "Understanding Who We Are Brings Self-Respect," *Ensign*, January 1974, 5.
5. Bruce R. McConkie, *A New Witness for the Articles of Faith* (Salt Lake City: Deseret Book, 1984), 512.
6. George Q. Cannon, *Journal of Discourses*, 26 vols. (London: Latter-day Saints' Book Depot, 1852–81), 11:230.
7. Bruce R. McConkie, *Doctrines of the Restoration: Sermons and Writings of Bruce R. McConkie* (Salt Lake City: Bookcraft, 1989), 197–98; emphasis added.
8. Joseph Smith, *History of The Church of Jesus Christ of Latter-day Saints*, edited by B. H. Roberts, 2d ed. rev., 7 vols. (Salt Lake City: The Church of Jesus Christ of Latter-day Saints, 1932–51), 6:364.
9. Spencer W. Kimball, "The Role of Righteous Women," *Ensign*, November 1979, 102.
10. Joseph F. Smith, *Gospel Doctrine: Sermons and Writings of Joseph F. Smith* (Salt Lake City: Deseret Book, 1986), 14.
11. Lee, "Understanding Who We Are," 5.
12. Gordon B. Hinckley, "Find the Lambs, Feed the Sheep," *Ensign*, May 1999, 110.
13. Kimball, "Righteous Women," 104.
14. Gordon B. Hinckley, "Our Responsibility to Our Young Women," *Ensign*, September 1988, 11.

15. Gordon B. Hinckley, "Live Up to Your Inheritance," *Ensign*, November 1983, 84.

WOMEN AND THE MORAL CENTER OF GRAVITY

Bruce C. Hafen

Today's culture is losing the vision of motherhood, marriage, and family life. As our Primary children sing in "Follow the Prophet," "Now we have a world where people are confused. If you don't believe it, go and watch the news."[1]

Church members aren't immune to this confusion. A Latter-day Saint mother, called to work with young single adults, was expecting a new baby. One by one, several of her young women privately asked her how she really felt about having another child. Sincere and trusting, they asked questions that reflected honest anxiety about being bound to husbands and assuming the burdens of motherhood. She was surprised to hear such concerns from young women who were believing, active Church members.

In response, she invited each of the young women to do what she had allowed only her husband and children to do. She tenderly placed the questioner's hand on her abdomen and invited her to feel the baby's movements. Then, with her hand on that young woman's, she lovingly taught each one in turn that, despite the relentless demands, she had discovered an exquisite happiness through being married and having children. These young women drank with deep reassurance from the wellspring of testimony. Unfortunately, too few young people today have such mentors.

Bruce C. Hafen, a member of the First Quorum of the Seventy, recently returned from service as the area president in Australia and New Zealand. A native of St. George, Utah, he earned a juris doctor degree from the University of Utah. He has served as president of Ricks College, dean of Brigham Young University Law School, and provost at BYU. He and his wife, Marie K. Hafen, are the parents of seven children and grandparents of ten.

What is happening to us? We are now living through the biggest attitude change about family life in five centuries. An *Atlantic Monthly* writer believes today's massive family disintegration is part of what he calls "the Great Disruption," a wave of history as big as the shift from the age of agriculture to the Industrial Revolution some two hundred years ago.[2] Many people today are skeptical about the very idea of "belonging" to a family. Family bonds were once seen as valuable ties that bind; some now see those ties as sheer bondage.

Vast forces are eroding our foundations of personal peace, love, and human attachments. Whatever held families together appears to be weakening. At times this feels like an ecological disaster, as if a vital organism in the environment is disappearing.

Patricia Holland has said, "If I were Satan and wanted to destroy a society, I think I would stage a full-blown blitz on women."[3] What did she mean? Men and women share the traits of human nature and often perform the same tasks. But some strengths are gender-specific; and we are losing what women have traditionally contributed to cultural stability. Like the mortar that keeps a brick wall from toppling over, women have held together our most precious relationships: our marriages and child-parent ties. But now we're seeing cracks in that mortar, which reveal some things we have too long taken for granted.

A salesman walked down a street past a group of boys playing baseball. No one answered the door of the house where he knocked. Through a side door, he saw a boy the age of those playing in the street, dutifully practicing the piano. Baseball gear leaned against the wall. He called, "Excuse me, Sonny. Is your mother home?" The boy glanced at his baseball gear and said glumly from the keyboard, "What do you think?"

More broadly, studies of third-world development show that of all the factors affecting a culture's social and economic growth, perhaps the most significant is the literacy of women. Women have always lifted entire cultures. Their influence begins in each society's very core—the home. Here women have taught and modeled what social historian Alexis de Tocqueville called "the habits of the heart," the civilizing "mores" or attitudes that create a sense of personal virtue and duty to the community, without which free societies can't exist.[4]

Shakespeare's *Macbeth* powerfully portrays the moral influence of women. Shakespeare coins the phrase "the milk of human kindness" when Lady Macbeth is persuading her husband to murder the king and take his throne. As Macbeth hesitates, his wife sneers, "Thy nature [is] too full o' th' milk of human kindness."[5] Then, in a haunting passage, from her balcony she commands the evil forces of the universe to "unsex me here" and "fill me . . . [with] direst cruelty. . . . Take my [woman's] milk for gall. . . . Come, thick night."[6]

Lady Macbeth's womanly heart makes her incapable of taking a life unless she renounces her female instinct to give and nurture life. Later, after they have killed the king, she goes insane, then dies—not just from guilt, but perhaps from renouncing her very nature.

"The milk of human kindness" is a symbol of female nurturing at many levels. Especially, it refers to the moral influence of women. Consider now four ways in which modern society has devalued that nurturing. Perhaps seeing more closely what we're losing will help us regain it. Let's look first at the devaluation of motherhood.

For most of our history, the very word *motherhood* meant honor, endearment, and sacrifice. Victor Hugo wrote, "She broke the bread into two fragments and gave them to her children, who ate with eagerness. 'She hath kept none for herself,' grumbled the sergeant.

" 'Because she is not hungry,' said a soldier.

" 'No,' said the sergeant, 'because she is a mother.' "[7]

Yet this spirit of self-sacrifice has become a contentious issue in recent years, making contentious the very idea of motherhood. For instance, an essay called "The Problem of Mothering" argues that women have been oppressed in society as a direct result of "the social assignment of mothering to women [because] women's oppression is in some way connected to mothering."[8] Others have blamed the sacrificing mother herself—for her selflessness that has allowed and encouraged male domination. Stereotyping the motherly role, they contend, forces women to accept a sexist division of labor everywhere, most especially in family relationships.[9]

These critics do have a point. Some people have exploited mothers' willingness to accept relentless demands. And some women have indeed felt undue pressure to conform to rigid roles that deny a woman's sense of self. But the critics have swung the pendulum too far. As *Newsweek* put it, they "sometimes crossed the line into outright contempt for motherhood."[10]

If being selfless means a woman must give up her own inner identity and personal growth, that understanding of selflessness is wrong. That was a weakness in some versions of the Victorian model of motherhood, which viewed women as excessively *dependent* on their husbands. But today's liberationist model goes too far the other way, stereotyping women as excessively *independent* of their families.

A more sensible view is that husbands and wives are *interdependent*. The Church's inspired Proclamation on the Family states that spouses are "equal partners" who "help one another" fulfill their individual responsibilities.[11] Marriage offers *each* partner the opportunity for spiritual development. I once said in frustration to Marie, "The Lord put Adam and Eve on the earth as full-grown people. Why couldn't he have done that with this boy of ours?" Marie replied, "God gave us that child to make Christians out of us." That is an equal-opportunity blessing for the growth of each parent.

The social critics who moved mothers from dependence to independence skipped the fertile middle ground of interdependence. Those who moved mothers from selflessness to selfishness skipped the fertile middle ground of self-chosen sacrifice that contributes to a woman's personal growth. Because of these excesses, the end result of debates about the value of motherhood have, ironically, caused many to discount not only mothers but women in general.

One woman's recent essay, "Despising Our Mothers, Despising Ourselves," reported that, despite many victories for women since the 1960s, the self-respect of American women is at an all-time low. Why? Because we've experienced not just a revolt against men's oppression but also a revolt against women: "Heroic women who [dedicated] their lives to . . . children—as mothers, teachers, nurses, social workers—. . . [have been] made to feel stupid and second rate because they [took] seriously the Judeao-Christian precept that it was better to do for others than for oneself." Devaluing motherhood devalues "the primary work of most women throughout history," which tells women they "aren't worth serious consideration."[12]

Then what happens? Society's bricks begin to crumble. Consider the unprecedented appearance of brutality in children. American schools have now witnessed several cases of children shooting other children, something the world had never seen before. The forerunner to these events was the world-shocking 1993 case of James Bulger, in which two ten-year-old boys murdered a two-year-old child. This crime prompted some British researchers to study how children learn the difference between right and wrong. They found that a child's understanding of good versus evil emerges emotionally long before it emerges rationally, so that the orientation of a child's conscience begins with its earliest relationship with its mother.[13]

A child is an echo chamber. If he hears the sounds of love from his mother, he will later echo those sounds to others. But if the mother's signals are confusing and hateful, that child is more likely later to sound confused and hateful.[14] Whether or not a mother feels support— from her husband, her family, and her society—profoundly influences whether she feels like a mother of hope, who values herself enough to nurture a child of hope with "the milk of human kindness." And children of hope create a society of hope.

A Latter-day Saint woman recently said that some mothers in the Church feel guilty when their children's needs make it impossible for them to do all the things they feel they ought to be doing in their ward and stake. Some mothers, she said, believe that Church service is the Lord's work, and mothering is, well, "home-work."[15] Not so. This misimpression is just one more example of how a confused society has sent women the false message that motherhood is a second-class activity. All of us need to do our part in the Church, but there is no higher example of the Lord's work than doing what good mothers and fathers do. Our two most sacred buildings are the temple and the home. A family dinner table, surrounded by parents and children who share their laughter and their lives, is a sacred setting—not just a place setting. Seek ye first the kingdom of heaven—and that kingdom is, first of all, in your home. "Home-work" is the Lord's work.

A second area where society is devaluing the gender-specific gifts of women is sexual behavior. Historically, the keystone of the archway of sexual fidelity was the intuitive sexual self-control of women. The sexuality of most women reflects an inner moral compass that can point true north, like a natural magnet. Of course, just as a natural magnet can lose its power through damage or trauma, women can also lose their natural moral magnetism. Many men have also demonstrated the capacity for moral self-direction. But throughout history, women have tended to be society's primary teachers of sexual mores.

As scientist Leon Kass put it, "A fine woman understood that giving her body, even her kiss, meant giving her heart, which was too precious to be bestowed on anyone who would not prove worthy by pledging himself in marriage to be her defender and her lover forever." Thus, "it is largely through the purity of her morals, self-regulated," he continued, "that woman wields her influence. Men will always do what is pleasing to women, but only if women suitably control and channel their own considerable sexual power."[16]

This view of female sexuality deplores abuse of women. It also celebrates the spiritual and emotional fulfillment of marriage for both women and men. Yet women have too long endured the unfairness of a cultural double standard that tolerated promiscuity in men while condemning it in women. Sociologist David Popenoe writes that "men the world over are more sexually driven and 'promiscuous,' while women are more concerned with lasting relationships." Thus women have been "expected to set limits on the extent of intimacy."[17]

A double standard that winks at this male laxness enough to excuse it is unequal and unfair. Society might have responded to this inequality by demanding fidelity of men. But instead, our generation has romped into history's most staggering sexual revolution, seeking male/female equality by encouraging women to imitate the habitual promiscuity of men. It is as if our culture had two hands, a female hand that was morally healthy, and a male hand that was morally withered. In the name of equality, we held up both hands and said, "Please make both my hands the same." And what happened? Both hands became withered.

This odd combination of sexual liberation and women's liberation has, with incredible irony, now liberated men—not only from a sexual conscience but also from the sense of family responsibility that women's higher sexual standards once demanded of them. The biggest losers in this process are, sadly, children and women—the very women who've lost their former power to demand lasting commitments from their children's fathers.

Despite the unfairness of the double standard, our culture's concept of marriage made serious demands of men. Men are simply not as "biologically attuned to being committed fathers as women are to being committed mothers."[18] So marriage was our culture's way of teaching men to provide for and protect their families. But our current culture of divorce shows us that because male commitment is often a learned behavior, it "is fragile and can disappear" when the culture no longer expects or teaches it.[19] Most men won't stay married in any society unless their culture requires it of them.[20]

By expecting men to marry, our culture sent men a message that controlled the damage of the double standard. But in the rush toward women's sexual liberation, we no longer seem to expect men to marry. So we've given up not only the double sexual standard but also the power of marriage to tame the male wanderlust. And the losers in this hasty bargaining were not men but women—and, even more so, children.

As a third area of devaluation, society has stopped prizing women's innate yearning for permanent marriage bonds. Our antimarriage culture now literally throws out our babies with the bath water of resentment toward the very idea of marital commitment. Rates of divorce and illegitimacy have raged out of control for years. We live in "father-less America," with nearly a third of all American children born out of wedlock and more than fifty percent of new marriages expected to end in divorce.

Two experts describe all this as a "remarkable collapse of marriage, leading to growing family instability and decreasing parental invest-ment in children."[21] After surveying the gale-force damage to children in this messy scene, sociologist Popenoe concludes that our only hope today is what he calls "the female predisposition toward permanent pair bonding."[22] What does he mean? Simply that women prefer permanent marriage. For instance, most young women once would have answered the early propositioning of a young man with forceful authority: "Not until you marry me."

And why is this a *female* predisposition? New evidence suggests that women have innate qualities that differ from men's, including a stronger desire for long-term marriage. "Women, who can bear only a limited number of children" and who must nurture them through years of dependency, "have a great [inner] incentive to invest their energy in rearing [their] children, while men, who can father [many] offspring, do not."[23] Because child-rearing is so demanding, women have found ways to keep their children's fathers nearby for long-term protection and support.

Women's desire for long-term mates has also made them more selective about whom they marry.[24] This female instinct, with all the social benefits that flow from raising secure, healthy children, has led women and civilized cultures to entice fathers to share the yoke of family responsibility through marriage bonds.

The chain of being that moves from a mother of hope, to a child of hope, to a society of hope gives our culture an enormous interest in permanent marriage. Thus the woman's greater desire for permanence really is the mortar holding together the bricks of social stability.

As the writer Wendell Berry said, "Marriage [is] not just a bond between two people, but a bond between those two people and their children, and their neighbors." When this bond weakens, we face "an epidemic of divorce, neglect, community ruin, and loneliness." That is why "lovers must turn from their gaze at one another back toward the community. The marriage of two lovers joins them to one another, to forebears, to descendants, to the community, to Heaven and earth. It is the fundamental connection without which nothing holds."[25]

Essential to the connection Berry describes is the female longing for permanent ties. When the marriage bond is secure, a wife stands at the center of moral gravity for her family's universe, holding her husband close with her gravitational pull. When he moves to the perimeter of the home and community to guard and to sustain his family, he is like a falcon and she is his falconer. If he strays too far, he will no longer hear her voice, ever calling him home. Poet William Butler Yeats tells us what happens then:

> *Turning and turning in the widening gyre*
> *The falcon cannot hear the falconer;*
> *Things fall apart; the center cannot hold;*
> *Mere anarchy is loosed upon the world.*[26]

Sadly, society's devaluation of the female center of moral gravity is creating just such disintegration.

The image of the falcon and the falconer suggests an important distinction between the roles of fathers and mothers. Psychiatrist David Gutmann found that in all successful societies, fathers have been "creatures of the perimeter," who provide for and protect their families, while mothers nurture young children.[27] The Church's Proclamation on the Family uses the terms *provide* and *protect* to describe fathers' primary tasks, and *nurture* to describe mothers' primary task.[28] "Strong mothers build secure homes," Gutmann says. "Fathers and fathers' sons maintain secure neighborhoods."[29]

Ideally, then, mothers first nurture children's feelings about right and wrong, and then fathers teach them the law of the family and community. This places fathers and other men into disciplinary roles, teaching sons with loving firmness to separate psychologically from their mothers until they internalize community norms within their own conscience. By this process, according to Gutmann, young men transform their aggression and resentment of authority into an internal sense of duty to protect and provide for their family and community. Then they can form their own homes as mature husbands, rather than childishly needing wives who behave like mothers to them.

Gutmann is distressed about radical feminist criticism of male authority in this long-standing pattern. That criticism undermines the male role, relegating fathers to being "second-fiddle mothers." This demeaning of men, says Gutmann, drives them from marriage into the "masculine default habitats" of "the bar and the adulterous bed," where they "feel like men, rather than failed mothers." Then men tragically turn their aggression against women and against the community, becoming their enemy instead of protector and provider.[30]

By contrast, the Proclamation on the Family states that "marriage between a man and a woman is ordained of God."[31] In that holy togetherness—the "equal partnership" of man and woman—each partner makes a unique and crucial contribution, but these two parts are not two solos. They are the interdependent parts of a duet. Both they and the larger society must assign equal value to each part.

A fourth category of women's undervalued moral influence is in their gift for nurturing human relationships. Recent research shows that women will often sacrifice an achievement for the sake of a relationship, while men will more likely sacrifice a relationship for the sake of an achievement.[32] And strong relationships hold both families and societies together.

Other studies tell us that the "feminine intuition" that values, sustains, and develops personal relationships blesses all intersections of community activity. Economists praise this female strength, with its emphasis on personal networks, as an asset in the economy of the future.[33]

The Church has long involved women in decision-making processes and personal ministering to local congregations. The Relief Society is a sisterhood for all adult women. Through this sisterhood, mothers and other women learn to strengthen not only family bonds but also an endless multitude of other relationships which are nourished—sometimes kept alive—by the touch of human kindness. Women's perspectives can profoundly enrich many fields of human endeavor without compromising the primary value of home and family.

I love the biblical story of Mary's relationship with her cousin Elisabeth, to whom she went to share, to talk, and to receive support. If LDS women criticize each other rather than connect with and support each other, the adversary wins the day by driving wedges into natural, womanly relationships of strength. Because women can give so much never-failing charity to each other in relationships, one curse of the modern world has been to isolate and alienate women—including LDS women—from one another by making them more competitive, like men. Once more, I pray for two healthy hands, for both genders, hands in gestures of compassion, not competition.

Can we love and support each other without judging each other harshly? So many of us are trying our hardest to live the commandments, often against great odds in our personal lives and unique family situations. Heaven knows, the world isn't giving us much support in these relationships. Let us support one another, even when—especially when—we differ on matters of personal choice and circumstance. Those are usually differences of preference, not principle.

In summary, consider a true story from Australian history that illustrates the power of women as mothers of hope, women of fidelity, wives of commitment, and nurturers of human ties. When first a British colony, Australia was a vast wilderness jail for exiled convicts. Until 1850, six of every seven "Brits" who went "down under" were men. The few women there were themselves often convicts or social outcasts. The men ruthlessly exploited them, leaving most of them as women without hope, powerless to change their conditions.

In 1840, a reformer named Caroline Chisholm suggested the idea that more women would stabilize Australian culture. She wrote to the British government about what she considered the best way to establish a "great and good" community: "All the clergy you can dispatch, all the schoolmasters you can appoint, all the churches you can build, and all the books you can export, will never do much good without 'God's police'—wives and little children—good and virtuous women." Caroline Chisholm searched for women to "raise the moral standard of the people." For twenty years she traveled to England to recruit young women and couples who shared commonsense principles of family life. Over time, these women tamed the men who tamed the wild land; and civil society gradually emerged, aided by new state policies that raised women's status and reinforced family life.[34] As one historian put it: "The initial reluctance of the wild colonial boys to marry was eroded fairly quickly." Eventually, thousands of new immigrants who shared the vision of these "good and virtuous women" established stable families as the basic unit of Australian society, and more quickly than it had occurred in any other western country.[35]

This striking story of women's moral influence grew from a deliberate plan to replace a "rough and wild" penal colony with "a more moral civilization" that capitalized on women's innate civilizing capacity.[36] Thus Australia became a promised land, flowing with a healthy environment of milk and honey. And the milk, literally and figuratively, was the milk of human kindness—the woman's touch, which nurtures those habits of the heart without which no civil society can exist.

Many radical feminists would probably reject the concept of women as civilizing agents, because they fear that accepting inherent differences between men and women will cause gender discrimination that places women in second-class roles. The evidence, however, shows that, despite many similarities, men and women do differ innately in some crucial ways. Hence the title of one popular book, *Men Are from Mars, Women Are from Venus*.

Psychologist Carol Gilligan's 1982 book *In a Different Voice* shows how women and men perceive the same things in different ways. Gilligan, for example, found that women have a stronger commitment to care-giving than men do.[37] If society can value this gender gift without creating discrimination against women, we just might experience, as Anne Summers put it, "a genuine breakthrough in our thinking about the qualities contemporary society now has the greatest need for."[38]

The recent women's movements opened many doors to women and awakened many men who had taken advantage of women's willingness to give their bread to others and keep none for themselves. But that pendulum has moved our attitudes too far, devaluing and damaging our culture's support for motherhood, sexual fidelity, marriage, and women's distinctive voices.

It is now time to swing back the pendulum, to find true north, the moral compass point that will nurture our children and communities with the touch of human kindness. Surely society can restore the confidence of today's women in their own instincts without coercing them into being nonentities. Surely we can invite men to follow the examples of compassion they see in their mothers, wives, and daughters. We have already learned the hard way that women, children, and the entire culture are worse off when we seek equality between men and women by encouraging women to adopt permissive male lifestyles.

Let us seek a more responsible form of equality that celebrates and preserves the natural moral influence of women, thereby encouraging both men and women to honor the equal yoke and lifelong commitments of marriage. That kind of progress will make civilization in the twenty-first century not only more equal but infinitely more civilized.

Let me add a concluding symbol for marriage. Marie and I were once in the gray-green beauty of Belfast, Ireland. We noticed that some Irish women wore wedding rings of unusual design called the Claddagh ring, named for a place near Galway. On top of the ring is a heart with two hands holding it—one on each side. A small crown rests on top of the heart.

The jewelers in Belfast weren't sure what the symbols meant. They said vague things about hearts and love and romance. Then a book on Irish wedding traditions told us that originally, the ring was made of three parts: The bride comes to the altar wearing a gold band on her ring finger. On this gold band is a heart, supported on one side by a cupped hand. This symbolizes the offering of her whole heart in marriage.

The groom brings to the altar a second gold band, which he places on the bride's ring finger. This second band also has on it a hand, which then cups the other side of the heart. This symbolizes the giving of his whole heart to her in marriage. They are now of one heart. The priest would then add a third thin band to the ring on the bride's finger. On this ring is a golden crown, which when placed on the heart, symbolizes God's blessing on the marriage.

With their hands on either side of the heart, and God's crown on top of it, the marriage is like a triangle—she and he pledge to each other, and both pledge themselves to God. The crowning blessing is that God also pledges himself to them.

In a covenant marriage, both men and women individually draw moral and spiritual strength from God. Then they bless each other, their family, the Church, and society by sharing that strength with others, in ever-expanding, concentric circles of spiritual influence.

The deepest wellspring that nourishes our sense of spiritual and moral direction, which gives us strength to help others, is God's influence on each of us individually. Each man and each woman is entitled to a direct relationship with him, with no intermediary. Even in a marriage, the wife does not go through her husband to make contact with the Lord, nor does he go through his wife to make that contact. As the prophet Jacob taught, "The keeper of the gate is the Holy One of Israel; and he employeth no servant there" (2 Nephi 9:41).

As we individually draw closer to God, that relationship empowers us also to draw closer to and lift one another. Fed by the springs of his love, we can then honestly be afflicted in one another's afflictions. When that happens, we will perhaps sense in a new way what it means that the Savior was afflicted in our afflictions. By taking the burdens of others upon us, we are emulating at our level the great miracle by which he took our burdens upon him. And the more our sacrifices approximate his, the better we will know him.

In Doctrine and Covenants 30:6, the Lord counseled one missionary regarding his companion, "Be you afflicted in all his afflictions." Marie and I first noticed this phrase while reading the scriptures together in Australia. I still remember how it lifted us when we looked through the concordance and found that Isaiah had used this same phrase in describing how Christ bore our afflictions: "In all their affliction he was afflicted, and the angel of his presence saved them: in his love and in his pity he redeemed them; and he [bore] them, and carried them all the days of old" (Isaiah 63:9).

Sisters and brethren, when we bear one another's burdens, we are doing something Christlike, and we will thereby become more like him.

The first time I became aware of Marie Kartchner was in a BYU religion class called "Your Religious Problems." She was leading a class discussion on following the guidance of the Lord's Spirit in life. She has continued seeking answers to that question over all the years since that day. As I have tried to merge my heart with hers, I have felt from her the pulse of a heart attuned to sing his grace. And when those feelings come to me, I can only say with Shakespeare's Cordelia, "How shall I live and work to match thy goodness?" Surely "my life will be too short, and every measure fail me."[39]

May God bless us, that his pure love will crown our marriages, our friendships, and our relationships of every kind, that our influence on each other will reflect his influence on us. I know the Savior lives.

Notes

1. "Follow the Prophet," *Children's Songbook* (Salt Lake City: The Church of Jesus Christ of Latter-day Saints, 1989), 111.
2. Francis Fukuyama, "The Great Disruption," *Atlantic Monthly* 283 (May 1999): 55.
3. Patricia T. Holland, "With Your Face to the Son," in Jeffrey R. Holland and Patricia T. Holland, *On Earth As It Is in Heaven* (Salt Lake City: Deseret Book, 1989), 85.
4. Alexis de Tocqueville, *Democracy in America*, ed. J. P. Mayer (Garden City, N.Y.: Doubleday & Co., 1969), 287, 590; see also Bruce C. Hafen and Marie K. Hafen, *The Belonging Heart: The Atonement and Relationships with God and Family* (Salt Lake City: Deseret Book, 1994), 255.

5. William Shakespeare, *Macbeth*, I, v, 16–17.

6. Ibid., lines 41–50.

7. Victor Hugo, as cited by Jeffrey R. Holland, "Because She Is a Mother," *Ensign*, May 1997, 35.

8. Quoted in Kathleen S. and Howard M. Bahr, "Another Voice, Another Lens: Making a Place for Sacrifice in Family Theory and Family Process," Virginia F. Cutler Lecture, Brigham Young University, 13 November 1997.

9. Anne Summers, *The Colonization of Women in Australia* (Ringwood, Victoria: Penguin Books Australia Ltd., 1975, 1994), 70.

10. "Feminism's Identity Crisis," *Newsweek*, 31 March 1986, 58.

11. First Presidency and Council of the Twelve Apostles, "The Family: A Proclamation to the World," *Ensign*, November 1995, 102.

12. Orania Papazoglou, "Despising Our Mothers, Despising Ourselves," *First Things* (January 1992): 11.

13. Richard Whitfield, "Sensitive Directions for Children's Moral Development," Presentation to World Congress of Families, Prague, Czech Republic, 20 March 1997.

14. Ibid.

15. Personal communication with author.

16. Leon Kass, "The End of Courtship," *Public Interest* (Winter 1997): 39.

17. David Popenoe, "The Essential Father," in *Life without Father* (The Free Press, 1996), 12 (manuscript version).

18. David Popenoe, "The Case for Marriage and the Nuclear Family: A Biosocial Perspective," unpublished manuscript, 6.

19. Quoted in Fukuyama, "Great Disruption," 72.

20. Popenoe, "Essential Father," 25 (manuscript version).

21. Jean Bethke Elshtain and David Popenoe, "Marriage in America," Institute for American Values, 1995.

22. Popenoe, "Case for Marriage and the Nuclear Family," 6.

23. Ibid.

24. Wilson, quoted in Popenoe, "The Essential Father," 13 (manuscript version).

25. Wendell Berry, *Sex, Economy, Freedom and Community* (New York: Pantheon Books, 1993), 125, 137–39.

26. William Butler Yeats, "The Second Coming," in *The Norton Anthology of English Literature*, ed. M. H. Abrams, 5th ed., 2 vols. (New York: W. W. Norton, 1962), 2:1948.

27. David Gutmann, "The Paternal Imperative," *The American Scholar* (Winter 1998): 118.

28. First Presidency, "The Family: A Proclamation," 102.

29. Gutmann, "Paternal Imperative," 118.

30. Ibid.

31. First Presidency, "The Family: A Proclamation," 102.

32. Studies reported in Carol Gilligan, *In a Different Voice: Psychological Theory and Women's Development* (Cambridge, Mass.: Harvard University Press, 1982).

33. Paul Gollan, "How Feminine Intuition Can Help the Profit Margin," *Sydney Morning Herald*, 28 July 1998, 13.

34. Summers, *Colonization*, 355.

35. Ibid., 337–53.

36. Ibid., 354–57.

37. Gilligan, *In a Different Voice*.

38. Summers, *Colonization*, 46.

39. William Shakespeare, *King Lear*, IV, vii, 1–3.

THE THURSDAY ISLAND STORY

Marie K. Hafen

While Bruce and I were serving in the South Pacific and Australia, we came to hear what we have affectionately dubbed "The Thursday Island Story." Thursday Island is a small island just off the northeast tip of Australia, nestled neatly between Wednesday Island and—you guessed it—Friday Island. (No, I'm not kidding.)

This story illustrates not only a woman's influence on a man, but also a man's equally important influence on a woman.

"Brian" grew up in New Zealand in tough circumstances. His mother lived with one man after another, each of whom Brian longed to call Dad. But not one of them ever was. When he was about ten, he often saw his mother's current boyfriend come home drunk and beat her. By the time Brian was twelve, this boyfriend had given him alcohol, and within a year or two he was into hard drugs. By his late teens, Brian left New Zealand for Australia where he joined a drug gang in Sydney and spent all his energy feeding his habit, which by then was the sole focus left in his life.

One day, with no money and desperate for his fix, he determined to rob a stranger. Ready for the first time to kill someone if he had to, Brian waited on a dark Sydney street near a train station. Taking a deep breath, he approached a well-dressed man and threatened him with a knife.

"Give me your money, or I'll kill you," he hissed. As the man

Marie Kartchner Hafen has served on the Young Women General Board and on the board of the Deseret News. She holds a master's degree in English from Brigham Young University and has taught courses at Ricks and at BYU in composition and Shakespeare. She and her husband, Bruce C. Hafen, a member of the First Quorum of the Seventy, are the parents of seven children and grandparents of twenty-three.

fumbled for his money, Brian caught a quick glimpse of a small family photo in his wallet. Seeing that photo made Brian's heart scream. "A family! How can I kill this man who has all I've ever wanted?"

Feeling shame burn through him, he bolted, throwing his knife into some nearby bushes. He ran and ran, until he fell, breathless and sobbing, to the grass in a city park. When the sobbing subsided, he still felt frantic, worthless, and without hope. As his mind wildly cast about for answers, he could think of only one thing. He would take his own life.

Impulsively, he climbed to the top of a nearby skyscraper to jump to his death. As he teetered on the brink, an odd thought stopped him cold. "If I jump, my last earthly act will be to leave a mess for somebody else to clean up." He stepped away from the edge, determined to find a better way to take his life. As he made his way back to his dingy apartment, an idea hit him. He would go to Thursday Island.

He remembered a very peaceful visit to that island years before. With almost his last dollar, he caught a flight from Sydney. Once on the island, he rented a boat, agreeing to return it to the owner the next morning at dawn. But actually, he planned to row himself to a tiny, uninhabited island, where he could end his life and leave no mess for someone to clean up.

As he vacantly ate his final supper in a local hotel, he noticed three women singing on a small stage. One of them had a very mellow voice. He stayed, listening, and later, grateful for a little comfort, offered the three of them a drink. Two said yes; "Lani," the one with the mellow voice, politely refused the drink but stayed after the other two left and talked with him.

They talked until the place closed, they talked as he walked her home, and they just kept talking until dawn broke on the horizon. He had not told her his plans, and when he saw the growing light, he nervously blurted, "I've got to go now. Thank you. This has been the most peaceful night of my life." Then he hurriedly turned to leave.

"Stop, Brian," Lani called. "I don't know where you're going . . .

but don't go." The light in her eyes matched the calming tones of her voice.

"It's too late. I've made up my mind." But his steps faltered. He looked back at her face; then, teetering again between death and life, he looked toward the sea. Something about the light in her eyes and her voice pulled him back through her door. She didn't ask him to explain; she just fixed him some breakfast. As he was finishing eating, two young men in white shirts appeared at the door. Lani was a new convert, and the missionaries were dropping by to see how she was doing.

Within a short time, they had taught Brian the discussions. He was baptized and decided to stay on Thursday Island. Not long afterwards, Brian and Lani were married. At last Brian had a family photo of his own.

Lani fed Brian spiritually and physically. Her spirit "sang" to him, calling to his heart. He heard the song and changed because of it, feeling true peace for the first time in his life. That was more than twenty-five years ago.

When we last saw them, Brian and Lani were serving together on a full-time mission in Australia. A few weeks later, Brian sent us a letter in which he looks back on how much Lani has helped him. But also notice how much *he* is helping her. He writes:

"Lani is always a blessing to me. In her humble way, she lives the gospel. She is currently going through a trial of memory loss, and it gives her much anguish. At times I feel helpless to put her at ease. Then I remember how she cared for me as I went through withdrawals from drugs and the nights she sat up till daylight comforting me as my mind wandered with its fears. Love and patience, selfless service, and faith in the Savior—that is how she helped me. I pray as often as I can. I love my wife and desire to be her strength. The Savior is helping us."[1]

A wife supports a husband. A husband sustains a wife. Each has held the other in comforting vigil. In a very real way, each is "afflicted" with the other's afflictions. These very words are used in counsel the Lord gave Peter Whitmer, as he and Oliver Cowdery were about to leave on a mission, "Give heed unto the words and advice of your brother, . . . and *be you afflicted in all his afflictions,* ever lifting up your heart unto me in prayer and faith, for his and your deliverance" (D&C 30:5–6; emphasis added).

In the Thursday Island story the progression looks like this: She calls to him in his afflictions with the love she feels from the Lord. He feels *her* love, and through her comes to know Christ's love for himself. Now with the love *he* feels from the Lord, he loves her even more and strengthens her in her affliction. The afflictions and the love become not just his or hers but theirs. Both, tethered to the Lord by their individual and now combined faith, are being drawn into the center by his love—into oneness with him.

This progression reverses the unraveling relationship between the falcon and the falconer, an image of anarchy from W. B. Yeats' well-known poem "The Second Coming." *This* center—his divine center, and the one Brian and Lani found—*will* hold. Anarchy is no more; for Christ's goodness, like a fetter, has bound up our wander-prone hearts—bound them to one another—and then to him. Paradoxically, *this* "turning gyre" that *seems* only to narrow actually opens into celestial worlds without end.[2]

The Thursday Island story tells me that a man can also call to a woman in ways that soothe and stabilize her. Recently I heard about a young man who was a catalyst in turning a young friend from her self-destructive ways.

"Michelle" wanted to turn her life away from the foolish choices she had been making. Her confidence was shaky, but she very much wanted to change. By "chance," one night she met Scott, a returned missionary, at a dance. They each liked how the other moved on the dance floor. (People don't talk much on dance floors these days, you know.) During breaks they did strike up a conversation and then a friendship. One night, after several weeks of phone calls and a few dates, they had a serious talk about what her past might mean to her future. She was afraid that by her mistakes she might have already forfeited her potential. He didn't say, "You dummy." He didn't say, "You should've" or "You should." He thought a second. He looked at her intently and said simply, "I see you. I know who you really are."

Could the priesthood be playing a role in Scott's wisdom? Perhaps there is a parallel between the civilizing influence of Caroline Chisholm's women on the male convict settlers of Australia and the Christianizing influence of the priesthood on the men of this Church.

While visiting a stake in Australia, Bruce met with three sister leaders. At that time, and since, Church leaders had been strongly encouraging women's full participation in stake and ward councils. Wondering if this participation was increasing as well as improving, Bruce asked these three women, "Are the men in your lives listening to you?" Their brows furrowed. "Do you mean our priesthood leaders or our husbands?"

Bruce made the question more specific. Could they estimate what percentage of the sisters in their stake would say their husbands do listen to them, and what proportion would say that their priesthood leaders listen to them? After a little private discussion, they estimated that the priesthood leaders listened a little better than the husbands, though neither estimate was much to brag about.

Sensing Bruce's dismay that the men—whether as priesthood holders or as husbands—were not better listeners, one of the sisters said, "I can tell, Elder Hafen, that you're disappointed, but things *are* getting better. More than that, I don't know of any organization on earth that begins to do what the priesthood does in teaching men to listen to— and to value—women, and children for that matter. The men in my life," she went on, "take me more seriously than they otherwise would because they hold the priesthood and the priesthood teaches them how to treat, and how to serve, others."

The priesthood can connect men to God and thereby to others, if they desire. And then their desire is not simply about leadership; it's about love, about "gentleness and meekness, and . . . love unfeigned" (D&C 121:41).

The young man who assures his new friend that he sees her for who she really is, and not for her mistakes, surely knows something of the love that comes when we are connected to God. Now her desire to find the Savior's love for herself is leading her to make better choices.

This discussion also applies to those who are single. When a single woman makes her own one-to-one connection with the Lord, she worries less about when, or if, she will marry. It doesn't matter whether being single results from never having married, being widowed, or being divorced; the principles are the same. Whatever else happens, we need to become celestial beings whose hope is based in Christ and who are sealed his (Mosiah 5:15).

As we were talking with a young married couple recently, someone observed that a woman can be haunted with self-doubt when the men in her life do not seem to value her. I like what our friend Sue said about that: "A woman's self-worth depends not on how much other people seem to value her but rather on how well she is spiritually grounded. To depend on what others think of us lets them determine our sense of worth. When our happiness is based on someone else's choices, rather than our own, we become prime candidates for 'deadly hope.' We hope someone will approve of us so we can approve of ourselves, but we simply cannot control other people's choices. We can, however, control our own choices and our own relationship with the Lord. I know from my own experiences that if we walk one step toward him, he will always run at least two steps toward us. Hope based in Christ is not deadly, but full of life and light."[3]

Lea Rosser, a country girl from Yass, Australia, obtained a university education and, placing herself in the Lord's hands, moved courageously to the big city. In Sydney, with still more grit, she got more education in city government and eventually was hired as the city manager for the shire where the Olympic games were held. After the Olympics were over, she said, "I cast my net into unknown waters to see if my bait [was] suitable." A job offering that matched her talents came several long months later. She reflects, "Here I was thinking [that] Heavenly Father wasn't going to 'plunk' me somewhere this time, but he did."[4]

A single woman, like Lea, may enjoy an especially meaningful relationship with Christ if she lives so as to become like him. Though she sorely longs for marriage, she feels after Christ's companionship in her aloneness. This binding tether brings stability no matter what gales about her. Because she is bound securely to him, she is free to have a buoying, strengthening influence on others, an influence that is uniquely hers, uniquely a woman's, and uniquely Christian.

Single or married, wife or husband, all have the self-same challenge of becoming celestial individually in order to be celestial together. "Tina," a wonderful young Aussie mum, felt discouraged and unworthy because of the "gap between the ideal of married life and the reality of her marriage," as she put it. "Geoff" had stopped attending church, and she felt bereft spiritually. Then on a temple trip to Sydney, she read a book on the Atonement. Its pages were for her "truth and hope and light being unfolded" and she set out to put her "spirituality back on track."

She prayed for changes in her marriage, in her husband's choices, and in her own choices. To her surprise, changes came not in big ways, but "in the most subtle ways and through obedience to promptings." She continued to work not on trying to force her husband to be active but rather on standing "faithful regardless of others' decisions" and on making herself "the kind of wife and person that Geoff wants to be with forever." Tina's new understanding of the Atonement and growing closeness to the Savior helped her be able to say, "[Even though] I have wanted to give up [many times, and] many times I questioned my testimony, [this trial] has been a good test for me. The Lord has blessed me with strength, understanding and healing. He has become my friend and my support."[5]

Now, speaking for myself, it's not my husband's inactivity in this Church that's been my affliction—it's his activity! Being assigned to Australia was one of the sweetest joys of our life *and* one of the hardest things I have ever done.

I could hardly stand (as one of many examples) to be away from our daughter Sarah when she had her first baby. Her pregnancy had been complicated by terrible morning sickness followed by a rare, intensely itchy rash that never stopped. She was afflicted! I took consolation in the care she was getting from her husband, Eric, and her older sister, Emily, who came from out of town to fill in for me. But still, *I* wasn't there. All I could do was give advice and empathy over the phone, mail baby clothes, and pray from the ache in my mothering heart.

My prayers changed when I was away from those I love so much—especially when they were in crisis. I prayed more honestly, more deeply, and with greater intent. The intensity of the ache caused me to stretch longer for him, pleading for blessings upon my family and friends. Somehow this stretching expanded—and expands—my heart to make more room for him. What I have experienced makes me want to urge every couple in the Church to serve a mission not only because you are needed so much but because your service and your sacrifice can expand your spiritual vision.

There is, of course, plenty more changing for me to do, more turning of my heart toward the call of the Falconer. Like any wife and mother, I need to learn to communicate better with my family, to be more patient with them while they are learning to be patient with me, to be restrained and not indulge in criticism. Together, as a family, the rough edges are getting smoothed as we struggle to forgive and repent—and to keep loving through it all. And in all of this, he is making better Christians of us.

I would not trade any of what I've come to feel for him, or the cost of this discovery, for the ease of no aching and no stretching. He is too precious to me now, and I feel too tender toward him. I yearn for nothing more than to be, in the long light at the end of this mortal day, at home with him.

Notes

1. Letter in possession of the author.
2. William Butler Yeats, "The Second Coming," in *The Norton Anthology of English Literature*, ed. M. H. Abrams, 5th ed., 2 vols. (New York: W. W. Norton, 1962), 2:1948. "Turning and turning in the widening gyre / The

falcon cannot hear the falconer; / Things fall apart; the center cannot hold, / Mere anarchy is loosed upon the world."

3. Letter in possession of the author.
4. Personal communication with the author.
5. Letter in possession of the author.

"HERE AM I, SEND ME"

꒰꒱

M. Russell Ballard

Sisters, it is an honor for me to be with you. I bring you the greetings of the First Presidency and the Quorum of the Twelve Apostles. I was with them this morning in the temple, and they send to you their love. Recently I spoke at a Brigham Young University devotional about the important role of women in the Church. I have been asked by the Women's Conference committee to share with you some of the same things that I told the students.

Sister Ballard and I have been married for fifty years this August. The most important day in my life was the day we were married in the Salt Lake Temple. We are the parents of two sons and five daughters. We now have forty-one grandchildren, of whom twenty-two are granddaughters. Now, with this many women around me all of the time, I count myself as an expert on the subject of women.

I received an outline called "A Woman's Lifeline" the other day that I can relate to because I've seen all these little girls grow up, and I thought you might be able to relate to it also.

Age 3: She looks at herself and sees a queen.

Age 8: She looks at herself and sees Cinderella.

Age 15: She looks at herself and sees an ugly duckling (Mom, I can't go to school looking like this today!)

Age 20: She looks at herself and sees "too fat/too thin, too

Elder M. Russell Ballard has been a member of the Quorum of the Twelve Apostles since 1985. He and his wife, Barbara Bowen, have been married fifty years. They are the parents of two sons and five daughters and the grandparents of forty-one, of whom twenty-two are granddaughters. He counts himself as an expert on the subject of women.

short/too tall, too straight/too curly" but decides she's going out anyway.

Age 30: She looks at herself and sees "too fat/too thin, too short/too tall, too straight/too curly" but decides she doesn't have time to fix it so she's going out anyway.

Age 40: She looks at herself and sees "too fat/too thin, too short/too tall, too straight/too curly" but says, "At least I am clean," and goes out anyway.

Age 50: She looks at herself and says "I am what I am" and goes wherever she wants to go.

Age 60: She looks at herself and reminds herself of all the people who can't even see themselves in the mirror anymore. Goes out and conquers the world.

Age 70: She looks at herself and sees wisdom, laughter, and ability and goes out and enjoys life.

Age 80: Doesn't bother to look. Just puts on a purple hat and goes out to have fun with the world.

The moral is, maybe we should all grab that purple hat a little earlier.

The reason I am concerned about you dear women of the Church, knowing how important you are to the Lord, is expressed in a letter that came to the Church offices a short time ago. A good sister wrote:

"I have a wonderful husband and children, whom I love deeply. I love the Lord and His Church more than I can say. I know the Church is true! I realize I shouldn't feel discouraged about who I am. Yet I have been going through an identity crisis most of my life. I have never dared utter these feelings out loud but have hidden them behind the huge, confident smile I wear to Church every week.

"For years I have doubted if I had any value beyond my roles as a wife and mother. I have feared that men are that they might have joy but women are that they might be overlooked. I long to feel that I as a woman matter to the Lord."[1]

If you have ever wondered, "Does the Lord respect women? Do

women matter to the Lord? Do women matter to the leaders of the Church?" The answer is a resounding YES!

Elder James E. Talmage stated that "the world's greatest champion of woman and womanhood is Jesus the Christ."[2] I believe that is a true statement. The first time the Lord acknowledged Himself to be the Christ was to a Samaritan woman at Jacob's well. He taught her about living water and proclaimed, simply, "I . . . am he" (John 4:26). And it was Martha to whom He proclaimed, "I am the resurrection, and the life . . . And whosoever liveth and believeth in me shall never die" (John 11:25–26).

And then, during His greatest agony as He hung on the cross, the Savior reached out to one person, His mother. In that terrible but glorious moment he asked John the Beloved to care for her as though she were his own (John 19:26–27).

Of this you may be certain: The Lord especially loves righteous women—women who are not only faithful but filled with faith, women who are optimistic and cheerful because they know who they are and where they are going, women who are striving to live and serve as women of God.

There are those who suggest that males are favored of the Lord because they are ordained to hold the priesthood. Anyone who believes that does not understand the great plan of happiness. The premortal and mortal natures of men and women were specified by the Lord Jehovah Himself, and it is simply not within His character to diminish the roles and responsibilities of any of His children.

As President Joseph Fielding Smith explained: "The Lord offers to his daughters every spiritual gift and blessing that can be obtained by his sons."[3] We also know that all of us, men and women alike, receive the gift of the Holy Ghost and are entitled to personal revelation. We may all take upon us the Lord's name, become the sons and daughters of Christ, partake of the ordinances of the temple from which we emerge endowed with power, receive the fulness of the gospel, and achieve exaltation in the celestial kingdom. These spiritual blessings are available to men and women alike, according to their faithfulness and their efforts to receive them.

The basic doctrinal purpose for the creation of the earth is to provide for God's spirit children the continuation of the process of exaltation and eternal life. God said to Moses, "And I, God, created man in mine own image, in the image of mine Only Begotten created I him; male and female created I them. And I, God, blessed them, and said unto them: Be fruitful, and multiply, and replenish the earth" (Moses 2:27–28).

The Proclamation on the Family confirms that God has not revoked or changed this commandment. The First Presidency and the Twelve Apostles "solemnly proclaim that marriage between a man and a woman is ordained of God and that the family is central to the Creator's plan for the eternal destiny of His children."[4]

This doctrine sometimes causes women to ask: "Is a woman's value dependent exclusively upon her role as a wife and mother?" The answer is simple and obvious—no! Motherhood and marital status are not the only measures of a woman's worth. Some women do not have the privilege of marrying or rearing children in this life. To the worthy, these blessings will come later. Women who do have the privilege of rearing children will, of course, be held accountable for that priceless, eternal stewardship. While there is simply not a more significant contribution you can make to society, to the Church, or to the eternal destiny of our Father's children than what you do as a mother, motherhood is not the only measure of goodness or of one's acceptance before the Lord. Every righteous woman has a significant role to play in the onward march of the kingdom of God.

I have a deep and abiding feeling about women and about the crucial role they make in every important setting, particularly in the family and in the Church. I have spoken boldly about the role women must play in the councils of the Church. We cannot fulfill our mission as a Church without the inspired insight and support of women.

For that reason I am concerned about what I see happening with some of our young women and some of our not-so-young women. The adversary is having a heyday distorting attitudes about gender and roles and families and individual worth. He is the author of mass confusion about values and roles, the contribution and the unique nature of women. Today's popular culture, which is preached by every form of media from the silver screen to the Internet, celebrates the sexy, saucy, socially aggressive woman. These distortions are seeping into the thinking of some of our own women in the Church.

My deep desire is to clarify how we in the presiding councils of the Church feel about the sisters of this Church, how our Heavenly Father feels about His daughters and what He expects of them. My dear sisters, we believe in you.

We believe in and are counting on your goodness and your strength, your propensity for virtue and valor, your kindness and courage, your strength and resilience. We believe in your mission as women of God. We realize that you are the emotional (and sometimes spiritual) glue that holds families and often ward families together. We believe that the Church simply will not accomplish what it must without your faith and faithfulness, your innate tendency to put the well-being of others ahead of your own, and your spiritual strength and tenacity.

Women live in homes under many different circumstances—married, single, widowed, divorced, with children and without. But where the women are righteous and good, love, peace, and joy abound in the home. When children are in the home, every effort should be made by mothers to be home for them. All righteous women are part of God's great plan for His daughters to become queens and to receive the highest blessings in time or eternity.

On the other hand, Satan's plan is to get you so preoccupied with the world's glitzy lie about women that you completely miss what you have come here to do and to become. Remember, he wants us to "be miserable like unto himself " (2 Nephi 2:27). Never lose your precious identity by doing anything that would jeopardize the promised eternal future your Heavenly Father has provided for you.

Women have labored valiantly in the cause of truth and

righteousness from before the foundations of the world. In President Joseph F. Smith's vision of the redemption of the dead, he saw not only Father Adam and other prophets but "our glorious Mother Eve, with many of her faithful daughters who had lived through the ages and worshiped the true and living God" (D&C 138:39).

Think about the incomparable role of Eve, whose actions set in motion the great plan of our Father, and about Mary, the "precious and chosen vessel" (Alma 7:10), who bore the Christ Child. Surely no one would question the contribution made by these majestic women.

Our dispensation is not without its heroines. Countless women from every continent and walk of life have made dramatic contributions to the cause of Christ. Consider Lucy Mack Smith, the mother of the martyred Prophet Joseph and Hyrum and the grandmother of President Joseph F. Smith. Her resilience and righteousness under the most emotionally and spiritually taxing conditions surely influenced her prophet sons and set them firmly on the path towards fulfilling their foreordained destiny.

At this point you may be thinking, "But what about me and my contribution? I'm not Eve or Mary or even Lucy Mack Smith. I'm just regular, plain old me. Is there something about my contribution that is significant to the Lord? Does He really need me?" Remember, the righteous who are not highly visible are valued too and, in the words of a Book of Mormon prophet, are "no less serviceable unto the people" (Alma 48:19).

President Spencer W. Kimball responded to that question this way: "Both a righteous man and a righteous woman are a blessing to all those whom their lives touch.

" . . . [In] the world before we came here, faithful women were given certain assignments while faithful men were foreordained to certain priesthood tasks. While we do not now remember the particulars, . . . [we] are accountable for those things which long ago were expected of us."[5]

Every sister in this Church who has made covenants with the Lord has a divine mandate to help save souls, to lead the women of the world, to strengthen the homes of Zion, and to build the kingdom of God. Sister Eliza R. Snow, the second general president of the Relief Society, said: "Every sister in this church should be a preacher of righteousness. . . . because we have greater and higher privileges than any other females upon the face of the earth."[6]

Every sister who stands for truth and righteousness diminishes the influence of evil. Dear sisters, every one of you who strengthens and protects your family is doing the work of God. Every sister who lives as a woman of God becomes a beacon for others to follow and plants seeds of righteous influence that will be harvested for decades to come. Every sister who makes and keeps sacred covenants becomes an instrument in the hands of God.

I have been drawn to an interchange between God the Father and His Eldest and Only Begotten Son, who is the ultimate example of living up to one's premortal promises. When God asked who would come to earth to prepare a way for all mankind to be saved and strengthened and blessed, it was Jesus Christ who said, simply, "Here am I, send me" (Abraham 3:27).

Just as the Savior stepped forward to fulfill His divine responsibilities, we have the challenge and responsibility to do likewise. If you are wondering if you make a difference to the Lord, imagine the effect when you make such commitments as the following:

"Father, if you need a woman to rear children in righteousness, Here am I, send me."

"If you need a woman to make a house, a home filled with love, Here am I, send me."

"If you need a woman who will shun vulgarity and dress modestly and speak with dignity and show the world how joyous it is to keep the commandments, Here am I, send me."

"If you need a woman who can resist the alluring temptations of the world by keeping her eyes fixed on eternity, Here am I, send me."

Between now and the day the Lord comes again, He needs women in every family, in every ward, in every community, in every nation who will step forward in righteousness and say by their words and their actions, "Here am I, send me."

My question today is, Will you be one of those women?

Now I know you want to. But how will you do it? How, in a world filled with deceptive messages about women and the family and knowing the significance of both to the Lord, will you perpetually respond to the Lord by saying, "Here am I, send me"?

For those who really want to live up to who you are, for those who at all costs want to repent, if necessary, and who want to see through Satan's deceptions, may I suggest that you listen to and follow those whom you sustain as prophets, seers, and revelators. I suggest that you learn to hear the voice of the Spirit, or the voice of the Lord as communicated by the power of the Holy Ghost.

I cannot stress enough the importance of listening to and following the prophet and the apostles. In today's world, where twenty-four hours a day the media's talking heads spew forth conflicting opinions, where men and women jockey for everything from your money to your vote, there is one unpolluted, unbiased, clear voice that you can always count on. And that is the voice of the living prophet and the apostles. Our only motive is "the everlasting welfare of your souls" (2 Nephi 2:30).

Think of it! Think about the value of having a source of information you can always count on, that will always have your eternal interests at heart, and that will always provide inspired truth. That's a phenomenal gift and guide.

Today I make you the same promise I made in general conference in April 2001. It is a simple one, but it is true. If you will listen to the living prophet and the apostles and heed our counsel, you will not go astray.[7]

If you want to avoid the snares of Satan, if you need direction when the choices in front of you are puzzling and perplexing, learn to hear the voice of the Lord as communicated through the Holy Ghost. And then, of course, do what it tells you to do.

Nephi taught clearly that the Holy Ghost is the "gift of God unto all those who diligently seek him" and that "he that diligently seeketh shall find" (1 Nephi 10:17, 19). The unquestionable reality, my dear sisters, is that you control how close you are to the Lord. You determine just how clear and readily available promptings from the Holy Ghost will be. You determine this by your actions, by your attitude, by the choices you make, by the things you watch and wear and listen to and read, and by how consistently and sincerely you invite the Spirit into your life.

As life progresses, how will you respond to challenges that will inevitably come? Will you know where to turn for peace and consolation if your marriage faces hard times or health challenges loom up or you are called upon to bury a child—as two of our own children have done—or if a child threatens to stray from the gospel path? How will you know what to do when you face financial reverses? Where will you turn for insight and inspiration when you are called upon to lead in your ward or stake? You dear mothers, where will you turn for strength to care for and lead your family on Sundays when your husbands are serving as priesthood leaders in your stake or ward?

My dear sisters, there is only one way to safely and confidently meet the obstacles and opportunities that are part of life's path: listen to the prophet and the apostles, study the principles we teach, and then take those principles to the Lord and ask Him how you should apply them in your life. Ask Him to influence your thoughts, temper your actions, and guide your steps. "Counsel with the Lord in all thy doings, and he will direct thee for good" (Alma 37:37). He will communicate with you through the power and the presence of the Holy Ghost.

There are several things you can do to greatly enhance your ability to understand the promptings of the Holy Ghost and thereby hear and respond to the voice of God. Let me tell you what they are.

First, fast and pray. When the sons of Mosiah were united with Alma the Younger, they rejoiced in their reunion and acknowledged that because they had "given themselves to much prayer and fasting" they had been given the spirit of prophecy and revelation, and when "they taught, they taught with power and authority of God" (Alma 17:3).

Second, immerse yourself in the scriptures. The word of God will "tell you all things what ye should do" (2 Nephi 32:3). The scriptures are a conduit for personal revelation. I urge you to intensify your study of them. I promise that your ability to hear the voice of the Lord as communicated through the Holy Ghost will increase and improve.

Third, prepare to spend time in the house of the Lord. When the appropriate time comes for you to go to the temple, you will leave the temple "armed with . . . power" (D&C 109:22) and with the promise that as we "grow up" in our knowledge of the Lord we will "receive a fulness of the Holy Ghost" (D&C 109:15). The temple is a place of personal revelation. If you are endowed, visit the temple regularly. If you are not, prepare yourselves to enter. Inside the doors of the temple rests the power that will fortify you against the vicissitudes of life.

Fourth, listen to the counsel of your parents and your husband. They are usually wise and experienced. Share with them your fears and concerns. Seek blessings from your father or your husband. If he has gone to the other side of the veil, or if for some reason he is not worthy or able, go to your bishop or your stake president. They love you and will count it a privilege to bless your life. If you haven't yet done so, you should also receive your patriarchal blessing.

Fifth, practice obedience and repentance. There are certain things you simply cannot do if you want to have the Holy Ghost with you. It is not possible to listen to inappropriate music, watch movies or soap operas filled with sexual innuendo, tamper with pornography on the Internet (or anywhere else for that matter), take the name of the Lord in vain, wear revealing clothing, or compromise in any way the law of chastity. Mothers, you particularly must set the example of modesty in dress and action. You cannot disregard the values of true womanhood and expect the Holy Ghost to remain with you. Whenever anyone participates in those kinds of activities, it should not be a surprise that feelings of loneliness, discouragement, and unworthiness follow. Do not make the choice to go it alone rather than have the Spirit of the Lord to guide, to protect, to prompt, to warn, and to fill you with peace. Repent if you need to so you can enjoy the companionship of the Spirit.

Women and men who can hear the voice of the Lord and who respond to those promptings become invaluable instruments in His hands.

Finally, my dear sisters, you have a profound, innate spiritual ability to hear the voice of the Good Shepherd. You need never wonder again if you have worth in the sight of the Lord and to the Brethren in the presiding councils of the Church. We love you. We cherish you. We respect you. Never doubt that your influence is absolutely vital to preserving the family and to assisting with the growth and spiritual vitality of the Church. This Church will not reach its foreordained destiny without you. We men simply cannot nurture as you nurture. Most of us don't have the sensitivity, spiritual and otherwise, that by your eternal nature you inherently have. Your influence on families and with children, youth, and men is singular. You are natural-born nurturers. Because of these unusual gifts and talents, you are vital to taking the gospel to all the world, to demonstrating that there is joy in living the way prophets have counseled us to live. I see many grandmothers here today, and I encourage you to never, never stop teaching, and never allow your wisdom of a lifetime of faithful dedication to the Lord to grow dim in your own families or your wards.

Today more than ever, we need women of faith, virtue, vision, and charity, as the Relief Society Declaration proclaims. We need women who can hear and will respond to the voice of the Lord, women who at all costs will defend and protect the family. We don't need women who want to be like men, sound like men, dress like men, drive like some men, or act like men. We do need women who rejoice in their womanhood and have a spiritual confirmation of their identity, their value, and their eternal destiny. Above all, we need women who will stand up for truth and righteousness and decry evil at every turn, women who will simply say, "Here am I, Lord, send me."

I bear my witness and testimony to you that each one of you is precious to the Lord and to His Church. Never doubt that this kingdom of God will continue to roll forward until it fills the entire earth. For the Church to accomplish its mission, we need every sister, young and old, to be beacons and banners to the entire world, to show the rest of the world there is a people who honor and uphold the role of women as daughters of God destined to receive every eternal blessing He has for His faithful children.

I testify to you, my dear sisters, that I know that Jesus is the Christ, that He lives, and that this is His Church. I plead with our Heavenly Father that He will bless you precious women of the Church in every way.

Notes

1. Letter in possession of author.
2. James E. Talmage, *Jesus the Christ*, 3d ed. (Salt Lake City: The Church of Jesus Christ of Latter-day Saints, 1916), 475.
3. Joseph Fielding Smith, "Magnifying Our Callings in the Priesthood," *Improvement Era*, June 1970, 66.
4. First Presidency and Council of the Twelve Apostles, "The Family: A Proclamation to the World," *Ensign*, November 1995, 102.
5. Spencer W. Kimball, *My Beloved Sisters* (Salt Lake City: Deseret Book, 1979), 37.
6. Eliza R. Snow, "Great Indignation Meeting," *Deseret Evening News*, 14 January 1870, 2.
7. See also M. Russell Ballard, "His Word Ye Shall Receive," *Ensign*, May 2001, 66.

INDEX

121; doing the basics and trusting in God's help, 121–22; and Church membership/activity, 122; factors contributing to, 122–23; hope as an antidote to worry, 123–24; Boyd K. Packer on having miserable days, 124; Dallin H. Oaks on getting help for, 124; using all available sources of help, 124; using counseling to treat, 124–25; indicators of a biological base for, 125; using medication to treat, 125; living with, 125–27. *See also* Mental illness

"Despising Our Mothers, Despising Ourselves," 293–94

Devenport, Billy, 8

Devon, England, 92

Dew, Sheri, 127

Dinesen, Isak, 93

Disobedience. *See* Obedience

Diversity: in the United States, 29–30; in the Church, 30. *See also* Religious tolerance/respect; Religious tolerance/respect, teaching children

Divorce: relying on the wisdom of man *vs.* God, 86–87; effect on children, 87; staying together in difficult times, 87; story of woman receiving direction from the scriptures during, 264; increase in the rate of, 296–97

Earthquake victims, story about visiting, 236

Enoch, 281

Evans, Richard L., on avoiding debt, 6

Eyring, Henry, 251

Eyring, Henry B., on bearing record of Christ, 26

Faith: and agency, 100–101; connecting the dots, 101, 102; essence of, 101; in the midst of a corrupt and tumultuous world, 102–3; and daily sacrifice, service, and commitment, 103; of Sarah Rich, 103; when your life doesn't fit the pattern, 103; of Bathsheba Bigler Smith, 103–4; moving on as doors close behind you, 104–5;

poem about, 105; as a force in family history work, 105–7; fear as the opposite of, 107; scriptures as a source of, 107; as the essence of earthly experience, 108; Joseph Smith's counsel to Emma on, 108; Bruce R. McConkie on gaining faith like the ancients, 191; of missionaries at Christmastime, 271; of African-American family at São Paulo Temple dedication, 271–72; of Mary Fielding Smith, 272–73; of Margaret McNeil Ballard, 273–74; M. Russell Ballard on finding spiritual safety, 274–75; in times of trial, 275–76

Families: bearing record of Christ to, 53–55; Proclamation on the Family on importance of home and family in the Lord's plan, 54; Christ as the foundation for building faithful, 101–2; Dallin H. Oaks on building unity in, 190; following the Lord's pattern for strengthening, 229–31; women as protectors and defenders of, in Church councils, 243; shift in society's attitudes toward, 291

Family history work: stories about, 105–7, 138–39, 139–40; Boyd K. Packer on, 136; Dallin H. Oaks on, 136; importance of, 136; Gordon B. Hinckley on, 137; Joseph Fielding Smith on, 137; Richard G. Scott on, 139. *See also* Temples and temple work

Family impact studies, 243

"Family, The: A Proclamation to the World," 54, 170, 293, 298, 299, 319

Family work: Gordon B. Hinckley on, 178; *vs.* play, 178; and becoming a Zion people, 179; selfishness and, 179, 180; *vs.* working elsewhere, 179; combating weariness with, 179–80; as a source of conflict, 180, 187; as a gift from God, 181; as part of the Lord's work, 181–82, 188; as the work of nurturing of life, 182; devaluation of, 182–84; running homes like businesses, 184, 186–87;